New Edition

PRE-INTERMEDIATE

Language in use

Teacher's Book

ADRIAN DOFF & CHRISTOPHER JONES

CAMBRIDGE
UNIVERSITY PRESS

PUBLISHED BY THE PRESS SYNDICATE OF THE UNIVERSITY OF CAMBRIDGE
The Pitt Building, Trumpington Street, Cambridge, United Kingdom

CAMBRIDGE UNIVERSITY PRESS
The Edinburgh Building, Cambridge CB2 2RU, UK
40 West 20th Street, New York, NY 10011–4211, USA
10 Stamford Road, Oakleigh, VIC 3166, Australia
Ruiz de Alarcón 13, 28014 Madrid, Spain
Dock House, The Waterfront, Cape Town 8001, South Africa

http://www.cambridge.org

First published 1991
New edition 2000
First printing 2001

Printed in the United Kingdom at the University Press, Cambridge

ISBN 0 521 77404 7   Teacher's Book
ISBN 0 521 77407 1   Classroom Book
ISBN 0 521 77406 3   Self-study Workbook
ISBN 0 521 77405 5   Self-study Workbook with Answer Key
ISBN 0 521 77403 9   Class Cassette Set
ISBN 0 521 77402 0   Self-study Cassette
ISBN 0 521 65461 0   Video (PAL)
ISBN 0 521 65460 2   Video (NTSC)

Contents

Introduction

How the course is organised

Who the course is for

This new edition of *Language in Use Pre-intermediate* is the second of the four levels in the *Language in Use* series. It can be used by students who have completed *Language in Use Beginner*, or who have studied English using another beginner's course. It is also suitable for students who are coming back to English after learning it at some time in the past.

The components of the course

The course contains 24 units, each designed to last for about three classroom hours, plus regular Study Pages spreads. The students' materials are divided into two major components: a Classroom Book and a Self-study Workbook. Both are accompanied by cassettes.

The syllabus

The course has a dual syllabus: a grammatical syllabus, which deals with the basic structures of English, and a topic syllabus, which deals with vocabulary. These two strands are reflected in Grammar units and Vocabulary units, which alternate through the course. For example:

Unit 7	The past	*Grammar unit*
Unit 8	A place to live	*Vocabulary unit*
Unit 9	I've done it!	*Grammar unit*
Unit 10	Clothes	*Vocabulary unit*

This alternation of Grammar and Vocabulary units allows systematic coverage of the two major content areas of English. It also allows a natural recycling of language through the course: structures are recycled in Vocabulary units and vocabulary is recycled in Grammar units.

The Classroom Book

The Classroom Book contains the main presentation and practice material of the course, as well as activities in speaking, writing, reading and listening.

Grammar

The Grammar units cover grammatical areas that are essential at this level; these include the main verb tenses, modals, mass and unit, quantifiers and comparison structures.

Our aim is to help students use grammar actively in communication, so the main activities in the unit provide opportunities for role-play, problem-solving, and exchange of information.

Each Grammar unit ends with a section called *Focus on Form*, which provides a summary of the main structures of the unit, together with more controlled practice. It also contains a pronunciation exercise focusing on rhythm and stress.

A typical Grammar unit is shown on page 3d.

Vocabulary

The Vocabulary units deal with key topic areas (e.g. family relationships, travel, food and drink, clothes, health, work and free time). As in the Grammar units, the activities in Vocabulary units provide opportunities for communicative uses of language.

Each Vocabulary unit ends with an integrated reading and listening activity, designed to develop receptive skills.

A typical Vocabulary unit is shown on page 3e.

Study Pages

After every two units, there is a double spread of Study Pages, which contains:

- a *Focus* exercise, presenting a small, self-contained area of language (e.g. place prepositions, likes and dislikes), which is then recycled in later units
- a *Pronunciation* exercise
- a *Phrasebook* exercise, presenting functional language used in everyday conversation (e.g. buying tickets, arranging to meet)
- *Consolidation* exercises, which bring together material from previous units
- *Review* exercises.

A typical Study Pages spread is shown on page 3f.

Other features

After Unit 24, there is a *Final Review* section.

There is also an illustrated *Reference Section*, which includes a full summary of each unit, and *Tapescripts* of the Classroom Book recordings.

The Self-study Workbook

The Self-study Workbook provides back-up for work done in class and opportunities for further self-study. Like the Classroom Book, it has units and Study Pages.

Each unit contains:

- a range of homework exercises
- a listening activity
- a *Words* section, focusing on useful new vocabulary.

Each Study Pages spread contains:

- an informal progress test
- a *Phrasebook* exercise
- a *Writing* exercise, which guides students towards writing sentences and simple paragraphs.

There is also a Final Review, in the form of a written test.

Skills development

Speaking skills

Because *Language in Use* is concerned with active use of grammar and vocabulary, oral fluency is developed through many of the exercises in the Classroom Book.

Writing skills

Writing is developed through both the Classroom Book and the Self-study Workbook.

In the Classroom Book, writing is often an integrated part of the classroom activity, and takes the form of sentence-writing and note-making.

In addition, the *Writing* exercises in the Self-study Workbook guide students towards writing simple paragraphs; these exercises form part of an independent *Writing skills* syllabus which runs through the course.

Listening and reading skills

In the Classroom Book, listening and reading are used in each unit as a basis for presentation or as a stimulus for a speaking or writing activity.

Each Vocabulary unit also contains an extended activity which integrates reading and listening. This is designed to develop receptive skills.

In the Self-study Workbook, each unit contains a short listening task designed to develop particular listening strategies.

Pronunciation

There are two separate strands of pronunciation exercises running through the course:

– *How to say it* exercises (in Grammar units). These focus on rhythm, stress and weak forms, and are linked to the structures taught in the unit.
– *Pronunciation* exercises (in Study Pages). These focus on consonant clusters, weak forms, and the pronunciation of difficult words that appear in the units.

Functions

The *Phrasebook* exercises in the Study Pages cover a range of situational functions, such as introducing people, buying and ordering things, renting a room, making an appointment and asking for information.

Interactional functions are also practised in many of the activities in the Grammar and Vocabulary units.

Other more general functions (such as describing, giving personal information and narrating) are widely practised throughout the course.

Underlying principles

Flexibility

Language in Use takes account of the fact that no two language classes are alike: students vary in ability, age and interests, and may have different cultural and learning backgrounds; classes vary in size, physical layout and formality; teachers have different teaching styles; and learners may have widely differing ideas about what and how they need to learn. The course caters for some of these variations by:

– providing open-ended activities, so that classes can find their own level, and so that both weaker and stronger students have something to contribute
– encouraging students to contribute their own ideas and draw on their own knowledge and experience
– providing activities that can be adapted to a variety of different teaching styles and types of class.

Clarity

In any language course, it is important that students understand clearly what they are doing and why they are doing it, and have a clear idea of what they have learnt. In writing *Language in Use*, clarity has been a major consideration, both in the material designed for the student and in the teaching notes.

Recycling

At Pre-intermediate level, it is very important for learners to encounter the same language over and over again, and recycling of language is a major feature of *Language in Use Pre-intermediate*. This is done in several ways:

– Within each unit, language which is introduced in one exercise is picked up and given further practice in later exercises.
– The main structures in Grammar units are summarised and recycled in the *Focus on Form* exercises.
– Language which is taught in one unit is reintroduced and integrated into activities in later units.
– The key structures and vocabulary from each unit are consolidated in the Workbook exercises.
– The *Consolidation* and *Review* exercises in the Study Pages (every two units) recycle language from earlier units.
– The *Final Review* sections in both the Classroom Book and the Workbook review language from the whole course.

In the teaching notes, there is a 'language box' at the beginning of each exercise, which indicates what new language is introduced and what language is recycled, and refers back to units in *Language in Use Beginner*.

Learning and acquisition

We believe that both 'learning' and 'acquisition' are important elements in learning a language. In other words, it is useful to spend time consciously focusing on particular language items, and it is also important to provide opportunities for natural language acquisition through fluency activities.

Both these elements are therefore incorporated in *Language in Use*. Some activities involve careful use of language and focus mainly on accuracy; in others, students develop fluency through freer, more creative use of language. Similarly, some reading and listening tasks focus on specific language items, while others are concerned with fluency and skills development.

In addition, the dual syllabus gives opportunity for acquisition of both grammar and vocabulary. In Grammar units, the focus is on learning grammatical structures, and this allows vocabulary to be acquired naturally. In Vocabulary units, the focus is on learning vocabulary, and this allows the natural acquisition of grammatical structures.

Using the course

The teaching notes

The teaching notes are designed to help you to make the most appropriate use of the Classroom activities with your students. They are in two columns.

The main notes for each activity (in the left-hand column) give a simple and straightforward route through the material, and include explanations for students and ideas for blackboard presentations.

In the right-hand column are a variety of options and alternatives which include:

- suggestions for homework both before and after the lesson
- optional phases within the lesson such as extra practice, sentence-writing, comprehension checks, vocabulary work and role-play
- alternative procedures suitable for
  - classes which are better/weaker than average
  - larger/smaller classes
  - monolingual/mixed-nationality classes
  - more formal / less formal teaching situations
- notes giving explanations and examples of further language points arising from the main presentation.

The teaching notes for each unit also contain cross-references to exercises in the Self-study Workbook.

Using the Focus on Form exercises

The Focus on Form exercises at the end of each Grammar unit provide a summary of the main structures of the unit, plus extra, more controlled practice. They can be used in various ways:

- *Basic structure practice*

  Main exercise → Focus on Form exercise

  After finishing an exercise, use Focus on Form to focus on the main grammar point and give quick extra practice.

- *Summarising the main points*

  Whole unit → Focus on Form exercises

  After finishing a unit, use the Focus on Form page to summarise the main grammar points, and to give extra practice if necessary.

- *Revision*

  Series of units → Focus on Form exercises

  Come back to Focus on Form exercises as a way of revising grammar from previous units.

- *Homework*

  Some Focus on Form exercises can be set as homework, in addition to or instead of Workbook exercises.

Using the Self-study Workbook

There are various ways of using the exercises in the Self-study Workbook. You will probably want to adopt a mixture of these approaches.

Homework
All the Workbook exercises can be used for homework. In the teaching notes for each classroom activity, there are cross-references to suitable exercises.

Independent self-study
Allow students to work independently, choosing exercises that suit their individual needs. Students can use the Answer Key to check their answers, or give in their books periodically to be marked.

Classwork
Some Workbook exercises are also suitable for use in class. Two possibilities are the *Listening* and *Writing* exercises, which are often closely linked to classroom activities.

Short cuts through the course

Language in Use is designed to provide plenty of material, and it is possible to cover the course without doing every single exercise. If you are short of time, or if you wish to move through the units quickly with a good class, there are various short cuts you can take through the book:

- With a good class, leave the Focus on Form exercises for self-study.
- In the combined reading and listening activities, give the reading for homework, and do the listening in class.
- Limit the time you spend in class on material from the Self-study Workbook. If students have the version with Answer Key, they can mark their own work.

Grammar units

Grammar units contain:

– three activities that introduce key structures

– a Focus on Form page. This provides a summary of the main grammar points of the unit, together with more controlled practice, and a pronunciation exercise.

Presentation of the future for making predictions. Students make sentences with *will* and *won't*.

Presentation of *might*, in the context of making suggestions.

Part 2 – students make suggestions and give reasons with *might*.

Parts 2 & 3 focus on questions with *will*.

Presentation of probability expressions. Students listen to someone's answers to a questionnaire about the future.

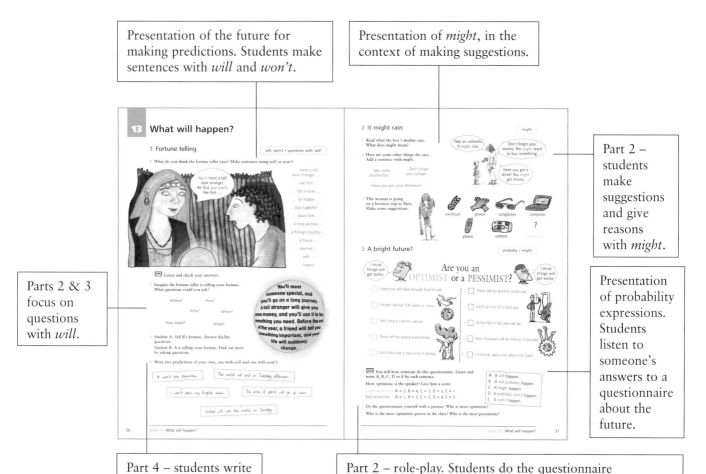

Part 4 – students write their own predictions.

Part 2 – role-play. Students do the questionnaire themselves, and find out if they are optimists or pessimists.

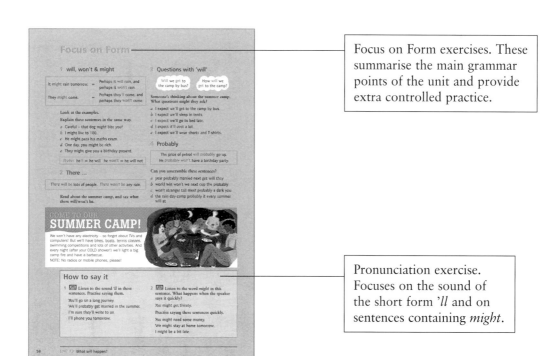

Focus on Form exercises. These summarise the main grammar points of the unit and provide extra controlled practice.

Pronunciation exercise. Focuses on the sound of the short form *'ll* and on sentences containing *might*.

Vocabulary units

Vocabulary units contain:

– three activities introducing a range of vocabulary linked by topic
– an integrated reading and listening activity, for skills development.

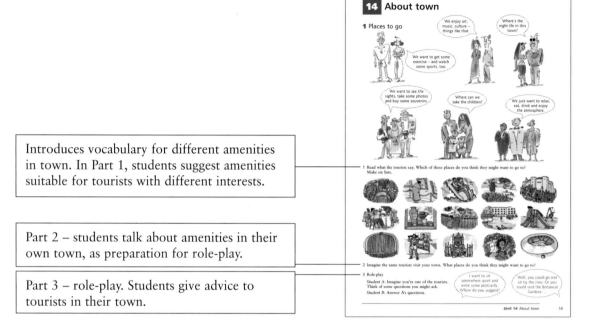

Introduces vocabulary for different amenities in town. In Part 1, students suggest amenities suitable for tourists with different interests.

Part 2 – students talk about amenities in their own town, as preparation for role-play.

Part 3 – role-play. Students give advice to tourists in their town.

Introduces vocabulary for talking about shops. Part 1 revises the names of shops introduced at Beginner level.

Integrated reading and listening activity.

Part 1 – reading. Students read about tourist attractions in Los Angeles and match them with photos.

Part 2 – useful ways of talking about goods and service in shops.

Part 3 – students write about a shop that they like.

Giving directions around town. Part 1 revises basic direction prepositions.

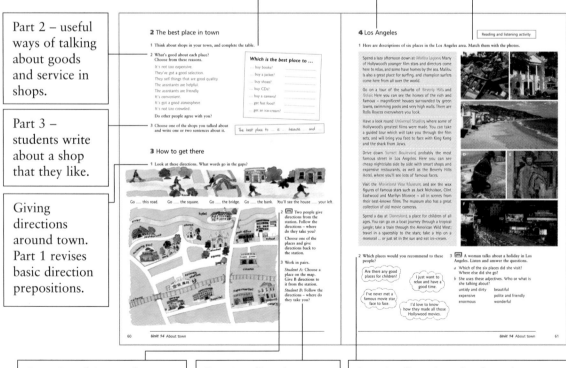

Parts 2 and 3 – students listen and follow directions on the map, then give directions themselves.

Part 3 – directions game. Can Student B follow Student A's directions?

Part 2 – listening. Students hear a woman talking about a holiday in Los Angeles, in which she visited some of the places in the reading text.

Study pages

Study Pages contain:

– a *Focus* exercise, presenting a self-contained area of language
– a *Pronunciation* exercise
  a *Phrasebook* exercise, presenting functional language
– *Consolidation* exercises, bringing together language from previous units
– *Review* exercises.

Focus exercise introduces future sentences with *If* (first conditional) and *When*.

Pronunciation exercise focuses on unusual words from earlier units.

Consolidation exercises:
– short answers for *yes/no* questions
– two-word phrasal verbs

Parts 2 and 3 – students make sentences from a table, then go on to freer practice.

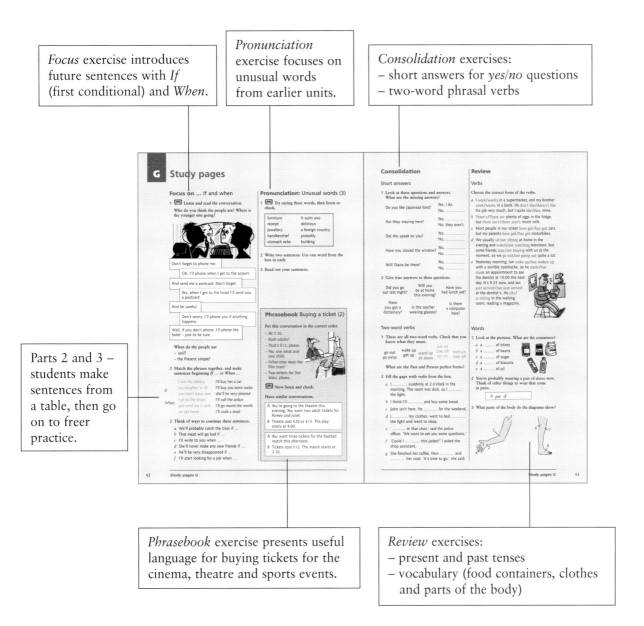

Phrasebook exercise presents useful language for buying tickets for the cinema, theatre and sports events.

Review exercises:
– present and past tenses
– vocabulary (food containers, clothes and parts of the body)

Guide to units

	Classroom Book	Self-study Workbook
1 **Things people do**	Saying what people do; saying how often you do things; talking about facts **Grammar:** Present simple tense; frequency expressions	Grammar exercises Listening: *The best time of the day*
2 **Family and friends**	Talking about family and other relationships **Vocabulary:** Family and friends; love and marriage	Vocabulary exercises Listening: *Relatives*
Study pages A	Focus on ... Personal data **Pronunciation:** Unusual words (1) **Phrasebook:** Introductions **Consolidation:** Possessives: *'s and s'*; *awake* and *wake up* Review	Check your progress Phrasebook Writing: *Joining sentences*
3 **Talking about places**	Describing places; saying what there is; asking about facilities **Grammar:** *There is/are*; *have/has got*	Grammar exercises Listening: *Rooms and flats*
4 **On the move**	Describing regular journeys; talking about public transport; asking for travel information **Vocabulary:** Arriving and leaving; ways of travelling; adjectives; times and costs	Vocabulary exercises Listening: *Trip to Stonehenge*
Study pages B	Focus on ... Where things are **Pronunciation:** Small words (1) **Phrasebook:** Buying a ticket (1) **Consolidation:** *early, in time, on time, late*; the time of day	Check your progress Phrasebook Writing: *Punctuation*
5 **Talking about now**	Talking about things happening 'now' and 'around now'; describing scenes **Grammar:** Present continuous tense; *There is/are + -ing*	Grammar exercises Listening: *We're busy*
6 **Food and drink**	Describing dishes and ingredients; saying what you eat; buying food **Vocabulary:** Food and drink; containers	Vocabulary exercises Listening: *Polish dishes*
Study pages C	Focus on ... Likes and dislikes **Pronunciation:** Clusters (1) **Phrasebook:** In a café **Consolidation:** Simple and continuous; *get* Review	Check your progress Phrasebook Writing: *Reference*

	Classroom Book	Self-study Workbook
7 **The past**	Talking about past events; saying when things happened **Grammar:** Past simple tense; time expressions	Grammar exercises Listening: *A man and a penguin*
8 **A place to live**	Talking about houses **Vocabulary:** Houses and flats; locations; rooms and furniture; adjectives	Vocabulary exercises Listening: *Favourite rooms*
Study pages D	Focus on ... *Both* and *neither* **Pronunciation:** Small words (2) **Phrasebook:** Finding a room **Consolidation:** Past time expressions; *very, quite ...* Review	Check your progress Phrasebook Writing: *Joining ideas*
9 **I've done it!**	Talking about things that have just happened; asking about preparations **Grammar:** Present perfect tense; past participles	Grammar exercises Listening: *What has happened?*
10 **Clothes**	Talking about clothes; buying clothes; saying when you wear things **Vocabulary:** Clothes; colours, sizes and prices	Vocabulary exercises Listening: *Working clothes*
Study pages E	Focus on ... *Mine, yours ...* **Pronunciation:** Unusual words (2) **Phrasebook:** Paying for things **Consolidation:** Present perfect and Past simple; *'s* Review	Check your progress Phrasebook Writing: *Sequence (1)*
11 **Quantity**	Talking about quantity; saying there is too much and not enough **Grammar:** *a/some/any*; quantity expressions; *How much/many ...?*; *too much/many* and *not enough*	Grammar exercises Listening: *A healthy diet*
12 **How do you feel?**	Talking about aches and pains; saying what you do when you're ill; going to the doctor **Vocabulary:** aches and pains; parts of the body; remedies; doctors and medicine	Vocabulary exercises Listening: *Ouch!*
Study pages F	Focus on ... *For* and *since* **Pronunciation:** Small words (3) **Phrasebook:** Making an appointment **Consolidation:** *a little, a few, very little, very few*; *well* Review	Check your progress Phrasebook Writing: *Lists*

Classroom Book		Self-study Workbook
13 **What will** **happen?**	Making predictions; giving advice **Grammar:** *will, won't* and *might*; *will probably* and *probably won't*	Grammar exercises Listening: *Giving blood*
14 **About** **town**	Where to go in towns; describing shops and restaurants; giving directions **Vocabulary:** Places to go in towns; shopping; direction prepositions	Vocabulary exercises Listening: *Living in London*
Study **pages G**	**Focus on ...** *If* (first conditional) and *when* **Pronunciation:** Unusual words (3) **Phrasebook:** Buying a ticket (2) **Consolidation:** Short answers; two-word verbs **Review**	Check your progress Phrasebook Writing: *Reason and contrast*
15 **Comparing** **things**	Making comparisons; expressing preferences; describing outstanding features **Grammar:** Comparative adjectives; *than*; superlative adjectives	Grammar exercises Listening: *The most and the fewest*
16 **Free time**	Talking about leisure activities; explaining how sports are played **Vocabulary:** Leisure activities; enjoyment and ability; sports	Vocabulary exercises Listening: *Rock climbing*
Study **pages H**	**Focus on ...** Ability **Pronunciation:** Clusters (2) **Phrasebook:** Asking where **Consolidation:** *more, less* and *fewer*; *go* and *play* **Review**	Check your progress Phrasebook Writing: *Sequence (2)*
17 **Rules and** **advice**	Giving rules; talking about obligation; giving advice **Grammar:** *have to* and *don't have to*; *can* and *can't*; *must* and *mustn't*; *should* and *shouldn't*	Grammar exercises Listening: *Radio phone-in*
18 **A day's** **work**	Talking about jobs; saying why you would(n't) enjoy different jobs; describing a career **Vocabulary:** Names of jobs; features of jobs; stages of a career	Vocabulary exercises Listening: *A security guard*
Study **pages I**	**Focus on ...** *Someone, anyone* **Pronunciation:** Words with *-ion* **Phrasebook:** Renting things **Consolidation:** Verbs with prepositions; *do* **Review**	Check your progress Phrasebook Writing: *Letter writing*

	Classroom Book	Self-study Workbook
19 **Telling stories**	Talking about past events and their circumstances; telling stories; describing a scene in the past **Grammar:** Past continuous tense; Past simple tense; *when* and *while*	**Grammar exercises** **Listening:** *The wedding video*
20 **People**	Describing people's physical appearance; saying roughly how old people are; describing people's character **Vocabulary:** Physical characteristics; age; character adjectives	**Vocabulary exercises** **Listening:** *Family picture*
Study pages J	**Focus on ...** Nationalities **Pronunciation:** Unusual words (4) **Phrasebook:** Personal questions **Consolidation:** *while* and *during*; *with* Review	**Check your progress** **Phrasebook** **Writing:** *Relative clauses (1)*
21 **Future plans**	Talking about intentions and plans; talking about future arrangements **Grammar:** *going to*; *will*; Present continuous tense; future time expressions	**Grammar exercises** **Listening:** *Plans for the evening*
22 **Around the world**	Saying where things are in the world; saying what places are like; asking about tourist destinations **Vocabulary:** Countries and continents; geographical features and location; climate	**Vocabulary exercises** **Listening:** *Living in a hot climate*
Study pages K	**Focus on ...** Nothing, no one, nowhere **Pronunciation:** Consonant links **Phrasebook:** Arranging to meet **Consolidation:** Using the Present continuous; *It's ...* Review	**Check your progress** **Phrasebook** **Writing:** *Relative clauses (2)*
23 **Past and present**	Talking about changes; talking about experiences **Grammar:** Present perfect tense; *still* and *yet*; *ever* and *never*	**Grammar exercises** **Listening:** *Have you ever ...?*
24 **Arts and entertainment**	Talking about cultural events; talking about TV programmes **Vocabulary:** Art and culture; writers, artists and performers; television programmmes	**Vocabulary exercises** **Listening:** *TV survey*
Final review		

1 Things people do

1 Couples

Present simple

1 Think of things people do in their free time. Use these verbs:

listen to ...   read ...   watch ...   visit ...   go (out) to ...

2 These three students are at a British university. Read what they say about themselves.

Joanna

Susanne

Tanya

I always get up early and I go to bed early too – I'm usually in bed by 11.00. I don't watch TV. I often go out in the evening with friends. Or sometimes friends come round to my flat, and we spend the evening there.

I often listen to pop music on the radio, and I watch TV a lot – films, mainly. I don't read very much – magazines sometimes, but not books. I like going out with friends. I usually go to bed late – around 12.00 or even later.

I really like staying at home. Sometimes I read or listen to music – classical music, mostly. I don't watch TV very much, but I usually watch the news, or sometimes films. And I often study in the evening.

Now read about their boyfriends. Can you match the girlfriends and boyfriends?

Mark goes out a lot. He visits friends or goes to parties or cafés. He doesn't like staying at home. When he's at home he usually studies, or he watches films or sport on TV. He usually goes to bed quite late.

John gets up very early and studies before breakfast. In the evening he usually stays at home. He reads a lot – books, newspapers and magazines. He sometimes listens to music, but he doesn't watch TV.

Richard likes rock music and jazz. He listens to music at home, and he often goes out to concerts and clubs. He goes to bed late, and he sleeps a lot at the weekend. He doesn't like getting up early!

Listen and check your answers.

3 You are going to interview another student. Look at the texts and think of some questions.

Work in pairs. Find out about your partner. Ask and answer questions.

4 Write a few sentences about your partner. Can other students guess who it is?

Do you watch TV a lot?

Do you get up late?

▬▬▬ likes listening to music. She likes pop music and classical music, but she doesn't like jazz. She often watches TV and

This unit covers the main uses of the Present simple tense, for talking about repeated activities and things that are generally true. It revises the basic forms of the Present simple (positive and negative sentences, *yes/no* questions and *Wh-* questions), and introduces frequency expressions.

1 Couples

In this exercise students read about three female students and their boyfriends, and match the couples according to their lifestyles. It focuses on the Present simple for talking about everyday activities.

> ➤ Focus on Form: Exercises 1, 2 & 3
> ➤ Workbook: Exercise A, Listening

> *Key structures:* Present simple tense (1st and 3rd person singular); negative forms; yes/no questions. *Vocabulary:* common verbs, leisure activities, types of music, TV programmes. (→ Beginner Units 7, 9, 22.)

1 Vocabulary elicitation; presentation of Present simple tense

- Look at the verbs and ask students to think of things people do in their free time. Possible answers:

listen to music, the radio	*visit* friends, relatives
read a magazine, a novel	*go (out)* to the cinema, a café, a concert
watch TV, a film, the news	

  If you like, build up a list of phrases on the board.

- If necessary, present the positive and negative forms of the Present simple:

I listen		I don't	
He listens	to music.	He doesn't	listen to music.

Note
This exercise assumes that students are already familiar with the Present simple tense; it aims to remind students of the basic forms and give practice in using them.

Language note
Some of the sentences include the frequency adverbs *usually* and *often*. Frequency adverbs are practised in Exercise 2.

2 Reading & matching; listening to check

- Look at the pictures of the three female students and read what they say. Present any new words or phrases (e.g. *early, late*).
- Give time for students to read the texts about the boyfriends. Then read through them together, explaining any new words (e.g. *rock music*). Ask students who they think the couples are, and why they think so.
- ⬛ Play the recording and check the answers. Answers:

  Joanna and Richard, Susanne and Mark, Tanya and John.

Vocabulary option
Use the texts to introduce vocabulary for types of music (e.g. *classical music, pop music, rock music, jazz*) and TV programmes (e.g. *the news, sport, film*).

⬛ The tapescript is on page T10.

3 Presentation of yes/no questions; pairwork practice

- Remind students how to form *yes/no* questions:

I <u>*like*</u> music.
<u>**Do**</u> you <u>*like*</u> music?

- Ask students to look at the texts (and the phrases on the board) and suggest other questions. Possible questions:

Do you listen to the radio?	Do you get up early?
Do you like pop/classical music?	Do you go to bed early/late?
Do you go out a lot?	Do you work/study in the evening?
Do you usually stay at home?	Do you often go to concerts/cafés/clubs?
Do you often watch TV?	Do you watch the news/films/sport on TV?

- To demonstrate the pairwork activity, choose one student and ask him/her a few questions. Then get the student to ask you similar questions.
- Students work in pairs. They take it in turn to ask each other questions. If you like, ask them to make brief notes in preparation for the writing stage (e.g. *TV – yes; music – sometimes, in the evening*).

Presentation option: better classes
If you like, show structures with *like* + noun or *-ing*, and get students to use them during this stage:

I like	music.
	listening to music.

These forms are practised in Study Pages C, Focus, page 30.

4 Writing sentences; guessing

- Students write a few sentences about their partner. Make sure students use the 3rd person forms correctly (they can use the texts about the boyfriends as a model).
- Collect the sentences, and read some of them out. See if the class can guess who they describe.

Homework option
Students write the sentences for homework. Collect them and read them out in the next lesson.

2 I usually …

This exercise introduces a range of frequency adverbs which are often used with the Present simple. Students use them to talk about habits.

▶ Workbook: Exercise B

> *Adverbs:* always, (not) usually, sometimes, never; How often? *Vocabulary:* walk, to work/school, make (a bed).   (→ Beginner Unit 7, Study Pages D.)

1 Presentation of frequency adverbs

- Read the examples, and get students to help make a list of frequency adverbs on the board, putting them in order of frequency:

> *always   usually   sometimes   not usually   never*

Point out that:
- these adverbs normally come just before the main verb.
- in the negative, we say *I don't usually, He doesn't usually …*, etc.

He	*usually has* *doesn't usually have*	*breakfast in bed.*

- Ask the question round the class. Students answer with complete sentences.

2 Personalisation: making true sentences

- Read through the items, and tell the class about yourself, adding a few comments (e.g. *I usually sleep with my window open – sometimes in very cold weather I close it, but I usually sleep with it open.*)
- Students do the exercise in pairs. As a round-up, ask students to tell you about their partner.

3 What do you know?

This exercise is in the form of a quiz, in which students read and answer Wh- *questions, then make up similar questions of their own from prompts.*

> *Key structures:* Wh- questions. *Vocabulary:* celebrate. (→ Beginner Unit 9.)

1 Reading & answering quiz questions; presentation of Wh- questions

- Ask the questions round the class, or let students work through them in pairs and then go through the answers. Answers:

Butcher: meat   *Chinese New Year:* January and February   *Penguins:* Antarctica
Sushi bar: rice and fish   *Valentine cards:* 14th February   *Balalaika:* Russia
Champagne: France

- Remind students how to form *Wh-* questions:

Where	*does he* *do they*	*live?*

2 Practice: asking & answering questions

- Give students letters, A or B, and ask them to look only at their own page, either 105 or 106. Establish what the questions should be (but without discussing the answers at this point):

A's questions: 1 Where do pandas come from? 2 What does a baker sell?
3 When do Americans celebrate Independence Day?
B's questions: 1 Where do elephants come from? 2 What does a greengrocer sell?
3 When do Americans celebrate Hallowe'en?

- In pairs, students ask their questions. Their partner tries to answer them. Then go through the answers together. Answers:

A: 1 China 2 bread 3 4th July
B: 1 India and Africa 2 fruit and vegetables 3 31st October

3 Extension: making up quiz questions

- Working alone or in pairs, students think up a question of their own.
- Students read out their questions and other students try to answer them.

Note
If you like, introduce *often* and *not often* here as well. Point out the slight difference in meaning between *often* and *usually*:
– I often go out in the evening. (= I go out a lot.)
– I usually go out in the evening. (= I go out most evenings.)

Option: How often …? questions
Present questions with *How often do you …?* and go through the items, asking students to make questions (e.g. *How often do you sleep with the window open?*). In the pairwork stage, they ask and answer questions.

Homework option
Students write the sentences for homework.

▶ Focus on Form: Exercises 2, 3 & 4
▶ Workbook: Exercise C

Background notes
On *St Valentine's Day* (14th February), people in Britain and the USA send cards (often without their name in) to people they admire or love.
On *Independence Day* (4th July), Americans celebrate the independence of the USA.
On *Hallowe'en* night (31st October) people used to believe that the spirits of the dead returned. Nowadays it is mainly a children's celebration.

Homework option
Students write questions for homework, and ask them in the next lesson.

2 I usually …

Frequency words

1 Read the bubbles. Who walks to work the most often? Put the people in order.

A I don't usually walk to work. I usually go by bike.

B I never walk to work – I live 25 kilometres away!

I always walk to work. My office is only in the next street.

C

D I sometimes walk to work, but I sometimes go by bus.

E I usually walk to work. It's a nice way to start the day.

What about you? How often do you walk to work or school?

2 Look at these sentences. Add frequency words so that they are true for you.

a I sleep with the window open.

b I make my own bed.

c I have a big breakfast.

d I sleep in the afternoon.

e I drink wine with my evening meal.

f I read in bed.

3 What do you know?

Questions

1 Read these quiz questions. Can you choose the right answers?

PEOPLE AND JOBS

What does a butcher sell?
- newspapers
- clothes
- meat

FESTIVALS

When do Chinese people celebrate New Year?
- January and February
- March and April
- May and June

ANIMALS

Where do penguins live?
- Antarctica
- Siberia
- Iceland

FOOD AND DRINK

What do people eat in a sushi bar?
- rice and fish
- burgers and chips
- pasta and chicken

FESTIVALS

When do people send Valentine cards?
- 14th January
- 14th February
- 14th March

MUSIC

Where do people play the balalaika?
- Greece
- Russia
- China

FOOD AND DRINK

Where does champagne come from?
- Italy
- France
- Spain

2 *Student A*: Turn to page 105. Ask B your questions.
Student B: Turn to page 106. Ask A your questions.

Where do kangaroos come from: Africa, Australia or America?

Australia.

3 Work with a partner. Write a quiz question of your own.

---

1 Verb + s

Complete the table, then read out the text.
Which verbs need -s?

play	→	plays
work	→	....
drive	→	....
speak	→	....
watch	→	watches
go	→	....
teach	→	....
wash	→	....
study	→	studies
fly	→	....
have	→	has

I (have) a sister and a brother.
My sister (work) for a big American company. She (drive) a Cadillac, and (fly) to New York every month.
My brother (speak) four languages. He (teach) Spanish at University and he (go) to Mexico for his holidays. He also (play) the piano in a band.
And me? I'm a student. I (study) during the day, and I (watch) TV in the evening. And at the weekend I (wash) dishes in a restaurant.

2 Negatives

Fish fly.

They don't fly – they swim.

The American President lives in the Kremlin.

He doesn't live in the Kremlin – he lives in the White House.

Correct these sentences.

a Lions eat fruit.
b In Mexico, people speak Portuguese.
c The British Prime Minister lives in Edinburgh.
d In America, people drive on the left.
e Kangaroos come from South Africa.

3 Yes/no questions

Do you walk to work?	Yes, I do. No, I don't.
Does she walk to work?	Yes, she does. No, she doesn't.

Does she like Chinese food?

Do you like Chinese food?

Yes, I do.

Yes, she does.

Work in threes. Use these ideas.

a ... drive a car?   d ... eat meat?
b ... play the piano?   e ... speak German?
c ... like cheese?   f ... work on Sundays?

4 Wh- questions

'X' is your partner. Ask questions to find the missing information.

a X lives in ...
b X gets up at ...
c X eats ... for breakfast.
d X goes to ... at weekends.
e X speaks ... languages.

Where do you live?

Where does (Bill Clinton) live?

Now ask about a famous person. Make up the answers!

How to say it

1 🔲 Listen to *doesn't* and *don't* in these sentences. Practise saying them.

He doesn't like staying at home.
She doesn't speak French.
They don't go out very often.
I don't play the piano.

2 🔲 Listen to the -s and -es endings.

drives	drinks	watches
reads	works	teaches
listens	gets	washes

Practise saying these sentences.

He drives a car.
She drinks Coca-Cola.
He watches TV every night.

Focus on Form

1 Verb + s

- Students complete the table. Answers:

  works, drives, speaks; goes, teaches, washes; flies.

  Point out the different groups:
  - verb + -s
  - verb + -es (after -ch, -sh, -ss, -x and vowels)
  - -y changes to -ies
  - have changes to has (irregular).

- Students decide the forms of the verbs in the text. Then read the text round the class. Answers:

  I have …
  My sister works … She drives … and flies …
  My brother speaks … He teaches … he goes … He also plays …
  I study … I watch … I wash …

2 Negatives

- Do the exercise round the class or as pairwork. Answers:

  a They don't eat fruit. They eat meat.
  b They don't speak Portuguese. They speak Spanish.
  c He doesn't live in Edinburgh. He lives in London.
  d They don't drive on the left. They drive on the right.
  e They don't come from South Africa. They come from Australia.

3 Yes/no questions

- Look at the picture and check that students understand what is happening: The woman asks a question with *Does she …?*, the boy changes it into a question with *Do you …?* over the phone, then passes the answer back.

- Establish what the questions will be:

  a Does she drive a car? Do you drive a car?
  b Does she play the piano? Do you play the piano?
  c Does she like cheese? Do you like cheese?
  d Does she eat meat? Do you eat meat?
  e Does she speak German? Do you speak German?
  f Does she go to church? Do you go to church?

- Either divide students into groups of three to do the exercise, or do it with the whole class, choosing three students each time. Students should give true answers (*Yes, I do* or *No, I don't*).

4 Wh- questions

- Establish what the questions should be:

  a Where do you live?
  b When (What time) do you get up?
  c What do you eat for breakfast?
  d Where do you go (to) at weekends?
  e How many languages do you speak?

- Pairwork. Students ask each other the questions, and note down the answers.

- As a round-up, ask students what they found out.

- Role-play. Choose a student, and ask him/her to take the role of a famous person. Other students ask the same questions again, and he or she makes up suitable answers.

How to say it

1 Pronunciation of 'doesn't' & 'don't' in sentences

- [cassette] Play the recording. Pause after each sentence and get students to repeat it. Focus on the link between the end of *doesn't* and *don't* and the next word:

  /dʌznt‿laɪk/, /dʌznt‿spiːk/, /dəʊnt‿gəʊ/, /dəʊnt‿pleɪ/.

2 Pronunciation of '-s' & '-es' endings

- [cassette] Play each group of words and focus on the different sounds:

  Group 1: the -s is pronounced /z/.
  Group 2: the -s is pronounced /s/.
  Group 3: the -es is pronounced /ɪz/.

- Play the sentences and get students to practise them.

[cassette] Tapescript for Exercise 1: *Couples*

1 Yeah, we like the same things, mostly. We both like music, so we listen to music a lot. Richard always goes to rock concerts, and I often go with him. And, yeah, we go out a lot together – we both like staying up late, so that's good.

2 Mark and I go out quite a lot – we have the same group of friends, so we all go out together usually. I get up early and go to bed early. Mark's more a late night person, I'd say – he often stays out really late.

3 John gets up early, which I don't do – I always get up late. And he usually works early in the morning, but I usually work late at night – so that's a bit of a problem, really.

2

This unit covers three areas of language used for talking about relationships:
– talking about members of your family and giving details about them
– talking about other people you know (e.g. *friends, neighbours, room-mates*)
– talking about events in a relationship (e.g. *meet, go out together, get married*).
The reading and listening activity is about identical twins.

1 Photo album

This exercise introduces basic vocabulary for talking about relatives and other people you know well, e.g. friends, neighbours.

> Key vocabulary: older/younger (brother), boyfriend/girlfriend, neighbour, flat-mate, parents, grandmother. (→ Beginner Unit 2.)

1 Matching task; vocabulary presentation

- Introduce some of the key vocabulary by asking a few questions round the class, e.g.

  – *Do you know your neighbours?*
  – *Do you live with your parents? Or have you got a flat-mate?*
  – *Who's got a brother? Is he older or younger than you?*

  Do not go into too much detail about the family at this point, as this is dealt with in more detail in Exercise 2.

- Look at the photos, and ask students to identify the young woman.

- Read through the list and establish which are relatives and which aren't. (Answers: older brother, younger brother, grandmother, parents.) Use this to present the word *relative*.

- In pairs, students identify the people in the photos. Then discuss the answers together.

2 Listening to check; detailed listening

- Play the recording, in which the woman describes four of the six photos. Pause after each description, and ask students to identify the photos and the people in them. Answers:

  Photo C: herself, her flat-mate and her boyfriend
  Photo D: her grandmother
  Photo E: herself, her younger brother
  Photo F: herself, her boyfriend, her older brother and his girlfriend, her flat-mate

- Discuss who the other photos show. Answers:

  Photo A: her neighbours
  Photo B: her parents

- [cassette icon] Ask students what they know about each of the other people (e.g. *her boyfriend is called David*). Then play the recording again to check.

3 Speaking activity: showing family photos

- Ask students who have family photos to show them to the class and say who the people are. If a lot of students have brought photos, they can show them to their partner first; then some students show their photos to the whole class.

Before the lesson
Ask students to bring a few photos of family or friends to the class, to talk about in Part 3.

Language notes
A *flat-mate* is someone who shares your flat. Similar words: *room-mate, class-mate*.

Your *boyfriend/girlfriend* is someone you have a special relationship with. For other friends we say *a friend (of mine)*.

Relative is a general word for someone in your family. We can also say *relation*: this means the same.

Optional lead-in
Bring in some photos of your family and friends, and show them to the class.

Alternative activity
If students can't (or forget to!) bring in photos, pass photos of your family and friends round the class. Ask students to guess who they are, then tell them something about them.

[cassette icon] Tapescript for Exercise 1: *Photo album*

This is Julie and David and me. That's David in the middle – he's my boyfriend. And that's Julie on the left. She's my flat-mate – she's a secretary.

Now this is my grandmother. She's nearly 80 now. This picture was at a wedding, I think.

Oh, then this one, this is another picture of my boyfriend, David. And that's my brother, in the black jacket – he's 23, he works for television. And next to him is his girlfriend – she's an actress.

And this is me with my younger brother – he's 13.

2 Family and friends

1 Photo album

1 These are photos of a young woman with some of her relatives and friends. Which person do you think she is?

Here are the other people in the photos. Which are relatives, and which aren't?

- her older brother
- her younger brother
- her boyfriend
- her grandmother
- her flat-mate
- her parents
- her brother's girlfriend
- her neighbours

Can you find them in the photos?

2 🔲 Listen to the tape.

Which photos does the woman describe? What does she say about each person?

3 Bring in a few photos of your family and friends. Show them to other students, and say who the people are.

This is my …

Her name's …

He works in a …

He's … years old.

She's a …

They live in …

2 Relatives

My sister's husband

My father's sister and her children

Male	Female
....	grandmother
uncle	....
nephew	....
....	sister-in-law
....	

My sister's daughter   ME AND MY PARENTS   My mother's father

1 **Who are the people in the picture? Complete the table.**

2 **How many relatives do you have? Make a list.**

> 0 grandparents
> 1 uncle
> 3 cousins

3 **Talk about members of your family. Who's …**

... the oldest?

... the youngest?

... the nicest?

... the richest?

... the most interesting?

3 Love story

1 **These expressions are all connected with love and marriage. Put them in a likely order.**

Do other students have the same answer?

have children   get engaged   meet

get divorced   get married

fall in love   go out together

2 **Look at this story. Can you fill the gaps?**

It's 1939. A young American, Philip, is travelling through France. He a Marie, and they b immediately.

They c for a few months, and then he asks her to marry him. She says yes, and they d .

The war starts. Philip goes back to the USA. He writes, but Marie doesn't receive his letters.

After the war, Philip e an American woman. They f and they g , two girls and a boy.

Marie gets a job in Paris. She h a man there, and they i . But they aren't happy together, and after two years they j . After that, Marie lives alone.

Philip's wife dies in 1980, and in 1985, he goes to Paris on holiday. He goes into a café and sees Marie at the next table. They k again …

… and a few months later, they l .

3 **Cover the text and try to tell the story yourself.**

2 Relatives

This exercise focuses in more detail on the vocabulary of the family, and gives students practice in talking about their own relatives.

> *Key vocabulary:* grandfather, grandmother, aunt, uncle, nephew, niece, brother-in-law, sister-in-law, cousin. *Recycled language:* basic 'family' vocabulary, superlative adjectives, possessive forms. (→ Beginner Units 2, 21, Study Pages A.)

1 Vocabulary presentation

- Write the table on the board. Then look at the picture, and establish who the people are. Answers (left to right):

  his brother-in-law, his niece, his grandfather, his aunt and his cousins

- Add the missing words to the table:

grandfather	grandmother
uncle	aunt
nephew	niece
brother-in-law	sister-in-law
	cousin

2 Making a list; comparing

- To show what to do, write a list of your own relatives on the board.
- Students make a list of their relatives. They then compare their list with their partner's.
- As a round-up, find out who has the most (living) grandparents, the most cousins, etc.

3 Speaking activity

- To introduce the activity, answer one of the questions yourself, e.g. *The oldest person in my family is my grandmother. She's 89 years old, but she still drives a car.* Then ask the same question round the class.
- In pairs or groups, students tell each other about members of their family.
- As a round-up, ask a few students to tell the class about their relatives.

➤ Workbook: Exercise A, Listening

> *Review option*
> Go through the basic words for the family, and write them on the board: *mother, father, brother, sister, parents, children, son, daughter.*

> *Language note*
> A *cousin* (male or female) may be the child of your aunt or uncle, or any more distant relative.

> *Note*
> This gives incidental practice of superlative forms. These are dealt with fully in Unit 15, page 65.

> *Alternative: writing*
> Students write two or three sentences about one of their relatives. They then read out their sentences in turn.

3 Love story

This exercise introduces a range of language connected with love, relationships and marriage.

> *Key phrases:* meet, get engaged, get married, get divorced, have children, go out together, fall in love.

1 Sequencing task; vocabulary presentation

- Look at the expressions with the class. Write them on the board, asking students to suggest what order to put them in. As you do this, check that students know what they mean. More than one answer is of course possible – discuss different possibilities.

2 Reading & gap-filling

- Give time for students to read the text and decide how to fill the gaps. They could do this alone or with a partner. Go through the answers together, and present any new words (e.g. *immediately, receive, alone*). Expected answers:

  a meets *b* fall in love *c* go out together *d* get engaged *e* meets
  f get married *g* have children *h* meets *i* get married *j* get divorced
  k fall in love *l* get married

3 Activation: telling the story

- Ask students to cover the text. Ask them to try telling the story round the class, with one student saying a sentence and then another continuing.

➤ Workbook: Exercise B

> *Language note*
> You *get engaged* to someone (action); then you *are engaged* (state). Similar pairs are *get married/be married, get divorced/be divorced.*

> *Pairwork option*
> Students think of a possible order in pairs. Then discuss the answers together.

> *Note*
> These verbs are used here in the 'historic present'. This is commonly used in English to tell informal stories, jokes, etc., and in cartoon strips. With a good class, you could also teach the Past simple forms (*met, fell in love, got married*, etc.).

4 Identical twins

This combined reading and listening activity is about identical twins. The reading is about twins who grow up separately but show similar characteristics. The listening is about one pair of identical twins who grew up apart.

> *New vocabulary (reading):* twins, identical, the same, grow up, both, after-shave, toothpaste, unusual, moustache, electrician, firefighter, frighten, sneeze.
> *New vocabulary (listening):* turn out, obviously, mechanic, incredible.

1 Introduction

- To introduce the topic, write the word *twins* on the board, and establish what it means. Then write *identical twins* on the board, and establish what that means (= twins from the same egg; they look almost exactly the same).

> **Optional discussion**
> Ask if anyone knows any identical twins; ask in what ways they are the same, and in what ways they are different.

2 Reading & matching

- Read the first part of the text, and ask a few questions to check, e.g. *What do identical twins do? What about food? What about clothes?* etc.
- Talk briefly about why identical twins do the same things. Get the class to give you the two possible reasons:

  1 Because they're twins, so they're naturally very similar.
  2 Because they grow up together; they're in the same family, they spend their time together.

  Ask students which reason they think is more important.
- Look at the pictures, and establish what they show. Use this to present key vocabulary, e.g.

  A a *pen*   B someone opening a *birthday present*   C *fingers* with *rings*
  D someone *sneezing*   E two boys giving *presents* to each other   F an *electrician*, with a *moustache* and *glasses*   G a *magazine*   H someone opening a *birthday present*   I someone *cleaning his teeth*, with *toothpaste*   J a *firefighter*

- Students read the text, and match the twins with the pictures.
- Go through the answers together, and present any other new words. Answers:

  Tony and Roger: A, I   *Tina and Jane*: C, E   *Jerry and Mark*: F, J
  Paula and Kitty: B, H   *Oscar and Jack*: D, G

3 Listening

- Look at the pictures of Jim Lewis and Jim Springer. Explain that they first met when they were 40. Some things about them are the same and some things are different.
- ▭ Play the recording, pausing from time to time. Students listen and write *S* or *D* in the boxes.
- Go through the answers together. Answers:

  a S (They're both called Jim)   g S (They were both called Toy)
  b D (Lewis and Springer)   h D
  c D (Twice and three times)   i D (Mechanic and shop assistant)
  d S (Linda and Betty)   j S (They both drive a Chevrolet)
  e S   k S (They go to the same beach in Florida)
  f S (They both had dogs)

> ▭ Tapescript for Exercise 4: *Identical twins*
>
> Did you read about these twins from Minnesota? They're 40 years old, and they just met for the first time. They grew up in different families, never saw each other until … a few weeks ago, I think it was. And it turns out that they both have the same name, they're both called Jim. One of them married twice, the other one married three times – but their first wives were both called Linda, and their second wives were both called Betty. And they both have sons with the same name, and they both had dogs at some time, and their dogs both had the same name, they were both called Toy. They live in different towns, obviously, and they have different jobs, I think – yeah, one's a mechanic and the other one's a shop assistant. But they both drive the same kind of car – Chevrolet, I think it was. Oh yeah, and they both go to the same place in Florida for their holidays, the same beach even – though they never met there. Absolutely incredible.

4 Identical twins

1 What are *twins*? What are *identical twins*?

2 Read the first part of the text. Why do you think identical twins often do the same things?

Now read about the twins in the text. Can you match them with the pictures? (There are two pictures for each pair of twins.)

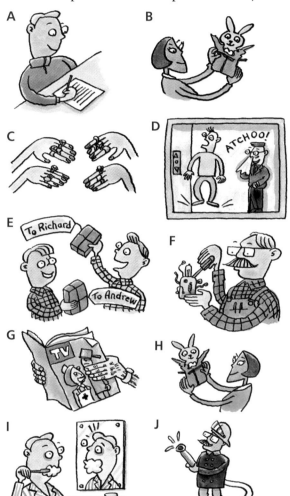

A B

C D

E F

G H

I J

Twin stories

Do you know any identical twins? Identical twins look the same, and they often do the same things – wear the same clothes, listen to the same music, eat the same food, and even do the same jobs.

But why? Because they're twins? Or because they grow up together in the same family?

Well, here are some twins who *didn't* grow up together. They went to live in different families when they were babies, and they met for the first time when they were adults.

• Tony and Roger met when they were 24. They both use the same after-shave, smoke the same cigarettes and use the same kind of toothpaste. And they both hold a pen in the same, unusual way.

• Tina and Jane were 36 when they first met. They wear seven rings on their fingers. One has a son called Andrew Richard, and the other has a son called Richard Andrew.

• Jerry and Mark are 40. They both have big moustaches, and wear the same kind of glasses. They're both electricians, and in their free time they work as firefighters.

• Paula is 26. After she met her twin Kitty for the first time, she sent her a birthday present. When she opened her own birthday present from Kitty, it was exactly the same thing.

• Oscar and Jack met when they were 65. They both read magazines from the back to the front, and when they're in a lift, they like to frighten the other people by sneezing loudly.

3 ▭ You will hear someone talking about Jim Lewis and Jim Springer.

Which of these are the same, and which are different? Write S (= same) or D (= different).

a ⟨S⟩ their first name

b ⟨D⟩ their last name

c ☐ number of times they married

d ☐ the names of their wives

e ☐ the name of their son

f ☐ the kind of pet they had

g ☐ their pet's name

h ☐ their home town

i ☐ their job

j ☐ their car

k ☐ where they go on holiday

Jim Lewis

Jim Springer

A Study pages

Focus on ... Personal data

1 🔊 Someone gives information about himself. Listen and complete the form.

Name: *Tim* ....

Nationality: ....

Date of birth: ....

Address: .... *Street* ....

....

Phone number: *0117* ....

Make of car: ....

Car number: ....

2 Answer these questions.

a How do you say these numbers?

 38   97   125   464   703

b How do you say this telephone number?

 01226 408199

c How do you say these dates?

 12th Dec 1987   31st Aug 2001

 9th Feb 1990   26th Nov 1975

d How do you spell these words?

 EDINBURGH MOSCOW BRAZIL

 TURKEY JAPAN GREECE

3 Work with a partner.

Student A: Give B information to fill in the form.
Student B: Write the information in the form.

Name: ....

Nationality: ....

Date of birth: ....

Address: ....

....

Phone number: ....

Make of car: ....

Car number: ....

Now check the form. Is everything correct?

Pronunciation: Unusual words (1)

1 🔊 Try saying these words, then listen to check.

often	January
listen	February
usually	breakfast
interesting	neighbour
languages	nationality

2 Write a sentence. Use at least two of the words from the box.

3 Read out your sentence.

Phrasebook: Introductions

Fill the gaps in the conversation.
Use these phrases.

nice to meet you

how do you do?

I'd like you to meet

this is

– Louise, ... my cousin Richard.
– Hello, Louise.
– Hello, ...
– And .... our neighbour, Mrs Green.
– Oh, ...

🔊 Now listen and check.

Work in groups of three. Practise introducing

– a neighbour	– your brother/sister
– an aunt/uncle	– a friend
– your boss	– a colleague of your father

Study pages A

Focus on ... *Personal data*

This exercise gives practice in giving personal information and completing forms. It revises numbers (including phone numbers), letters and dates.

> *Key language:* numbers; dates; letters of the alphabet.
> *New words:* nationality, date of birth, make.

1 Introduction: listening & completing a form

- Read the items on the form. To establish what they mean, ask a few questions around the class, e.g. *What's your nationality? What's your date of birth? What make is your car (your parents' car)?*
- 📼 Play the recording. Students listen and complete the form. Then check the answers together:

Name: Tim Dalton   *Nationality*: English   *Date of birth*: 28th June 1982   *Address*: 163 Cannery Street, Bristol, England.   *Phone number*: 0117 650991   *Make of car*: Honda Civic   *Car number*: W376 SBY

Use this stage to check how well students know numbers, dates, etc. You can then focus on areas of weakness in the next section.

2 Practice of numbers, dates & letters

- Either ask the questions round the class, or let students answer the questions in pairs, then go through the answers together. Answers to numbers and dates:

  a thirty-eight, ninety-seven, a hundred (or one hundred) and twenty-five, four hundred and sixty-four, seven hundred and three

  b oh one double two six – four oh eight one double nine

  c the twelfth of December, nineteen eighty-seven
    the thirty-first of August, two thousand and one
    the ninth of February, nineteen ninety
    the twenty-sixth of November, nineteen seventy-five

In Part d, check that students can spell using the names of the letters (see *Language in Use Beginner*, Study Pages A Focus, where the letters are also recorded.)

3 Personalisation: exchanging information

- As an introduction, give information about yourself and get a student to write it on a 'form' on the board.
- Pairwork. In turn, students give information about themselves and complete the form for their partner. They should spell any difficult words.

  Note: For *Make of car*, students should either talk about their own car or their parents' car, depending on their age.

> 📼 Tapescript for Focus on ... *Personal data*
>
> OK, my name's Tim Dalton, that's D-A-L-T-O-N, Dalton. I'm English, and I was born on 28th June, 1982. My address is 163 Cannery Street – that's C-A-double N-E-R-Y, Cannery Street, and that's in Bristol, B-R-I-S-T-O-L, England. My phone number is oh-1-1-7-6-5-oh-9-9-1. My car is a Honda Civic, C-I-V-I-C, Civic, and it's number is W376 SBY, I think. Yes, it is. W376 SBY.

Pronunciation: *Unusual words (1)*

> Words from Units 1 and 2 which may cause pronunciation problems.

1 Listening & practice

- 📼 Ask students to try saying each word, then play the recording of the word and get them to practise. Focus on:
  - the silent *t* and the /ə/ sound in /ˈɒfən/, /ˈlɪsən/.
  - the diphthong /ʊə/ in /ˈjuːʒʊəli/, /ˈdʒænjʊəri/, /ˈfebrʊəri/.
  - the reduced /ə/ sound in /ˈbrekfəst/, /ˈneɪbə/.
  - the stress in /ˈlæŋgwɪdʒɪz/, /ˈɪntrestɪŋ/, /næʃəˈnælɪti/.

2 Writing sentences

- Students write a sentence using words from the box, and including any other words they like, e.g.

  I often listen to the radio at breakfast time.
  Japanese and Chinese are interesting languages.

3 Reading sentences aloud

- Students read out their sentences in turn. Focus on the pronunciation of the key words.

  Alternative: Dictation. Students dictate their sentence to the person next to them. As a check, ask students to read out the sentence they wrote down.

Phrasebook: *Introductions*

This exercise teaches ways of introducing yourself and other people.

> *Key language:* How do you do? Nice to meet you. This is ... I'd like you to meet ...
> *Recycled language:* cousin, neighbour.

- Look at the expressions beside the picture and ask students to fill the gaps.
- 📼 Play the dialogue to check. Make these points:

  - If someone introduces you, you can say *Hello, Nice to meet you*, or *How do you do?* (more formal: used when meeting an older person or someone important).

  - If you want to introduce other people, you can say *This is ...* or *I'd like you to meet ...* (more formal).

- Ask students to imagine they are meeting the people listed. 'Introduce' them to the class and ask students to respond appropriately.
- In groups of three, students practise introducing the people in the list to each other.

> 📼 Tapescript for Phrasebook: *Introductions*
>
> A Louise, I'd like you to meet my cousin, Richard.
> B Hello, Louise.
> C Hello, nice to meet you.
> A And this is our neighbour, Mrs. Green.
> C Oh, how do you do?

Consolidation

Possessives: 's & s'

This exercise focuses on the two kinds of possessive -s. It builds on language introduced in Exercises 2.1 and 2.2.

1 Look at the examples and establish that:
   – after singular nouns, we add *'s* (*mother → mother's*).
   – after plural nouns ending in *-s*, we just add *'* (*parents → parents'*).
   – after plural nouns that don't end in *-s*, we add *-'s* (*children → children's*).

2 ● Do the exercise round the class, or give time for students to work through it themselves and then go through the answers together. Answers:

a Peter's	*d* butcher's	*g* women's
b grandparents'	*e* teachers'	*h* Italy's
c children's	*f* girlfriend's	

   ● Discuss Question *i* together. Answer:

   i student's (if there is one student in the flat) *or* students' (if there are more than one)

awake and wake up

This exercise focuses on opposite pairs of verbs and adjectives for talking about waking, sleeping, getting up, etc. It builds on language introduced in Exercise 1.1.

● Read the text and complete the table on the board, getting students to tell you what to write:

(be) awake	*(be) asleep*
wake up	*go to sleep*
get up	*go to bed*
get dressed	*get undressed*

● Give other examples of your own to show the differences in meaning (e.g. *I go to bed at 11, then I go to sleep, then ... I'm asleep*).

● Students complete the sentences. Expected answers:

   a Get up, get dressed   *b* asleep, wake up
   c awake, go to sleep   *d* go to bed / go to sleep

Review

Telling the time

Review of language from the Beginner level, Study Pages D, and from Unit 1 and Study Pages A Focus.

1 Look at the clocks and establish what times they show. Answers:

   a quarter to three, a quarter past nine, seven o'clock, five to four, twenty past six, half past ten

   If necessary, give more practice of the expressions *o'clock, (a) quarter past, half past, (a) quarter to*, etc., by drawing more clock faces on the board.

2 Ask the questions round the class, and get students to ask you the same questions.

   If you like, let students ask and answer the questions again in pairs.

Countries

Review of language from the Beginner level, and from Exercise 1.3.

1 ● Look at the acrostic, and do the first item with the class (Answer: Spain). Then let students do the acrostic, working alone or in pairs.

   ● Go through the answers together, asking students to spell the names of the countries. Answers:

   Spain, Poland, Brazil, Italy, Russia, Greece, Japan, England
   Yellow squares: Portugal

2 Do this as a game round the class. Start with the beginning of a sentence (e.g. *New York is in ...*), and see who can complete it. The student who gives the correct answer thinks up the next question, and so on.

   Alternative: Give time for students to write sentences down. Then students read out their sentence beginnings in turn and other students try to complete them.

Consolidation

Possessives: 's and s'

my mother's car

my parents' dog

the children's bikes

Fred's hat

the boys' room

the men's toilet

1 When do we use 's? When do we use s'?

2 Add an apostrophe (') to these sentences.

  a Is that Peters new computer?

  b You can stay at my grandparents house.

  c Where shall I put the childrens toys?

  d He works in a butchers shop.

  e Please do not park in the teachers car park.

  f What is your girlfriends name?

  g Do you sell womens clothes?

  h Juventus is one of Italys best football teams.

What about this sentence?

  i The students flat isn't very big.

awake and wake up

> I'm always awake before everyone else in our family. I usually wake up very early – around 6 o'clock. Then I read the paper in bed and drink tea, and I get up at about 7 o'clock and get dressed …
>
> … In the evening, I get undressed and go to bed at about 11 o'clock, and then I read in bed, but not for very long. I'm usually so tired that I go to sleep very quickly, and I'm always asleep by midnight.

1 **Read the text and write opposites in the table.**

(be) awake	(be) asleep
wake up	....
get up	....
get dressed	....

2 Fill the gaps in these sentences.

  a .... and .... quickly! You'll be late for school.

  b Ssh! They're .... Don't make a noise, or they might ....

  c Are you still ....? It's nearly midnight – time to .... now.

  d I'm tired. I think I'll .... now.

Review

Telling the time

1 **Look at the clocks and watches. What times do they show? Here are some useful expressions.**

  … o'clock

  (a) quarter …

  half …

  … to …

  … past …

2 **What time do you usually …**

  … wake up?

  … get up?

  … start work/school?

  … have lunch?

  … have dinner?

  … go to bed?

  … go to sleep?

Countries

1 **What are the names of the countries? Write them in the diagram.**

  a Madrid is in →

  b Warsaw is in →

  c São Paulo is in →

  d Rome is in →

  e Moscow is in →

  f Athens is in →

  g Tokyo is in →

  h London is in →

What is the country in the yellow squares?

2 **Test your partner with other countries.**

  Ankara is in …   … Turkey.

3 Talking about places

1 Behind the door

There is/are • has got

1 Look at these two doors. What rooms do you think are behind them?

Read the sentences in the box. Which room do they describe? Could any sentences describe both rooms?

a There's a map on the wall.
b There's an ashtray.
c There's a video in the corner.
d There are two phones.
e There are flowers by the window.
f The room has got a blackboard.
g The room has got a thick carpet.

What else do you think there is in each room?

2 Now look at these doors. Where do you think they are?

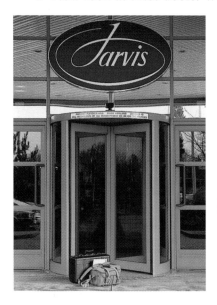

3 Choose one of the other doors, and imagine what's behind it. Write a few sentences about it. You can use these ideas, and add ideas of your own.

bed	menu	table	chair	television
picture	sofa	clock	lift	phone
fax machine	magazine	shower	computer	reception desk

4 Show your sentences to another student. Did you imagine the same things?

3

This unit is concerned with describing rooms and buildings, and focuses on two main areas of language:
– saying what *there is* and what *there isn't*
– describing features, using *have/has got.*

1 Behind the door

This exercise uses the context of rooms to introduce the two key structures of the unit: there is/are and have/has got. The doors shown on the page suggest certain kinds of rooms, but leave students free to imagine exactly what there is in each room.

▶ Focus on Form: Exercises 1 & 3
▶ Workbook: Exercise A

> *Key structures:* there is/are; has got. *Vocabulary:* school, classroom, hotel, lobby, restaurant, office, bedroom; furniture, objects in rooms. (→ Beginner Units 5, 6.)

1 Introduction: matching task; vocabulary & grammar presentation

● Look at the first two doors. Ask students what kind of doors they are. Answers:
the door of a classroom; the door of a manager's office, in an office building.

● Read the sentences and establish which of the rooms they describe. If possible, get students to give reasons. Expected answers:

a Both rooms
b The manager's office
c Probably the classroom
d The manager's office
e Probably the manager's office (but could be a classroom for young children)
f The classroom
g The manager's office

● Write these basic structures on the board:
Point out that:
– we use *there is* with singular nouns, *there are* with plural nouns.
– *It's got …* = The room has got …
– before plural nouns, we often use *some*.

> **There's a …**
> **There are (some) …**
> **It's got …**

● Check that students can use the structures by asking them to imagine other things in the two rooms, e.g.
Classroom: There are chairs; it's got big windows; there's a computer; there are some posters on the walls.
Office: There's a computer; it's got a coffee table and two armchairs; there's a fax machine; there are pictures on the walls.

2 Preparation for Stage 3: discussion

● Look at the other doors, and discuss where they are and what rooms might be behind them. Answers:
a hotel lobby/reception area; a restaurant; a hotel bedroom.

3 Writing sentences

● Working alone or with a partner, students choose one of the doors and write sentences about the room behind it. They should start with the words which are given, but then use their own ideas. Encourage them to imagine the room in some detail (e.g. what colour and size things are, how many there are, etc.).

4 Reading out sentences & comparing

● Choose doors in turn, and ask students to read out their sentences.

> *Note*
> Instead of *has got/hasn't got* we can also say *has/doesn't have*. For the sake of simplicity this unit only includes the form *has got/hasn't got.*

> *Language note*
> *There is/are* and *has got* are closely related in meaning: *The classroom has got a blackboard – There is a blackboard in the classroom.*
> We use *has got* mainly for describing permanent features, e.g. walls, blackboard (e.g. we say *There are some flowers in the classroom* but not ~~The classroom has got some flowers~~).

> *Optional lead-in*
> Look at the words together and ask students to match them with the rooms (e.g. *There are beds in the hotel bedroom. There are probably chairs in all the rooms. There's a lift in the hotel lobby*).

> *Alternative: guessing game*
> Students read out their sentences. Other students guess which room they're describing.

2 Good points and bad points

This exercise introduces negative forms, and practises using these structures to talk about rooms, buildings, towns and countries.

> *Key structures:* there isn't, there aren't; hasn't got.
> *Vocabulary:* share (v.), worst, unusual. (→ Beginner Unit 5.)

1 Reading & guessing; presentation of negative forms

● Look at the three letters. Establish what they are about, and ask students to suggest possible continuations:

A (a language school): … café / … library   B (a seaside resort): … good restaurants/ places to go out   C (e.g. a student hostel): a kitchen / curtains

● Focus on the negative forms. Ask students to complete the table, and write sentences on the board:

> **There isn't a bathroom.**
> **There aren't any computers.**
> **The classroom hasn't got a video.**
> **It hasn't got any beaches.**

2 Activation: continuing sentences

● Working alone or in pairs, students add one or two sentences to each remark, using positive or negative forms of *there is/are* or *has got*.

● Look at each remark in turn, and ask students what continuations they thought of. Possible answers:

a There aren't any good cafés. It's only got one cinema.
b It's got 5 floors. It hasn't got a front door. There's a garden on the roof.
c It's got very small windows. It hasn't got a desk. There isn't a telephone.
d It hasn't got any books for children. There aren't any chairs.
e There's only one village on it. It hasn't got any roads.

3 Is there a swimming pool?

This exercise gives practice in asking questions about hotels and their facilities. The main focus of the exercise is on question forms.

> *Key structures:* Is there a …? Are there any …? Has (the hotel) got …? Have (the rooms) got …?   *Vocabulary:* features of hotels.   (→ Beginner Unit 5.)

1 Presentation of question forms

● Read the questions, and point out that they are of three types: *Is …?* and *Are …?*, *Is there …?* and *Are there …?*, and *Has … got …?* and *Have … got …?*

● Students think of other questions. Write notes on the board in different groups, e.g.

Is it …	Is there …	Have the rooms got …
expensive?	a lift?	showers?
quiet?	a café?	televisions?

2 Listening & discussion

● 🔲 Play the recording and establish which questions the speakers answered.

● Play the recording again. This time, discuss what type of person the hotel is suitable for. Ask students to say why. Expected answers:

Students: No. The rooms are expensive. The restaurant's expensive.
Business trip: Yes. There's a business centre. It's near the airport. There's a bar.
Retired couple: Yes. The rooms have got comfortable beds. There's a garden.

3 Role-play

● Students work in pairs. One student asks questions, the other answers. They can either limit themselves to the language you have practised, or add other ideas of their own.

➤ Focus on Form: Exercises 1 & 3
➤ Workbook: Exercise B

> *Alternative*
> With books closed, write each letter phrase by phrase on the board. After each phrase, pause and ask students to guess what the letter is about and what will come next.

> *Language note*
> After *there aren't* we often add *any*: *There aren't any chairs.* *Some* and *any* are focused on in Unit 11, page 48.

> *Extension ideas*
> 1 Students write sentences about their own home, school, office, town, etc.
> 2 Guessing game. Students write some true and some false sentences about their own house or flat. Other students guess which sentences are true.

➤ Focus on Form: Exercises 2 & 4
➤ Workbook: Exercise C

> 🔲 The tapescript is on page T18.

> *Language note*
> *Is there* is followed by singular nouns (*Is there a bar?*), *Are there* by plural nouns (*Are there any single rooms?*) *Has … got* can of course be followed by singular or plural nouns:
>
> Has the hotel got a bar?
> Has the hotel got single rooms?

> *Whole class option*
> Choose pairs of students to act out a conversation in front of the class.

2 Good points and bad points

1 Here are parts of three letters. What are they about? How do you think they continue?

What are the negative forms? Complete the table.

Positive	Negative
There's a bathroom.	
There are some computers.	
The classroom has got a video.	
It's got some beaches.	

Negative forms

A It hasn't got a computer room, but there are some computers in one of the classrooms, and every classroom has got a video. The building's quite small, so there isn't a

B It's a beautiful place, and it's got some lovely beaches. Unfortunately, it's a bit quiet in the evenings. There aren't any

C I have to share my room with two other people, and there's only one bathroom on each floor. The worst thing is, it hasn't got

2 Look at these sentences. What do you think comes next? Add one or two sentences to each one.

a It isn't a very interesting town to live in.

b They live in a really unusual house.

c I don't like my office at all.

d It isn't a very good library.

e It's a very, very small island.

3 Is there a swimming pool?

1 Here are some questions about this hotel.

Is it near the airport?

Is there a bar?

Are the rooms warm?

Has the hotel got a swimming pool?

Have the rooms got phones?

Are there any single rooms?

Think of some other questions.

Questions

2 🔲 Three people talk about the hotel. Which questions do they answer?

Is this a good hotel for

– a group of students?
– someone on a business trip?
– a retired couple?

3 Role-play

Student A: You're thinking of staying at the hotel. Ask B questions.

Student B: You work at the hotel. Answer A's questions.

Focus on Form

1 there is & there are

In the picture ...

... there's a school.
... there isn't a church.

... there are some shops.
... there aren't any trees.

Look at the picture on page 104 for 10 seconds.

What can you remember about it? Talk about these things using *There is/isn't* and *There are/aren't*.

– lighter	– magazines	– watch
– books	– video	– pens
– camera	– cigarettes	– keys

2 Is there ...?

There's a school.
Is there a school?

There are some shops.
Are there any shops?

Ask questions about the picture on page 104.
Ask about these things:

– bag	– books	– TV
– shoes	– cards	– phone
– CDs	– apple	– glasses

What are the answers?

3 have got & has got

Look at these people and correct the sentences.

a The man's got long hair.   He hasn't got long hair. He's got short hair.
b He's got black eyes.
c The woman's got fair hair.
d She's got blue eyes.
e They've got a six-year-old child.
f They've got a cat.

> They've got = They have got
> She's got = She has got

4 Have they got ...?

Have they got a dog?

Has he got long hair?

Ask other questions about ...

... the woman (dark hair?)
... the man (green eyes?)
... the man and the woman (baby? cat?)

How to say it

1 🔊 Notice the sound of *there* in these sentences.

a There's a phone on the desk.
b There are some flowers on the table.
c Is there a television in the room?
d Are there any shops near here?

Practise saying them.

2 🔊 Practise the sound of *has got*.

a He's got a green car.
b The hotel has got three lifts.
c It's got a swimming pool.
d The house has got a big garden.

Focus on Form

1 there is & there are

● Read the examples, and check that students know these forms:

 – *there is* + singular, *there are* + plural
 – *there are* + some, *there aren't* + any

● Tell the class they will have 10 seconds to look at a picture. Then ask them to turn to page 104, and count 10 seconds. Then ask them to close their books.

● Students try to remember the picture and make sentences from the prompts. Expected answers:

There isn't a lighter.	There aren't any cigarettes.
There aren't any books.	There's a watch.
There's a camera.	There aren't any pens.
There are some magazines.	There are some keys.
There isn't a video.	

2 Is there …?

● Look at the examples, which show the structure of questions with *Is there …?* and *Are there …?*

● Look at the prompts and establish what questions you can ask (e.g. *Is there a bag? Are there any shoes?*).

● Pairwork. One student has the book open, and asks questions. The other student answers. Then they change round.

3 have got & has got

● Read the sentences and ask students to correct them. Answers:

 b He hasn't got black eyes. He's got blue eyes.
 c She hasn't got fair hair. She's got black hair.
 d She hasn't got blue eyes. She's got green eyes.
 e They haven't got a six-year-old child. They've got a baby.
 f They haven't got a cat. They've got a dog.

4 Have they got …?

● Students ask questions about the picture. Questions and answers:

 Has she got dark hair? (Yes, she has.)
 Has he got green eyes? (No, he hasn't.)
 Have they got a baby? (Yes, they have.)
 Have they got a cat? (No, they haven't.)

How to say it

1 *Pronunciation of 'there' in sentences & questions*

● ▭ Play the recording, pausing after each sentence. Focus on the way *there* links with the words that follow, and also on the reduced /ə/ sound in questions:

 /ðɛz_ə fəʊn/, /ðɛr_e səm flaʊəz/
 /iz_ðər_ə/, /ɑː ðər_eni/

● Practise saying the sentences.

2 *Pronunciation of 'has got'*

● ▭ Play the sentences. Pause after each item and get students to repeat them. Focus on the reduced /ə/ sound in /ðə həʊtel həz gɒt/, /ðə haus həz gɒt/.

▭ Tapescript for Exercise 3: *Is there a swimming pool?*

1 Oh yes, well, I love this hotel. I always go there. There's a very good restaurant. There's a nice bar, where you can sit and talk to people. And there's a good business centre in the hotel, with computers. And it's near the airport, so it's very convenient.

2 Well, it's not bad. The rooms are comfortable, but they're quite expensive. It's a long way from the centre of town. And there's a nice garden to sit in, but no swimming pool. And the restaurant's good, but again I think it's quite expensive.

3 Yes, I like staying there. The rooms are comfortable, they have big bathrooms. The beds are comfortable, too, which is good. You can also have breakfast in bed. I always have a room at the back, so it's nice and quiet. And there's a lovely garden at the back, too.

4

This unit is about travel and transport. It focuses on three main vocabulary areas:
– verbs for talking about journeys (e.g. *arrive, leave, cost, take*)
– types of transport (e.g. *bus, plane, taxi, underground*)
– adjectives describing transport (e.g. *safe, fast, expensive, comfortable*).
The reading and listening activity is about Heathrow Airport in London.

1 How to get there

This exercise is about ways of travelling from Washington to New York, and introduces common verbs used for talking about journeys. It also introduces adjectives and phrases (e.g. comfortable, on time) *which are picked up again and practised in Exercise 2.*

➤ Workbook: Exercise A

> *Key verbs:* cost, leave, arrive at, get to, take (an hour).   *Adjectives and phrases:* expensive, fast, slow, convenient, reliable, comfortable.   *Recycled language:* basic transport vocabulary, times.   (→ Beginner Unit 18, Study Pages D.)

1 Reading & gap filling; presentation of verbs

- Look at the map, and establish the three ways of getting from Washington to New York: by plane, by bus and by train.

- Give time for students to read the texts and decide what verbs should go in the gaps. Then read through the texts together. Answers:

  1 ... which *gets to/arrives* at La Guardia ... the whole journey *takes* less than three hours ... it *costs* about $300 return ...

  2 It *leaves* Washington ... and *gets to/arrives* at New York ... it only *costs* about $85 ...

  3 The journey *takes* about four hours ... which *gets to/arrives* at New York ...

- Point out that *arrive at* and *get to* have the same meaning:

> | The plane | arrives at
gets to | New York at 6.00. |

Optional pre-reading activity
Ask the class which they think is the best way to travel from Washington to New York, and why. Introduce some of the adjectives (e.g. *fast, comfortable*) at this point.

Note
The verb *leave* can be followed directly by a noun. We can say *The train leaves at 6.00* or *The train leaves Washington at 6.00.*

2 Speaking activity; presentation of adjectives

- Discuss what is good about each form of transport. Use this to focus on key adjectives for describing transport. Answers:

  Plane: It's quick.   *Bus:* It's cheap and convenient.   *Train:* It's reliable and comfortable, and it's always on time.

Note
These adjectives are practised further in Exercise 2, *Public transport.*

3 Personalisation: sentence writing & speaking

- To demonstrate the activity, tell the class about a journey you often make. If you like, write sentences on the board, giving prompts and getting the class to help you (e.g. *30 minutes – What can I say? The journey takes 30 minutes*).

- Students write sentences about a journey they often make (or one that someone in their family makes).

- Students read out their sentences.

Idea for further practice
Give situations, and ask students to work out the missing information, e.g. *I leave home at 7.00, and arrive at work at 8.30.* (= The journey takes an hour and a half). *My bus journey takes 10 minutes. I arrive at school at 8.00.* (= I leave home at 10 to 8).

🔲 Tapescript for Exercise 3: *Tourist information*

1 A How can I get to the airport?
   B The airport? You can get there by bus or by taxi.
   A How much does it cost?
   B The bus is £5, and a taxi is about £25.

2 A Excuse me, how can I get to the National Theatre?
   B The best way is by underground.
   A Right. How long does it take?
   B About 15 minutes. It isn't very far.

4 On the move

1 How to get there

1 Three people say how they get from Washington to New York. Fill the gaps with these expressions.

leaves   gets to   costs
takes   arrives at

66 I usually fly. If I leave home at 6.30 in the morning, I can catch the 7.30 flight, which .... La Guardia Airport at about 8.30. I'm in the centre of New York by 9.15, so the whole journey .... less than three hours. It's expensive – it .... about $300 return – but it's very quick. 99

66 I usually take the Greyhound bus. It .... Washington at 9 in the morning, and .... New York at 1.40 in the afternoon. The New York bus terminal is in Manhattan, so it's very convenient, and it only .... about $85 return on weekdays. 99

66 I usually go by train: it's only a bit slower than the plane and it's more reliable. It's about $100 return. The journey .... about four hours. I usually catch the 10.30 train, which .... New York at ten past two. It's comfortable, and it's always on time. 99

2 What's good about:

– going by plane?   – going by bus?   – going by train?

3 Write sentences about a journey you make regularly.

It arrives at …
I go by …   It leaves …   The journey takes …   It costs …
It gets to …

2 Public transport

1 Think about the place where you live. What kinds of public transport are there? Make a list.

2 Together, choose one kind of transport.

Complete the table. Which sentences do you think are true? Write ✓ or ✗.

	They're comfortable.		You don't have to wait long.
	They're expensive.		They're slow.
10:00	They usually come on time.		It's a pleasant way to travel.
	They're often crowded.		It's a safe way to travel.

3 Tell other people your answers. Do you all agree?

3 Tourist information

1 🔲 Listen to the conversations. What are the questions?

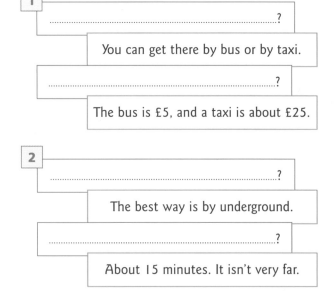

1
....?
You can get there by bus or by taxi.
....?
The bus is £5, and a taxi is about £25.

2
....?
The best way is by underground.
....?
About 15 minutes. It isn't very far.

What other questions could the tourists ask?

2 Imagine tourists coming to your area. Make a list of some places to visit.

3 Role-play

Student A: You're a tourist. Choose a place from the list. Find out how to get there.
Student B: You work at the tourist information office. Answer A's questions.

2 Public transport

In this exercise students give opinions about public transport in their own area. It focuses on types of public transport and adjectives used to talk about them.

> **Adjectives and phrases:** comfortable, expensive, crowded, slow, pleasant, safe; on time, wait long.
> **Recycled language:** Transport vocabulary. (→ Beginner Unit 18, Study Pages D.)

1 Introduction: vocabulary presentation

- Look at the picture. Use this as a basis to 'brainstorm' types of transport in your area. Get students to help you build up a list on the board, e.g. *bus, tram, plane, train, taxi, underground, ferry*. Present words for particular forms of transport that might be important, e.g. *suburban railway, cable car, minibus*.
- To activate this language, find out how many students use each of the forms of transport and how often.

2 Completing a table

- Together choose one form of transport to focus on.
- Read through the table, explaining any new words, e.g. *on time, crowded* (= lots of people), *pleasant* (= nice, you can enjoy it).
- Working alone, students complete the table.

3 Comparing answers

- Students turn to the person next to them. They go through the table and compare their answers
- As a round-up, go through the table with the class, and find out if everyone agrees.

3 Tourist information

This exercise focuses on common questions about travel and transport, and also consolidates language from Exercises 1 and 2. Students listen to dialogues and then act out an improvised role-play.

> **Questions:** How can I get to ...? How long does it take? How much does it cost?
> **Recycled language:** Present simple questions (Unit 1).

1 Listening & gap-filling; presentation of questions

- Look at the picture, and establish what it shows. (Answer: It's a tourist information office; people are asking how to get to places.)
- 🔲 Play the recording. Pause after each conversation and establish what the questions are. Write them on the board:

> **How can I get to the airport?** **How can I get to the National Theatre?**
> **How much does it cost?** **How long does it take?**

If you like, ask students to practise the two conversations in pairs.

2 Preparation for the role-play

- Ask students to suggest places to visit in your area. These can include places in the town where you are (e.g. *public buildings, sports facilities*), places in the region (e.g. *local beauty spots, nearby towns*) and places further away (e.g. *tourist resorts, national parks*). Build up a list on the board.

3 Role-play: asking about places to visit

- To demonstrate the role-play, take the part of B, and choose students to ask you questions.
- Pairwork. Students ask and answer questions.
- As a round-up, ask a few students who were A what they found out.

> ➤ Workbook: Exercise B, Listening

> *Language note*
> *On time* = at the correct time, e.g. *The train never arrives on time.*
> *In time (for)* = early enough e.g. *You're just in time for the news* (it's just starting).

> *Alternative*
> Students complete the table with a partner. Then discuss the answers with the class.

> *Mixed nationality classes*
> Students sit with someone from a different country, and they simply tell each other about transport in their own country.

> ➤ Workbook: Exercise C, Listening

> 🔲 The tapescript is on page T19.

> *Mixed nationality classes*
> A thinks of a place he/she would like to visit in B's country. B explains how to get there, and any other relevant information about it.

> *Whole class option*
> Ask students in turn to come to the front and take the role of B. Other students ask about places on the board.

4 Airport

This combined reading and listening activity is about airports. The reading gives statistics about Heathrow Airport in London. In the listening, three people say how they feel and what they do at airports.

> *New words (reading):* handle (v.), item, baggage, take off, land (v.), passenger, mobile phone, duty-free, smell (v.), drugs, heart attack, trolley, direct, destination, flight, population, illness.
> *New words (listening):* nervous, notice board, announcement, bored, exciting, far-away.

1 Reading sentences; guessing statistics; reading to check

● Ask students to cover the text and look only at the sentences *a–j*. Read through the sentences with the class, presenting new words as you go. Ask the class to guess what number goes in each gap, and write the guesses on the board.

● Give time for students to read through the text and check the answers. Then go through this together. Answers:

a 75,000,000 items of baggage	f 26,000 cups of tea
b 57,000 people	g 14 dogs
c 1,200 planes	h 40 heart attacks
d 20 mobile phones	i 9,500 baggage trolleys
e 500 bottles of whisky	j 85 countries

Note
This gives practice in saying large numbers. Point out that we use the singular form of *hundred, thousand* and *million*: *nine thousand five hundred, twenty-six thousand, 75 million.*

2 Listening & matching; discussion

● To introduce this part, ask students either how they feel when they're at an airport or (if they haven't been to one) how they think they would feel. Use this to introduce key adjectives, e.g. *nervous, bored, excited, frightened*.

● 🔲 Play the recording, pausing after each speaker. Match them with the feelings and with the photos, and establish what each speaker does at an airport. Answers:

1 Feels nervous; photo C. Sits near the notice boards, listens to the announcements
2 Feels bored; photo A. Looks around the duty-free shops, reads, listens to music
3 Feels excited; photo B. Walks around, looks at the planes, looks at other people

● Discuss which of the people students would most like to travel with, and why.

Optional extension
If students in your class often travel by plane, ask them how they spend their time at airports.

> 🔲 Tapescript for Exercise 4: *Airport*
>
> 1 Well, I don't like flying very much, so I'm usually a bit nervous at airports. I like … I like to sit near the notice boards and listen to all the announcements, because I'm always worried that I'm going to go to the wrong place, or miss the plane.
>
> 2 I get a bit bored at airports. The flights are always late, and there isn't much to do, you just have to sit and wait. Sometimes I look around the duty-free shops, but usually I just take a good book to read, or listen to music, maybe, on my Walkman.
>
> 3 I always find airports very exciting places to be. I like the feeling of people travelling, going to far-away places. Yeah, it's really exciting. I like to walk around, see the planes taking off and landing, and just look at all the other people, see where they're going, what they're doing. Yeah, I really enjoy it.

4 Airport

1 Can you match the sentences with the numbers? Fill the gaps, then check your answers in the text.

a Heathrow Airport handles over .... items of baggage every year.	14
b More than .... people work at Heathrow Airport.	20
c Every day, around .... planes take off and land at Heathrow.	40
d Passengers lose .... mobile phones every day at Heathrow.	85
e The duty-free shops sell more than .... bottles of whisky every hour.	500
f Passengers buy .... cups of tea at Heathrow every day.	1,200
g Heathrow's police station has .... dogs that can smell drugs.	9,500
h Every year, around .... people die of heart attacks travelling to or through Heathrow.	26,000
i There are .... baggage trolleys for passengers to use.	57,000
j You can fly direct from Heathrow to .... countries.	75,000,000

How many did you guess right?

Welcome to Heathrow

HEATHROW AIRPORT is the busiest international airport in the world.

More than 90 airlines use Heathrow. They fly direct to around 200 destinations in 85 countries around the world.

Every year, Heathrow handles 430,000 international flights. That's an average of 1200 every day – more than one a minute from six o'clock in the morning till midnight.

57,000 people work at Heathrow – that's the population of a small town.

Heathrow handles around 75,000,000 items of baggage every year.

There are 9,500 baggage trolleys for passengers – more than at any other airport.

Passengers lose 20 mobile phones every day.

Passengers buy 26,000 cups of tea and 6,500 sandwiches at Heathrow every day.

The duty-free shops sell a bottle of whisky every seven seconds – that's more than 500 bottles an hour.

Heathrow police station has 14 dogs that can smell drugs, and 300 police officers.

The most common illness among passengers is heart attack. Every year about 40 people die in this way while travelling to or through Heathrow.

2 Three people answer these questions.

How do you feel when you're at an airport?

What do you do while you're waiting for your flight?

a Match the speakers with the feelings.

b Match the speakers with the photos. What else does each person do?

c Imagine you're going on a plane journey. Which person would you like to travel with?

Focus on ... Where things are

1 Look at the people. Which person is

– opposite the cinema?   – beside the post box?
– above the café?   – between the cinema
– in front of the café?   and the bookshop?
– behind the tree?

2 Look at the pictures on page 105. Can you find places to

a post a letter?   e go to the toilet?
b make a phone call?   f change money?
c buy a newspaper?   g buy a plane ticket?
d have coffee?

Where is each place?

3 Can you remember where the places are? Ask and answer questions.

> Excuse me. Is there a post box near here?

> Excuse me. Where can I post a letter?

> Yes. There's one opposite the cinema.

> Well, there's a post box opposite the cinema.

4 Ask and answer questions about places in the town where you are now. Where can you do the things in Part 2?

Pronunciation: Small words (1)

1 🔲 Listen to the words in the box. They have the sound /ə/ when they are not stressed.

at	at six o'clock
for	for five hours
of	a packet of tea
to	listen to music
from	from Japan
some	some coffee
and	brothers and sisters
them	I don't like them

2 You will hear eight sentences. Each sentence contains one word from the box. Write the word you hear.

3 Practise saying the sentences.

Phrasebook: Buying a ticket (1)

Put this conversation in the correct order.

At 6.30, from
Platform 3.

Return.

That's £45, please.

Single or return?

When does the
train leave?

A ticket to
Cambridge, please.

🔲 Now listen and check.

Have similar conversations.

A You're going by train to London. You want two return tickets.
B The train leaves at 1.00 p.m. from Platform 10. The tickets cost £96.

A You're going by bus to Heathrow Airport. You want a single ticket.
B The buses leave every half hour. The ticket costs £5.

Study pages B

Focus on ... *Where things are*

This exercise focuses on place prepositions, and also on expressions for common activities (e.g. post a letter) and places in towns (e.g. post box, kiosk).

> *Prepositions:* in front of, behind, opposite, beside, above, between. *Activities:* post a letter, make a phone call, go to the toilet, change money. *Places:* post box, travel agent, exchange office. (→ Beginner Unit 10.)

1 Presentation of place prepositions

- Look at the picture and ask students to locate the people. Use this to check whether students understand the place prepositions. Present any that students do not know. Answers:

  opposite the cinema: woman with a dog
  above the café: girl in a red dress
  in front of the café: woman with a blue coat
  behind the tree: small boy
  beside the post box: boy with a letter
  between the cinema and the bookshop: man with a hat

2 Vocabulary presentation; practice of place prepositions

- Look at the pictures on page 105, and establish where you can do each activity. As you do this, present new vocabulary (activities and places).
- Ask students to say where each place is. Answers:

  a post box: opposite the cinema
  b telephone: in front of the station
  c kiosk: in front of the hotel
  d café: above the bookshop
  e toilets: behind/beside the station
  f exchange office: between the clothes shop and the music shop/beside the clothes shop
  g travel agent: beside the bookshop

3 Practice

- Look at the bubbles, and point out that there are two ways to ask the same thing. Ask students to give you questions for the other items (e.g. *Where can I make a phone call? Is there a telephone near here? Where can I buy a newspaper? Is there a kiosk near here?*).
- Ask students not to look at the pictures on page 105. In pairs, students ask questions as in the example, and answer from memory.

4 Extension: asking about real places

- Ask the same questions again, but this time get students to give real answers about the local area.

Pronunciation: *Small words (1)*

> Common words which have the reduced sound /ə/ when unstressed.

1 Listening & practice

- 🔲 Play the recording and ask students to repeat the phrases. Focus on the /ə/ sound.

2 Recognition task

- Play the sentences. Students write the word they hear.
- Play the sentences again and check the answers:

  1 and 2 for 3 of 4 at 5 to 6 from 7 them
  8 some

3 Practice

- Practise saying the sentences round the class. Focus on the pronunciation of the 'small words'.

Phrasebook: *Buying a ticket (1)*

This exercise practises language for buying tickets when travelling by train or bus. It picks up on language from Unit 4.

> *Key vocabulary:* single, return, ticket, platform, leave.

- Ask students to put the conversation in the correct order.
- 🔲 Play the dialogue to check.
- Look at the two situations with the class, and establish what the people will say. If you like, build dialogues up on the board.
- Either let students practise the dialogues in pairs, or ask two students to have each conversation in front of the class.

> 🔲 Tapescript for Pronunciation: *Small words (1)*
>
> 1 It has tomato and onion in it.
> 2 She works for an American company.
> 3 It's in front of the café.
> 4 The plane leaves at midday.
> 5 Nice to meet you.
> 6 I come from London.
> 7 Tell them your name.
> 8 There are some magazines on the table.

> 🔲 Tapescript for Phrasebook: *Buying a ticket (1)*
>
> A A ticket to Cambridge, please.
> B Single or return?
> A Return.
> B That's £45, please.
> A When does the train leave?
> B 6.30, from Platform 3.

Consolidation

early, in time, on time, late

This exercise focuses on expressions used for saying when people arrive. It builds on language introduced in Exercises 4.1 and 4.2.

- Use the examples to establish the differences in meaning between the expressions:
  - *early* = before the expected time.
  - *late* = after the expected time.
  - *on time* = exactly at the expected time.
  - *in time* = 'early enough' – at or before the expected time. (We often use it in expressions like *arrive in time for the party*; *arrive in time to catch the train.*)

- Do the exercise round the class, or give time for students to work through it themselves and then go through the answers together. Answers:

a in time	*d* late
b on time	*e* on time, late
c early	

The time of day

This exercise focuses on the use of on, in *and* at *with time expressions. It builds on language introduced in Exercise 4.1.*

- Look at the examples, and establish that:
  - we use *on* before the names of days (also before phrases like *Tuesday morning*).
  - we use *in the* before parts of the day (morning, afternoon, evening).
  - we use *at* before times, and also in the expression *at the weekend.*

  If necessary, give other examples of your own.

- Students add *in, on* or *at* to the sentences. Answers:

  a She usually visits me *on* Sunday afternoon.
  b The film finishes *at* 10 o'clock *in* the evening.
  c The plane leaves *at* 8 o'clock *on* Friday evening.
  d Are you still awake? It's 2 o'clock *in* the morning.
  e I usually go to bed *at* midnight *at* the weekend.

Idea for further practice
Give phrases (e.g. *the evening, Sunday evening, 7 o'clock*), and ask students to add *in, at* or *on.*

Review

Verbs and nouns

Review of language from the Beginner level and from Unit 1.

1 Ask students to find phrases using the verbs and the nouns. Expected answers:

   drive a lorry /a car
   have a shower/breakfast
   listen to the radio/music
   play cards/tennis
   read a magazine/the paper
   ride a bike/a horse
   speak French/English
   watch TV/cartoons
   wear jeans/a jumper

2 Ask students to suggest other nouns for each verb. You can use this as a general vocabulary expansion activity (reviewing sports, languages, clothes, etc.). If you like, build up phrases on the board. Possible answers:

   drive a bus/a taxi/a train
   have lunch/dinner/a bath/a party/a good time
   listen to a song/the Beatles/the news
   play chess/the piano/the guitar/football/basketball ...
   read a book/a notice/a letter/a poem
   ride a motorbike/a donkey
   speak German/Italian ...
   watch a football match/a film
   wear a dress/trousers ...

3 Students write sentences about themselves, using some of the verbs. As a round-up, ask students to read out their sentences.

Relations

Review of language from Exercises 2.1 and 2.2 and Study Pages A Consolidation.

- Ask students to continue the sentences. Make sure they use possessive -'s. Answers:

   Grandmother: she's my mother's mother (or father's mother).
   Uncle: he's my mother's brother (or father's brother).
   Aunt: she's my mother's sister (or father's sister).
   Cousin: she's my uncle's daughter (or aunt's daughter).
   Nephew: he's my brother's son (or sister's son).
   Niece: she's my brother's daughter (or sister's daughter).

Consolidation

early, in time, on time, late

It was my sister's wedding last Saturday at 11 a.m.

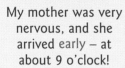

My mother was very nervous, and she arrived early – at about 9 o'clock!

I started late, but I arrived just in time – at about 10 to 11.

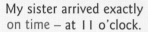

My sister arrived exactly on time – at 11 o'clock.

The wedding started, and then at 11.30 my brother arrived – late as usual.

Fill the gaps in these sentences.

a You're just .... The film starts in a few minutes.

b The bus arrives at exactly midday – it's always ....

c I usually come to class .... , so I have time to do my homework before the lesson.

d We always go to bed quite .... – usually around 12 or 1 o'clock.

e Please come to the meeting .... If you're .... , everyone has to wait for you.

The time of day

on I play football on Wednesday.
He has a piano lesson on Tuesday morning.

in I'm usually at home in the morning.
She often sleeps in the afternoon.

at We have dinner at 8.30 (in the evening).
They usually go away at the weekend.

Improve these sentences. Add *in*, *on* and *at*.

a She usually visits me Sunday afternoon.

b The film finishes 10 o'clock the evening.

c The plane leaves 8 o'clock Friday evening.

d Are you still awake? It's 2 o'clock the morning.

e I usually go to bed midnight the weekend.

Review

Verbs and nouns

1 **What can come after these verbs? Find two nouns in the box for each one.**

drive …
have …
listen to …
play …
read …
ride …
speak …
watch …
wear …

French	jeans	a shower
cards	TV	the paper
a bike	a car	a jumper
the radio	English	cartoons
a lorry	tennis	a horse
a magazine	music	breakfast

2 **What else can come after each verb?**

You can drive a taxi.

You can have a party.

3 **Write one or two true sentences about yourself and people in your family.**

I don't watch cartoons, but my little brother watches them all the time.

Relations

 This is my grandson – he's my daughter's son.

Talk about these people in the same way.

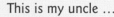 This is my grandmother …

This is my uncle …

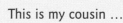 This is my aunt …

This is my cousin …

This is my nephew …

This is my niece …

5 Talking about now

1 Imagine ...

Present continuous

1 Imagine that you are in this plane.

What are you doing? Try to imagine the scene.

I'm travelling to ...

I'm wearing ...

I'm eating ...

I'm drinking ...

I'm feeling ...

I'm ...

2 🔲 You will hear someone imagining the same scene. What does he say about

– himself?   – his girlfriend?   – other people on the plane?

3 Choose one of these pictures. Imagine you are in the picture. Think about these questions.

What are you wearing?

Are you eating? drinking? reading? talking? ... ?

Is anyone else with you? What are they doing?

Are you listening to music? What kind of music?

How are you feeling?

4 Ask other students questions.

Are you eating?

Are you listening to music?

5

This unit covers two major uses of the Present continuous tense:
– for talking about events at the moment of speaking
– for talking about current activities going on 'around now'.
The unit also introduces expressions with *there is/are + -ing*.

1 Imagine …

In this exercise, students imagine a scene with themselves in it. This practises statements and questions using the Present continuous.

> **Key structures:** Present continuous tense: statements, *yes/no* and *Wh-* questions.
> **Vocabulary:** activity verbs. (→ Beginner Unit 11.)

➤ Focus on Form: Exercises 1 & 2
➤ Workbook: Exercise A

1 Imagining a scene; presentation of Present continuous (I'm …)

- If necessary, show the form of the Present continuous with *I'm*:

> **I 'm + verb + -ing**
> **I'm rea*ding*.**

- Ask students to imagine they are on the plane in the picture. Ask them to continue the sentences, getting a number of different suggestions for each. Possible answers:

I'm travelling to Australia. I'm wearing a white dress. I'm eating ice-cream. I'm drinking champagne. I'm feeling excited.

Then get students to think of other verbs. Possible answers:

I'm talking to the stewardess. I'm looking out of the window. I'm reading a book. I'm watching a film. I'm sleeping. I'm listening to music.

Presentation option: weaker classes
If students are completely unfamiliar with the Present continuous tense, turn to Focus on Form before you do this exercise, and present sentences and questions.

2 Listening; presentation of Present continuous (3rd person)

- 🔲 Play the recording. Pause after each section and ask students to make sentences using *He's*, *She's* or *They're*. If necessary, show these forms on the board:

> **He's**
> **She's** | reading.
> **They're**

Answers:

He's wearing a white T-shirt with a yellow sun on it. He's looking out of the window. His girlfriend is sitting next to him. She's reading a book. She's drinking a glass of fruit juice.
The other people are wearing grey suits. They're reading.

3 Preparation for pairwork; presentation of Present continuous questions

- If necessary, show Present continuous question forms on the board:

> **Are you rea*ding*?**
> **What are you rea*ding*?**

- Divide the class into pairs. Ask students in each pair to look at one picture each (so Student A looks at one picture, Student B at the other). Then read through the questions and ask students to think about the answers silently.

Optional lead-in
Choose one of the pictures yourself, and get students to ask you the questions.

4 Pairwork: asking & answering questions

- Pairwork. Students take it in turn to imagine that they are in the picture they have chosen. They describe what they are doing, and the other student prompts by asking questions.

- As a round-up, ask a few students what their partner said.

Homework option
Students write their description for homework.

> 🔲 Tapescript for Exercise 1: *Imagine*
>
> I'm in a plane, up above the clouds, and we're travelling to South Africa. And I'm with my girlfriend, she's sitting next to me, and I'm looking out of the window – I can see mountains, far below us. And my girlfriend is reading a book, and she's drinking a glass of fruit juice. And the other people on the plane are reading, and they're all wearing grey suits. But I'm wearing a white T-shirt with a big yellow sun on it.

2 There's a woman riding a bike

This exercise introduces the structure there is/are + -ing, *used for describing scenes where people are doing things. It also practises a range of verbs.*

> Key structures: there's a ... + -ing, there are some ... + -ing.   Verbs: buy, lie, play, sell, paint, sit, stand, climb, buy, smoke, walk, listen to, read, drink.

➤ Focus on Form: Exercise 3
➤ Workbook: Exercise B

1 Describing a picture; vocabulary & grammar presentation

- Look at the picture and ask students to describe what the people are doing. (e.g. *Look at the boys. What are they doing? They're playing football.*)
- Read the examples, which show how we can combine *There is/are* sentences with Present continuous sentences, to make *There is/are + -ing.*

  Ask students to make sentences about the picture. Expected answers:

  There are some boys playing football.   There's a man selling ice-cream.   There's a girl climbing a tree.   There's a girl standing by the tree.   There are some people sitting in a café.   There's a man smoking a pipe.   There are some children buying ice-cream.   There's a woman painting a picture.   There's a man sitting on the grass, playing a guitar.

Presentation option

Show on the board how these structures can be combined:

> There's a woman.
> ~~She's~~ riding a bike.
> ~~She's~~ singing a song.
>
> → *There's a woman riding a bike, singing a song.*

2 Pairwork game

- Turn to page 106. To check that students know the verbs needed for the game, ask them to describe the first picture.
- To demonstrate the game, choose another picture and describe it. Students guess which picture you chose.
- Divide the class into pairs or small groups to play the game.

Note

The verbs needed for the game are: *sit, read, drink, walk, listen to, stand (or wait), ride.*

3 Postcards

This exercise introduces the extended use of the Present continuous to talk about things going on 'around now'.

> Key structures: Present continuous, statements and yes/no questions.

➤ Workbook: Exercise C, Listening

1 Reading & grammar presentation

- Read the postcards and ask students what they can tell about the two writers. Possible answers:

  Phil: He's a chemistry student, he's got an exam soon, he hasn't got much money, Kate is possibly his girlfriend.
  Steve: He probably lives in a small town, he doesn't like it, he has a girlfriend called Chloe, his friend Tony is in Australia.

- Ask students to find Present continuous forms in the texts. Answers:

  I'm studying, I'm working, I'm looking (for), is happening, I'm not going, I'm working, are still going out.

  Explain that these verbs are not about things happening exactly at this moment, but in the period 'around now'.

Presentation option

If you like, contrast this use with the Present simple:

He's a student. He studies chemistry. (= in general).

At the moment, he's studying for his exam. (= around now, these days)

2 Practice: asking & answering questions

- To introduce this part, tell the class your own answers to the questions.
- Pairwork. Students ask each other the questions.
- As a round-up, ask a few students what they found out about their partner.

Alternative

Give time for students to think about the questions and note down answers (*Yes* or *No*). They then tell their partner (or the rest of the class) what they are doing these days, e.g. *I'm doing quite a lot these days, I'm not working very hard, but I'm going out a lot ...*

3 Writing a postcard

- If you like, write a short 'postcard' on the board, based on some of your answers in Part 2. Get students to help you by making suggestions.
- Students write a postcard, based on some of the things they said in Part 2.

2 There's a woman riding a bike

There is/are + -ing

1 Look at the picture.

> There's a woman.
> She's riding a bike.
> ▼
> There's a woman riding a bike.
>
> There are some people.
> They're lying on the grass.
> ▼
> There are some people lying on the grass.

Talk about other people in the picture. Use these verbs.

play	buy	paint	climb
sell	sit	stand	smoke

2 Look at the pictures on page 106.

Student A: Choose a picture. Talk about the people and what they're doing.
Student B: Which picture is A describing?

3 Postcards

'Around now'

1 Look at these postcards. What can you tell about the writers?

> Dear Kate
>   Sorry I didn't write before, but I'm really busy at the moment. I'm still studying hard for my chemistry exam, and I'm also working in a café in the evenings. Not a very good job – I'm looking for something that makes more money!
>   See you in the holidays.
>   With love,
>   Phil

> Hi, Tony!
> Thanks for your card. Australia sounds really good. Nothing's happening here. I'm not going to art college any more – I gave it up, and I'm working in a garage. Chloe and I are still going out together.
>
> Keep in touch.
>
> Steve

Which verbs are in the Present continuous? Make a list.

2 What are you doing these days? Are you ...

... doing a lot?	... eating a lot?	... earning a lot of money?
... working hard?	... having a good time?	... going out with anyone?
... going out a lot?	... watching TV a lot?	... looking for a job?

3 Write a postcard to someone you know. Say what you're doing (and what you aren't doing).

1 Present continuous

> He's wearing jeans.   He isn't wearing a suit.
> They're eating.   They aren't drinking.

All of these people are doing something wrong. Say what they're doing (or not doing). Here are some verbs:

drink   play   smoke   wear

listen   read   talk   work

A

B

C

D

E

F

2 Wh- questions

> Are you studying maths? Chinese? English?
> ▼
> What are you studying?

Ask *Wh-* questions. Use these question words.

What   Where   Why   How   How many

a Are you drinking wine? lemonade? water?
b Are they staying at a hotel? with a friend?
c Is she wearing one ring? two rings? three rings?
d Are you feeling tired? happy? unhappy?
e Is the baby crying because he's unhappy? because he's hungry? because he's tired?

3 There is/are + -ing

Someone is describing a street scene.

> There's a policeman standing at the corner.
> There's a car coming down the road.
> There are some people waiting at a bus stop.

Add more sentences. Use these ideas:

man	look in a shop window
children	run across the road
bus	wait at the traffic lights
dogs	lie in the road
women	sit in the sun
girl	carry a bag of shopping

How to say it

1 🎧 Listen to these sentences. Notice how the *-ing* ending links to the next word.

We're travelling to France.
She's writing a letter.
I'm looking for a job.
She's painting the wall.

Practise saying the sentences.

2 🎧 Listen to this sentence. What happens when the speaker says it quickly?

What are you doing?

Practise saying these sentences quickly.

Where are you going?
Are you staying at a hotel?
Why are you wearing a suit?

Focus on Form

1 Present continuous

● Look at the pictures and ask students what the people are doing wrong. Expected answers:

A He isn't wearing a hard hat.
B She isn't listening to the teacher. She isn't working. She's reading a magazine in the lesson.
C They're talking.
D They're wearing jeans. He isn't wearing a suit. She isn't wearing a dress.
E He's drinking beer. She's smoking.
F He's playing a computer game. He isn't working.

2 Wh- questions

● Check that students can form Wh- questions. If necessary, show how they are formed on the board:

> **He is studying.**
> 1   2
>
> **Is he studying?**
> 2   1
>
> **What is he studying?**

● Students make questions, working alone or in pairs. Then go through the answers:

a What are you drinking?
b Where are they staying?
c How many rings is she wearing?
d How are you feeling?
e Why is the baby crying?

3 There is/are + -ing

● Students make sentences. Answers:

There's a man looking in a shop window.
There are (some) children running across the road.
There's a bus waiting at the traffic lights.
There are (some) dogs lying in the road.
There's a woman sitting in the sun.
There's a girl carrying a bag of shopping.

How to say it

1 Links between words

● ▭ Play the recording, pausing after each sentence. Focus on the way the words link together, and also on the reduced vowel in /ʃɪz/:

/wɪə trævlɪŋ‿tə/, /ʃɪz raɪtɪŋ‿ə/, /aɪm lʊkɪŋ‿fər‿ə/, /ʃɪz peintɪŋ‿ðə/

● Practise saying the sentences.

2 Rhythm of rapid speech

● ▭ Play the sentence, and discuss what happens when it is said more quickly:

– there is more difference between the stressed sounds (What, do) and the unstressed sounds (are, you, ing).
– the unstressed sounds become shorter, and some sounds are reduced (/ɑː/ → /ə/).

● Play the other sentences and get students to repeat them quickly. Focus on the rhythm and reduced vowel sounds:

/wɛər ə ju gəʊɪŋ/
/ə ju steɪɪŋ ət ə həʊtel/
/waɪ ə ju wɛərɪŋ ə suːt/

6

This unit deals with three areas of language connected with food and drink:
– dishes and ingredients
– saying what you eat and whether it is good or bad for you
– containers (e.g. *a packet of*, *a jar of*).
The reading and listening activity is about unusual restaurants.

1 Dishes

In this exercise, students practise ways of talking simply about what dishes have in them. This recycles basic food vocabulary and introduces new items.

➤ Workbook: Exercise A, Listening

> *Meat:* beef, lamb, pork, chicken. *Vegetables:* onion, carrot, potato, pepper, mushroom, tomato, garlic, aubergine. *Other food:* sausage, noodles, prawn, rice, cheese, spices. *Phrases:* is made/cooked/filled with. (→ Beginner Unit 8.)

1 *Reading; vocabulary presentation*

● Read the two descriptions, and ask students to find:
– the kinds of meat.
– nine things shown in the small pictures.

Then ask what the other small pictures show. Focus on any new items, and build up vocabulary on the board. Answers:

Meat: lamb, beef, pork, chicken
The nine items in the pictures: h aubergine l onions b tomato g cheese
a prawns m peppers e garlic k mushrooms j spices
Other items in the pictures: c carrots d rice f potatoes i sausage

Language note
Most of the vegetables can be used here as count or non-count nouns. So we can say *It has potato in it* or *It has potatoes in it*; *It's made with tomatoes* or *It's made with tomato.*
Spices is a general word to cover e.g. pepper, cinnamon, chilli, coriander.

2 *Pre-listening discussion; listening to check*

● Look at the other dishes in turn. Ask students to suggest what they think might be in them. Build up lists of possible ingredients for each dish on the board.

● [cassette icon] Play the recording, pausing after each dish. Establish what the actual ingredients are. Answers:

Murgh Korma: chicken, yoghurt, onion, garlic, spices (bread, rice)
Spaghetti Bolognese: beef, pork, tomato, onions, garlic, wine
Töltött Paprika: peppers, pork or beef, rice, onions, spices, tomato
Irish Stew: lamb, potatoes, carrots, onions
Jambalaya: rice, onions, peppers, tomato, prawns, chicken, pork, sausage

Note
The idea of this is not, of course, that students are expected to know the answers; it is simply a preparation for the listening.

3 *Activation: guessing game*

● Write these phrases on the board (they were all in the recording):

> It has ... in it.   It's filled with ...
> It's made with ...   You eat it with ...
> It's cooked with ...

● To show what to do, think of a dish yourself. Tell the class what it has in it, and see if they can guess what it is.

● Working alone or in pairs, students think of a dish they know, and write a list of ingredients.

● Using their list, students describe the dish, using the phrases on the board. Other students guess what the dish is.

Note
It's made with, It's cooked with, and *It's filled with* are passive forms. Teach them here as set phrases.

Homework option
Students write a description of the dish they chose for homework, using the texts as a model.

[cassette icon] Tapescript for Exercise 1: *Dishes*

This is Murgh Korma, it's a curry dish from India. It's made with chicken, with yoghurt, onion, garlic and lots of spices. And you eat it with bread or rice.

Now this is Spaghetti Bolognese, a very well-known dish from Italy. The Bolognese sauce is made with minced beef and pork, tomato, onions, garlic and red wine.

This is Töltött Paprika, which is a very popular dish in Hungary. It's made with peppers, they're filled with minced

meat – pork or beef, usually – rice and onion, and spices. And it's cooked with tomato.

And this is Irish Stew – it's a popular dish in Ireland. It's made with lamb cooked with potatoes, carrots and onions.

This is Jambalaya, it's a dish from the USA. It's made with rice, onions, peppers and tomatoes. And it can have prawns, chicken, pork or pieces of sausage in it.

6 Food and drink

1 Dishes

This is a Mediterranean dish called Moussaka. It has aubergines, onions and tomato in it, with lamb or beef, and there's also cheese in it.

Singapore Stir-fried Noodles is a Chinese dish. The noodles are cooked with prawns, pieces of pork or chicken, peppers, garlic, mushrooms and spices.

1 Read the two descriptions and find
– four kinds of meat
– nine things that are in pictures a–m.

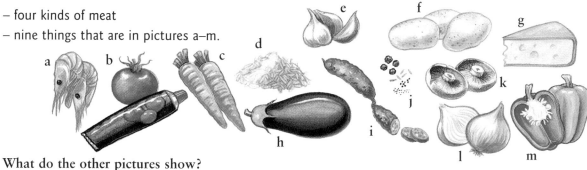

What do the other pictures show?

2 Look at these dishes. What do you think they have in them?

Murgh Korma (India)

Jambalaya (USA)

Spaghetti Bolognese (Italy)

Töltött Paprika (Hungary)

Irish Stew (Ireland)

🎞 Someone describe the dishes. Listen and check your answers.

3 Choose a dish you know. What does it have in it?
Can other students guess what it's called?

2 Good for you?

1 What kinds of food and drink can you see?

2 Which are good for you? Which are bad for you? Make two lists.
  Read out your lists. Do you all agree?

3 *Student A*: Ask B about the things in each list.
  Student B: Answers A's questions. How often do you eat or drink each thing?
  – every day?   – quite often?   – not very often?   – never?

  Is Student B a healthy eater?

How often do you eat fruit?

Not very often.

3 A packet of ...

1 You can buy food and drink ...

  ... in packets   ... in cans   ... in bottles
  ... in bags   ... in cartons   ... in jars

  Match the words with the pictures.

2 Here is somebody's shopping. What can you see?

There's a packet of sugar ...

3 Role-play

  Student A: You're a shopkeeper. You have *ten*
  of the things in the picture Make a list.

  Student B: Make a shopping list. You want to
  buy *five* of the things in the picture.

  Now go shopping. How many things can you buy?

I'd like a jar of honey, please.

OK. Here you are.

And a packet of sugar, please.

Sorry. We haven't got any sugar.

2 Good for you?

In this exercise, students find out from each other what they eat and drink, and whether they eat healthily or not.

> *Key expressions:* good for you, bad for you.   *Recycled language:* food vocabulary; frequency expressions (Unit 1).   (→ Beginner Unit 8.)

1 Introduction: vocabulary elicitation

- Look at the pictures and ask students what they show. Present any new items. Answers (left to right):

  wine, beer, cakes, fish, olive oil, fruit (apples, bananas, a lemon, an orange), chocolate, sweets, ice-cream, drinks (Coca-Cola, lemonade, Pepsi), coffee, meat (chicken, beef, salami), vegetables (cabbage, aubergines, carrots)

2 Writing lists; discussion

- Present the expressions *It's good for you* (= it's healthy) and *It's bad for you* (= it's unhealthy).

  Working alone or in pairs, students write the items in two lists: those that are good for you and those that are bad for you.

- Ask students to read out their lists, and see if the others agree. If you like, try to build up a collective list on the board that the class agrees on.

3 Pairwork: survey on healthy eating

- To introduce this part, get the class to ask you questions about the items in the lists, as in the example. Give them true replies, and then ask the class if they think you are a healthy eater or not.
- Pairwork. Students take it in turn to ask each other.
- As a round-up, ask a few students to tell you what they found out.

3 A packet of …

This exercise introduces words for containers (a packet of, a bottle of, etc.). It also gives practice in asking for things in shops.

> *Containers:* packet, bag, can, carton, bottle, jar.   *Recycled language:* words for food; I'd like …; We haven't got any …   (→ Beginner Study Pages E, Unit 13.)

1 Matching task; vocabulary presentation

- Ask students to match the words with the pictures. Use this to present words for containers. Answers:

  A jars   B cans   C packets   D bottles   E cartons   F bags

  If you like, ask students what they think the containers are made of and what might be inside them.

2 Activation: identifying objects in a picture

- Look at the picture and ask students to say what the items are. Answers:

  some bottles of beer, a bottle of orange juice, a bottle of milk, some packets of cigarettes, a bag of sweets, some packets/bags of flour, a jar of honey, a jar of jam, some packets of tea, some cans of fish, a can of Coke, some cans of tomatoes, a packet of spaghetti, some packets of chewing gum, a packet/bag of sugar, a bag of apples, some jars of coffee, some bottles of water, some bottles of wine

3 Role-play: asking for things in shops

- Preparation. Give each student a letter, A or B. A will be shopkeepers, B will be customers. Student A writes ten of the items in the picture in a list; Student B writes down five of the items.
- Divide the class into pairs, one A and one B. Student A asks for the things in his/her list, as in the example.
- As a round-up, find out if anyone was able to buy all the items on their list.

➤ Workbook: Exercise B

> *Language note*
> The collective word for wine, beer, etc. is *alcoholic drinks*; and for lemonade, Coca-Cola, etc. is *soft drinks* or *fizzy drinks*.

> *Option*
> Students to give their partner a score out of 10 (0 = very unhealthy, 10 = very healthy).

> *Optional extension: class survey*
> Find out how many students often eat or drink each of the items. Establish whether the class are healthy eaters or not.

➤ Workbook: Exercise C

> *Language note*
> A *jar* is usually made of glass; it is like a bottle with a wide top.
> A *bag* is usually made of paper, plastic or cloth.
> A *carton* is like a box, made of cardboard or plastic.
> A *packet* is a small container made of paper or cardboard.
> A *can* is made of metal.

> *Pairwork option*
> Students work out what the items are in pairs. Then go through the answers together.

> *Option: memory game*
> Ask students to cover the picture. See how many items they can remember.

4 Unusual places to eat

This combined reading and listening activity is about four unusual restaurants, three of which are real and one of which is invented.

> *New words (reading):* cocktail, graveyard, ghost, terrifying, course, cabaret, surrounded by, coral, strange, flowing, fantastic, fishy, tablecloth, guest, owner, double, stool, sign (v.). *New words (listening):* cook (n.), real.

1 Reading for information

● Read through the items in Question 1, and present the words *tablecloth* and *graveyard*. Then give time for students to read the texts and find the information.

● Go through the answers together, and focus on the part of the text which gives each answer. Answers:

    a Colours ('Yellow Night … a lemon sauce')
    b Red Sea Star ('fishy furniture')
    c Dracula's ('get on the ghost train for the dark, terrifying journey …')
    d Colours ('On Saturday the food is red, … the tablecloths …')
    e Twins ('… identical twins. They work together at the same tables')
    f Dracula's ('dancing in the Graveyard Disco')

2 Reading & discussion

● Discuss what is unusual about each restaurant. Expected answers:

    Dracula's: the atmosphere, probably the waiters/waitresses
    Red Sea Star: the view through the windows, the furniture
    Colours: the food, the waiters/waitresses, the customers
    Twins: the waiters/waitresses, the customers, the furniture

3 Discussion

● Ask students which restaurant they think is not real, but do not tell them the answer yet.

4 Listening

● 🔲 Play the recording. Students complete the sentences. Then go through the answers:

    Twins: You couldn't find so many identical twins.
    Colours: You couldn't have only purple food.
    Dracula's: The picture doesn't look real.
    Red Sea Star: The picture could be anything. You couldn't get to the restaurant.

● Take a class vote on which restaurant isn't real. Then tell them the answer: Colours isn't real.

🔲 Tapescript for Exercise 4: *Unusual places to eat*

A Well, I don't think *Twins* is real. How could you find so many identical twins to be waiters, waitresses, cooks? It says 'All 80 people who work there are twins'.
B Well, New York's a very big city.
A Yes, I know, but even so …
C Well, I think *Colours* isn't a real restaurant.
A Why not?
C Well, it says 'On Wednesdays everything is blue and purple'. What food do you know that's blue or purple?
A Fruit.
B Aubergines.
C Hmm. You can't just have fruit and aubergines on the menu.
A No, that's true. Well, what do you think?
B I think they're all real except *Dracula's*.

C Why?
B Because of this picture. I don't think it's a real restaurant.
C But it says 'restaurant' in the picture.
B Yes, I know, but I think it's from a film.
A Yes, a Dracula film.
B I don't think it's a real place. It doesn't look real, does it?
C But what about the *Red Sea Star Restaurant*? That's a bit strange, too.
A Why's that strange? There's a photo of it. That must be real.
C Yes, but who says it's a photo of a restaurant? It could be anything.
B Yeah, and the other thing is, it says it's 35 metres from land. So how do you get there? By boat or what?
A Well, they all seem rather strange, don't they? Maybe none of them are real.

4 Unusual places to eat

1 Read about the four restaurants. Where can you find these things?

a fish served in a yellow sauce

b tables and chairs that look like fish

c a train to take you to the restaurant

d red tablecloths

e two waiters to serve you instead of one

f a disco that looks like a graveyard

2 What is unusual about each restaurant?

– the food?
– the atmosphere?
– the waiters/waitresses?
– the customers?
– the furniture?
– the view through the windows?

3 Three of the restaurants are real places, but one is invented. Which one do you think isn't real?

4 [cassette] You will hear three people discussing which restaurant isn't real.

What do they say about each restaurant? Complete the sentences.

Twins
You couldn't find …

Colours
You couldn't have …

Dracula's
The picture …

Red Sea Star
The picture …
You couldn't …

Do you still think the same? Write your choice on a piece of paper.

Now find out the answer. Did you guess right?

DRACULA'S RESTAURANT

• *Melbourne, Australia*

Dinner is different at Dracula's. Start your evening with an interesting cocktail in the Graveyard Bar, then get on the ghost train for the dark, terrifying journey into Dracula's Restaurant. There you can enjoy a four-course meal and a two-hour cabaret, followed by dancing in the Graveyard Disco. Dracula's is great for just two people but also for birthday parties, office parties – even wedding parties. Dress: black is best!

Red Sea Star Restaurant

• *Eilat, Israel*

Do you enjoy eating by the sea? How about *under* the sea? The Red Sea Star Restaurant lies seven metres under the sea and 35 metres from land, and is surrounded by coral and colourful fish. The restaurant is lovely inside, too, with its strange, flowing windows, and fantastic fishy furniture. This is a wonderful place to have a meal. And the best thing on the menu? The fish, of course.

Colours Restaurant

• *London, England*

Colours Restaurant has a different colour for each night of the week. Friday is Yellow Night, and all the food is yellow or orange. You might have carrot soup, then fish in a lemon sauce, then a fruit salad. Other things change, too. On Saturday the food is red, and so are the waiters' jackets, the tablecloths, and even the flowers. On Wednesdays, everything is blue and purple. So find out the day's colour before you go, as most guests like to choose clothes that go with their meal.

Twins Restaurant

• *New York, USA*

All 80 people who work at Twins Restaurant are identical twins. They work together at the same tables, and they wear the same clothes. The owners are twins, too. Lots of other things here are in pairs: there are double lamps, double mirrors and, of course, double bar stools. You don't have to be a twin to eat here, but if you are, come along together: you can sign our twin guest book, we'll put your photo on the wall – and you get two drinks for the price of one!

C Study pages

Focus on ... Likes and dislikes

1 Look at these verbs. We can use them

  – to talk about *things*:
  I love *burgers*.
  I don't mind *cold weather*.
  I hate *football*.

  – to talk about *doing* things:
  I don't like *cooking*.
  I like *travelling* by train.
  I love *playing computer games*.

I love …
I like …
I don't mind …
I don't like …
I hate …

2 Make true sentences about yourself. Talk about these things:

chips	washing dishes	shopping
swimming	hot weather	Coca-Cola
dogs	cycling	learning English

3 Do this quiz with your partner. Score up to 5 for each answer (1 = *I hate* … 5 = *I love*).

Do you like an EASY life or a HARD life?

Do you like …
1 … chocolate? ....
2 … watching cartoons on TV? ....
3 … staying in bed till midday? ....
4 … sunbathing? ....
5 … relaxing in a hot bath? ....
6 … having breakfast in bed? ....
  TOTAL ....

7 … having cold showers? ....
8 … going for long walks? ....
9 … cleaning your room? ....
10 … getting up at dawn? ....
11 … long bus journeys? ....
12 … revising for exams? ....
  TOTAL ....

Which is bigger, the blue score or the red score?

Pronunciation: Clusters (1)

1 🔲 These words and phrases have two or more consonants together.
Try saying them, then listen to check.

clothes	bookshop
street	get dressed
get engaged	chemistry
friend	strawberry
postcard	at the next table

2 Write a sentence. Use at least two of the words or phrases from the box.

3 Read out your sentence.

Phrasebook: In a café

Match the remarks with the pictures.

I'd like a strawberry ice-cream.
What would you like?
Could we see the menu, please?
Could we have the bill, please?
Let's sit here.

🔲 Now listen and check.

Work in threes. Have similar conversations.

You're in a café. Order a coffee, a tea and some chocolate cake.	You're in a pizza restaurant. Order two pizzas, a salad and a Coca-Cola.

Study pages C

Focus on ... *Likes and dislikes*

This exercise focuses on verbs for expressing likes and dislikes, all of which are followed by a noun or -ing form.

> **Key structures:** love, like, don't mind, hate + noun/-ing.
> **Activities:** sunbathing, relaxing, cleaning, revising.
> **Recycled language:** everyday activities.

1 Presentation of key structures

- Look at the verbs in the box, and make sure students understand what they mean. Then read through the examples, and show these structures on the board:

| I like | books.
music. | | I like | reading.
listening to music. |

2 Practice

- Say the prompts, and get different responses from several students (e.g. *chips – I love chips, I don't mind chips, I don't like chips*).

3 Pairwork: quiz

- Read through the quiz, which shows whether you like an easy or a difficult life. Present any new vocabulary (e.g. *cartoons, relax, clean, dawn, revise*).
- Students do the quiz in pairs. One student asks the questions and notes down his/her partner's score, then they change round.
- As a round-up, find out which students like an easy life and which students like a hard life. Ask a few students to tell you about their partner (e.g. *She likes an easy life: she hates having cold showers and she hates revising for exams. She loves sunbathing and having breakfast in bed*).

> 🔲 Tapescript for Phrasebook: *In a café*
>
> 1 A Let's sit here.
>   B Oh, yes.
> 2 B Excuse me. Could we see the menu, please?
>   C Yes, of course. Just a moment.
> 3 C Now, what would you like?
>   A I'd like a strawberry ice-cream.
>   C Strawberry ice-cream.
>   B And I'd like a coffee, please.
> 4 A Could we have the bill, please?
>   C The bill. Yes, certainly. I'll bring it.

Pronunciation: *Clusters (1)*

> Consonant clusters in words from previous units.

1 Listening & practice

- 🔲 Play the words and ask students to repeat them. Focus on the consonant clusters in each word (underlined below):

/kləʊðz/	/ˈbʊkʃɒp/
/striːt/	/get drest/
/get ɪŋˈgeɪdʒd/	/ˈkemɪstri/
/frend/	/ˈstrɔːbəri/
/ˈpəʊstkɑːd/	/ət ðə nekst teɪbl/

2 Writing sentences

- Students write a sentence using words from the box, and including any other words they like, e.g.
  You can't buy clothes in a bookshop.
  You can see my street on this postcard.

3 Reading sentences aloud

- Students read out their sentences in turn. Focus on the pronunciation of the consonant clusters.

  Alternative: Dictation. Students dictate their sentence to the person next to them. As a check, ask students to read out the sentence they wrote down.

Phrasebook: *In a café*

This exercise practises expressions that can be used in a café: choosing and ordering food, and asking for the menu and the bill. It picks up on language from Unit 6.

> **Key expressions:** I'd like ..., What would you like?
> Could we ...?, Let's ...

- Ask students to match the remarks with the pictures.
- 🔲 Play the dialogue to check.
- If necessary, present the key expressions and do some quick practice (e.g. *Ask for a coffee – I'd like a coffee. You want to go out – Let's go out*).
- Look at the two situations with the class, and establish what the people will say. If you like, build dialogues up on the board.
- Either let students practise the dialogues in groups of three, or ask three students to have each conversation in front of the class.

Consolidation

Simple & continuous

This exercise focuses on the contrast between the Present simple and continuous tenses. It builds on language introduced in Unit 1 and Unit 5.

1 Read the two texts and establish that:
   - the first text is about what Jane Barrett does *in general*: what her job is and what it involves. The verbs are in the Present simple tense.
   - the second text is about what she and her son are doing *at the moment*: how they are spending their time now (on Saturday afternoon). The verbs are in the Present continuous tense.

2 Do the exercise round the class, or give time for students to work through it themselves and then go through the answers together. Answers:

   a I buy, I read, I usually finish, I'm reading, I'm enjoying
   b my brother is working, he is doing, he isn't watching, he usually watches

get

This exercise focuses on the use of the verb get. *It builds on language introduced in Units 1, 2 and 4, and Study Pages A Consolidation.*

- Look at the sentences, and build up a list of phrases with *get* on the board:

get up	*get on (a bus)*	*get engaged*
get dressed	*get off (a bus)*	*get married*
	get into (a car)	
	get to (work)	

   If necessary, give other examples of your own.

- Students make sentences from the pictures. Answers:

   The bride is getting into the car. She's getting married.
   The man is getting up and getting dressed.
   Some people are getting on the train, some are getting off the train.

Review

There is / have got

Review of grammatical structures from Unit 3.

- Ask students to make equivalent sentences with *there is/are* or *have/has got*. Answers:

   The hotel has got a swimming pool.
   There are seven cinemas in this town.
   This shop hasn't got any onions.
   Is there a toilet in this café?
   These classrooms haven't got any windows!

Things in rooms

Review of vocabulary from Unit 3

- Ask students to make lists from each picture. Then go through the answers, and build up lists on the board. Possible answers:

   Classroom: desks, chairs, blackboard/whiteboard, map, pictures, cassette player, video, cupboard, bin, books
   Office: computer, telephone, desk, chair, coffee table, bin, chairs, sheets of paper, shelves

Adjectives

Review of adjectives from previous units, especially Units 3 and 4.

1 Ask students to give the opposites of the adjectives. Answers:

   - They're very poor.
   - Is the shop closed?
   - He's got dark hair.
   - She's got short hair.
   - Their car's really slow.
   - Is it dangerous at night?
   - That jacket's expensive.
   - My father's quite young.

2 Students unscramble the adjectives. Then go through the answers and write the adjectives on the board. Answers:

   a convenient
   b single, double
   c crowded
   d reliable
   e pleasant
   f comfortable

Consolidation

Simple and continuous

1 Read the two texts. How are they different?

Jane Barrett is a writer. She writes children's books. She uses a computer a lot in her work. She uses the Internet to find information for her books, and she writes the books on the computer, too.

Today is Saturday, and Jane isn't working. She's sitting on her balcony reading a magazine. Her son David is inside – he's playing a computer game on his mother's computer.

2 Put the verbs in the correct form. Use the Present simple and Present continuous tenses.

a Every Monday I ⬚ buy ⬚ a new book. I ⬚ read ⬚ it every day on the train, and I usually ⬚ finish ⬚ it on Friday. At the moment I ⬚ read ⬚ Goldfinger, by Ian Fleming. It's very good – I ⬚ enjoy ⬚ it very much.

b This week, my brother ⬚ work ⬚ very hard, because he ⬚ do ⬚ his school exams. So he ⬚ not watch ⬚ much TV at the moment. That's good, because he usually ⬚ watch ⬚ four or five hours a night!

get

Here are some sentences with *get*.

He gets up at 8 o'clock, gets dressed and has breakfast. Then he gets into his car and drives to work. He gets to work at 9 o'clock.

Some people got off the bus and some got on.

They got engaged in June and got married in July.

What is happening in these pictures? Make sentences with *get*.

Review

There is/have got

What are the missing sentences?

there is/are		have/has got
There's a swimming pool in the hotel.	↔	....
....	↔	This town's got seven cinemas.
There aren't any onions in this shop.	↔	....
....	↔	Has this café got a toilet?
There aren't any windows in these classrooms!	↔	....

Things in rooms

What would you expect to find in these places?

a classroom   an office

Make two lists.

Adjectives

1 What are the opposites of these adjectives?

– They're very rich.   – Their car's really fast.
– Is the shop open?   – Is it safe at night?
– He's got fair hair.   – That jacket's cheap.
– She's got long hair.   – My father's quite old.

2 Can you unscramble the adjectives in these sentences?

a My office is in the centre of town, so it's very ceeinnnotv for the shops.

b – Have you got a egilns room?
   – Sorry, sir. We've only got bdelou rooms.

c The station's very cddeorw in the mornings.

d The train's always on time – it's very abeeillr.

e I like them. They're very aaelnpst people.

f This is a really abceflmoort chair.

7 The past

1 Famous firsts

Past simple

1 Look at the table. What are the missing past forms?

Now read about Charles Lindbergh. Fill the gaps with verbs from the table.

When Charles Lindbergh .... from New York to Paris in 1927, he .... much food with him. He .... New York in his plane 'Spirit of St Louis' with several bottles of water and five sandwiches. During the flight he .... the water, but he .... all the sandwiches – he still .... three of them when he .... in Paris 33 hours later. 'I .... hungry,' he told reporters.

Positive	Negative
was	wasn't
arrived	didn't arrive
ate	
	didn't drink
flew	
	didn't have
took	
	didn't leave

2 Look at these verbs. What are their past forms?

be   call   cut   explode   go   kill   like   **put**   say   take   use

Here are two more stories about 'famous firsts'. Can you complete them?

THE FIRST POTATO CRISPS

One day, a customer in an expensive New York restaurant .... the waiter and told him that he .... his chips, because they were too thick. The waiter .... very annoyed. He .... into the kitchen, took a potato, ... it into very thin slices, and .... the slices into a pan of very hot oil. Then he .... them back to the customer. To his surprise, the customer .... that they tasted delicious. They .... the world's first potato crisps.

THE FIRST TRAFFIC LIGHT

In 1868, the City of London set up the world's first traffic light outside the Houses of Parliament. The traffic light .... electricity – instead it .... gas lamps behind red and green glass. Unfortunately, it .... very successful: after a few days, it .... and .... a policeman. It was almost 50 years before they built another traffic light!

3 Choose one of the three stories. Cover the text, and try to tell the story yourself.

In this unit, students practise talking and asking about past events, using the Past simple tense. It focuses on three main areas:
– Past simple positive and negative
– Past simple questions
– past time expressions with *ago*.

7

1 Famous firsts

This exercise uses three gapped texts to focus on positive and negative forms of the Past simple. The texts are all true accounts of 'famous firsts': Lindbergh's flight across the Atlantic, the invention of potato crisps and the first traffic light.

➤ Focus on Form: Exercises 1 & 2
➤ Workbook: Exercise A & B

> Key structures: Past simple tense, positive and negative (regular and irregular verbs). *New verbs:* call, cut, explode, kill, use. (→ Beginner Units 17, 22.)

1 Presentation of Past simple positive & negative; reading & gap-filling

- Look at the table, and use the first two items to show positive and negative forms of the Past simple:
  Establish that to form the negative, we use *didn't* + infinitive.

Verb	Past	Past negative
arrive	arrived	didn't arrive
eat	ate	didn't eat

- Ask students to complete the table. Answers:

  didn't eat, drank, didn't fly, had, didn't take, left

- Look at the newspaper headline, and establish who Charles Lindbergh was (he was an American, and made the first non-stop solo flight across the Atlantic).

- Give time for students to read the text and decide what verbs should go in the gaps. Then read through it with the class, asking students to give the missing verbs, choosing between positive or negative forms. Answers:

  flew, didn't take, left, drank, didn't eat, had, arrived, wasn't

Presentation option: weaker classes
If students are unfamiliar with the Past simple tense, give other examples of regular verbs (e.g. *play – played, watch – watched, like – liked, live – lived*), then look at the irregular verbs in Focus on Form Exercise 1.

2 Presentation of past verb forms; reading & gap-filling

- Look at the verbs, and present any that students don't know (e.g. *call, cut, explode, use*). Build up the past forms on the board:

Regular:		Irregular:	
call	called	be	was
explode	exploded	cut	cut
kill	killed	go	went
like	liked	put	put
use	used	say	said
		take	took

- To introduce the texts, establish the meaning of *potato crisps* and *traffic light*, and also the words *slice* (= a thin piece, e.g. *a slice of bread*), *electricity* and *gas*. Students read the texts alone or in pairs, and fill in the correct verb forms (positive or negative).

- Go through the texts together. Answers:

  Potato crisps: called, didn't like, was, went, cut, put, took, said, were
  Traffic light: didn't use, used, wasn't, exploded, killed

Language note
Differences between British and US English:

British English	US English
(potato) crisps	potato chips
chips	(French) fries

3 Re-telling the stories

- Ask students to cover the stories, but to look at the verbs (either in their books or on the board). Students re-tell the story round the class, taking turns to say a sentence or two. They should not of course try to repeat the stories word for word; the idea is to tell the main facts and to use the verbs in the Past simple tense.

Pairwork option
Students practise re-telling the stories in pairs, choosing one story each.

2 Did you have a good time?

This exercise introduces Past simple questions, for asking about details of events in the past.

> **Key structures:** Past simple yes/no and Wh- questions.　(→ Beginner Unit 17.)

➤ Focus on Form: Exercise 3
➤ Workbook: Exercise C

1 Elicitation of questions; presentation of Past simple question forms

- Look at the picture. Make sure students know where Austria and Vienna are.
- Ask students to suggest possible questions. Use this to check whether students can ask questions using the Past simple. Possible questions:

Where did you go? Where did you stay?	How did you go (there)?
Did you stop on the way?	Did you have a good time?
Did you visit/go to Vienna?	When did you leave/get back?

- If necessary, present question forms on the board:

> *I stopped on the way.*　*I went by car.*
> *Did you stop on the way?*　*Did you go by car?*
> *Where did you stop?*　*How did you go?*

2 Listening & identifying questions

- ▭ Play the recording. Establish what the actual questions (and answers) are (see tapescript).

▭ The tapescript is on page T34.

3 Practice: making up questions

- Look at each remark, and ask students to suggest suitable questions, e.g.

  a Where did you go? Did you enjoy it? Who did you go with?
  b Did you have a party? Who did you invite? Did you get many presents?
  c What did you see? Who did you go with? Did you enjoy it?

> *Role-play option*
> Students come to the front of the class in turn, and say one of the sentences. Other students ask questions. Alternatively, students could do this in pairs.

4 Speaking activity: asking & answering questions

- Give students time to think of something they did recently. If you like, ask them to write a sentence about it.
- Call students in turn to read out or say their sentence. Other students ask them questions.

3 Three days ago

This exercise is in the form of a questionnaire which establishes how much people go out. It focuses on the use of ago *for saying when things happened.*

➤ Focus on Form: Exercise 4

> **Key structures:** Past simple + … ago; When did you last … ? time expressions.
> **Vocabulary:** leisure activities.　(→ Beginner Units 17, 22.)

1 Presentation of 'ago'; listening & completing a table

- To present *ago*, write a sentence on the board:
  Point out that *ago* tells us the *length of time* before now that something happened.

> *He arrived* | *on Saturday.*
> | *three days ago.*

> *Single nationality classes*
> If possible, give equivalent expressions in students' own language (e.g. *il y a 3 jours, vor 3 Tagen, hace 3 dias*).

- ▭ Play the recording. Students complete the table. Then go through it together, and discuss where the woman should come on the scale. Answers:

  b two days ago　*c* six days ago　*d* five days ago　*e* a week ago　*f* two hours ago
  (*Position on the scale:* Towards the right)

> *Practice option*
> Give time expressions, and ask students to change them into phrases with *ago: in February = two months ago; in 1991 = ten years ago; at 12 o'clock = three hours ago.*

2 Pairwork: asking & answering questions; completing a table

- Students interview each other, and complete the table for their partner. They then mark their partner's position on the scale.
- As a round-up, find out who was at number 9, number 8, etc. on the scale. Ask a few students what they found out about their partner.

▭ The tapescript is on page T34.

2 Did you have a good time?

Past simple questions

1 This person recently got back from a visit to Austria. What questions could you ask him?

2 🔲 Some friends ask him about his trip.

Are their questions the same as yours?
What answers does he give?

3 What could you ask these people? Think of one or two questions.

4 *Student A*: Think of something you did recently. Tell B.
Student B: Ask some questions.

3 Three days ago

... ago

1 🔲 You will hear someone answering these questions. Write her answers in the table.

When did you last ...	The speaker	Your partner
a ... go away for the weekend?	Two months ago	
b ... go out for a drink or a meal?	ago	
c ... go to the theatre, the cinema or a concert?		
d ... go out for a walk, a run or a swim?		
e ... go to a party, a club or a disco?		
f ... visit friends or relatives?		

How much does she go out? Mark her position on the scale.

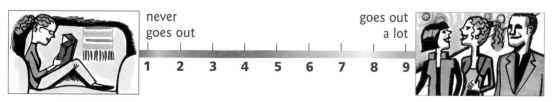

2 Now interview your partner, and mark his/her answers on the table.

Where does your partner come on the scale? What is the most interesting thing you found out?

Focus on Form

1 Irregular past forms

drink	give
eat	see
fly	find
have	drive
leave	read
take	come
go	sing
buy	put
make	wear
tell	write

What are the past forms of these verbs?

Student A: Choose a verb and make a sentence in the past. Say *buzzed* instead of the verb.

Student B: What's the missing verb?

Yesterday I *buzzed* a good film.

saw

He *buzzed* me his name.

told

(There's a list of irregular verbs on page 128.)

2 Positive and negative

She	washed / didn't wash	her hair.	He	had / didn't have	a shower.

Imagine three things your partner did yesterday, and three thing he/she didn't do yesterday. Write them down.

Read out your sentences, and see if you were right.

> You had a big breakfast.   You didn't cook a meal.
> You sang a song.   You didn't make your bed.
> You watched the news.   You didn't drive a car.

3 Wh- questions

Did you invite John to the party? Jane? Alice?

▼

Who did you invite to the party?

Ask *Wh-* questions. Use these question words.

What   Where   Why   When   How much

a Did they go to a restaurant last night? a theatre? a cinema?

b Did he leave because he was ill? because he was bored? because he was tired?

c Did you spend £5? £10? £20?

d Did she say 'Hello'? 'Go away'? 'Goodbye'?

e Did your mother arrive yesterday? two days ago? last week?

f Did you study French at university? maths? economics?

4 ago

They arrived about three hours ago.
He bought a new car six months ago.
I last washed my hair two days ago.

How long ago did these things happen?

a We went for a drive *on Saturday*.

b They got married *in 1996*.

c I had breakfast *at 6 o'clock this morning*.

d He left school *last June*.

e She spoke to me *at the start of the lesson*.

How to say it

1 🔲 Listen to *didn't* and *wasn't* in these sentences. Practise saying them.

He didn't go to school today.

I didn't spend any money.

I wasn't very hungry.

She wasn't there yesterday.

2 🔲 Listen to these *-ed* endings.

arrived	washed	visited
killed	liked	waited
used	watched	exploded
called	asked	

Practise saying these sentences.

I think she liked the film.

He washed the dishes.

I watched television.

Focus on Form

1 Irregular past forms

- Check whether students know the past forms of the verbs. If you like, write them on the board. Answers:

  drank, ate, flew, had, left, took, went, bought, made, told, gave, saw, found, drove, read, came, sang, put, wore, wrote

- Make a few sentences as in the example, and ask students to give the missing verbs.
- Give time for students to make up a sentence. Then ask students to say their sentence. Other students give the missing verb.

2 Positive and negative

- Check that students know how to form the Past simple negative: *didn't* + infinitive.
- If you like, introduce the activity by choosing a student, then writing a few sentences about him/her on the board. Then check if your guesses were right.
- Pairwork. Students write three positive and three negative sentences about their partner. They then read out their sentences to see if they were right.

  Whole class alternative: Students choose someone else in the class, and write sentences about him/her. Then ask students in turn to read their sentences aloud.

3 Wh- questions

- Either do the exercise round the class, or let students work through it in pairs and then go through the answers together. Answers:

  a Where did they go last night?
  b Why did he leave?
  c How much did you spend?
  d What did she say?
  e When did your mother arrive?
  f What did you study at university?

4 ago

- Do the exercise round the class. The answers will of course depend on when you do the exercise. Example answers:

  a We went for a drive three days ago.
  b They got married five years ago.
  c I had breakfast three hours ago.
  d He left school eight months ago.
  e She spoke to me twenty minutes ago.

How to say it

1 Pronunciation of 'didn't' & 'wasn't' in sentences

- 🔲 Play the recording. Pause after each sentence and get students to repeat it. Focus on the pronunciation of *didn't* and *wasn't*, and the way they link with the next word:

  /dɪdnt‿gəʊ/, /dɪdnt‿spend/, /wɒznt‿veri/, /wɒznt‿ðɛə/.

2 Pronunciation of '-ed' endings

- 🔲 Play each group of words and focus on the different sounds:

  Group 1: the *-ed* is pronounced /d/.
  Group 2: the *-ed* is pronounced /t/.
  Group 3: the *-ed* is pronounced /ɪd/.

- Play the sentences and get students to practise them.

🔲 Tapescript for Exercise 2: *Did you have a good time?*

A Oh hello! (Hi. Hello.) When did you get back?
B This morning. About 3 o'clock in the morning.
A Did you have a good time?
B Yeah, really good, yeah.
C How did you get there? By plane?
B No, I drove there.

C It's a long way to drive. Did you stop on the way?
B I stopped twice, for something to eat. That was all.
D Did you go to Vienna?
B Yeah, I spent about three days in Vienna.
D Where did you stay?
B Well, I had some friends there, so I stayed with them. They showed me round – it was really good.

🔲 Tapescript for Exercise 3: *Three days ago*

A OK. When did you last go away for the weekend?
B Go away? Probably two months ago. I went to Scotland.
A And when did you last go out for a drink or a meal?
B Two days ago – on Wednesday. I went out to a Chinese restaurant.
A OK. When did you last go to the theatre, the cinema or a concert?
B Oh, well – I went to a rock concert at the weekend, so that was six days ago.

A And when did you last go out for a walk, a run or a swim?
B Well, again at the weekend. I went for a walk on Sunday – so that was five days ago.
A Right. When did you last go to a party, a club or a disco?
B Exactly a week ago. I went to a party last Friday.
A OK. And when did you last visit friends or relatives?
B Oh, about two hours ago. I went to a friend's house.
A OK. Thank you.

8

This unit deals with two areas of language connected with homes:
– talking about types of houses and flats, and their position
– talking about rooms and furniture.
The reading and listening activity is about haunted houses and ghosts.

1 Houses

This exercise introduces expressions for talking about houses and flats and their location.

➤ Workbook: Exercise A

> *Types of home:* house, flat, block of flats, cottage. *Other key phrases:* in the suburbs, in the city centre, in the country; faces, looks out on, has a view of. *Adjectives:* dark, sunny, spacious, noisy, quiet. (→ Beginner Unit 6.)

1 Reading; vocabulary presentation

● To introduce the activity, ask a few questions round the class, e.g. *Who lives in a flat? What floor is it on? How many rooms has it got? Does anyone live in a house?* Use this to introduce basic vocabulary:

> house   cottage   flat   **block of flats**
> **it's on the third floor**   **it's a third-floor flat**
> **it's got four rooms**   **it's a four-room flat**

Language note
In British English we say *flat, block of flats*. In US English we say *apartment, apartment block*.

● Students read the texts and match them with the pictures. Then go through the answers together, and ask students what words helped them to identify each picture. Answers:

1 B (house, large garden)   2 C (flat, big block, main road)   3 D (cottage, in the country, lake)   4 A (flat, old part of town, balcony)

2 Reading & completing a table

● Working alone or in pairs, students read the texts again and complete the table. The purpose of this is to focus on key words and expressions. Expected answers:

cottage	in the country	on the edge of a small lake
flat	near the city centre	on a main road, has a view of the park
house	in the suburbs	faces south
flat	in the old part of town	looks out on a square

● Focus on:
– the prepositions *in* and *on*: *in the suburbs, in the country*; *on a main road, on the edge of*.
– the phrases *has a view of* and *looks out on*, which mean roughly the same.
– the verb *faces* (*north/south/east/west*).

Presentation option
Give other examples, e.g. *Through the window, there's a garden = the room looks out on a garden. You can see the sea from the room = it has a view of the sea.*

3 Asking & answering questions; making notes; writing sentences

● Pairwork. Students find out about their partner's home and make notes in the table.
● Students write sentences about their partner's home, using their notes.
● As a round-up, ask a few students to read out their sentences.

Optional lead-in
Show what to do at each stage by using your own home as an example; tell the class about it, show how to make notes on the board, then expand the notes into sentences.

T 35

8 A place to live

1 Home

1 Match the descriptions with the pictures. How do you know?

1 We've just moved to a house in the suburbs. It's got three bedrooms and a large garden. It's very spacious and there's lots of room for the children. The living room faces south, so it's fairly sunny.

2 I've got a four-room flat in a big block near the city centre. It's on the 5th floor, and has a lovely view of the park. Unfortunately it's on a main road, so it's fairly noisy.

3 They've got a little cottage in the country. It's in a lovely position, right on the edge of a small lake, but it doesn't get much sun, so it's rather dark inside.

4 I've found a quiet flat in the old part of the town. It's a bit small – just two rooms – but it's got a balcony which looks out on a square.

2 Now complete the first part of the table.

	What type?	Where is it?	More about its position
		in the country	
	flat		
			faces south
Partner's home			

3 Find out about your partner's home. Write notes in the table. Using your notes, write one or two sentences on a piece of paper.

Tony lives in a small flat in the city centre. It

2 Rooms

1 What rooms are these? How can you tell?

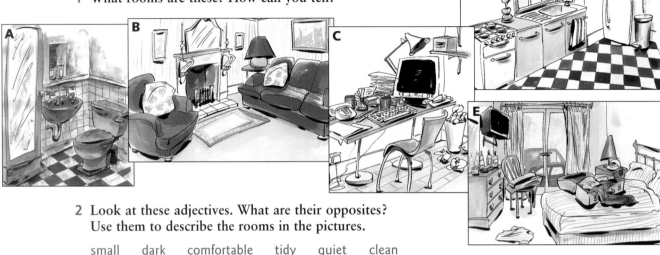

2 Look at these adjectives. What are their opposites?
Use them to describe the rooms in the pictures.

small   dark   comfortable   tidy   quiet   clean

3 [cassette] Three people describe a room they were in recently. What kind of rooms are they?

Now think of a room you were in recently. What was it like? What was there in it?
Can other students guess what room you are describing?

3 Everything in its place

1 This is Mike's new room. What things can you see in it?

2 Where could he put things in the room?

> He could put the sound system on one of the shelves.

> The rug could go by the window. Or he could put it in the middle of the room.

3 Work in pairs.

Student A: Look at the picture of Mike's room on page 105.

Student B: Look at the picture of Mike's room on page 106.

Say where things are in your picture. Can you find seven differences?

2 Rooms

This exercise introduces a range of adjectives for describing rooms.

➤ Workbook: Exercise B, Listening

> *Adjectives:* small, big, dark, light, comfortable, uncomfortable, tidy, untidy, quiet, noisy, clean, dirty.   *Recycled language:* rooms and furniture (Unit 3).

1 Describing pictures: rooms & furniture

● Look at the adjectives and ask students to give you the opposites. Build up two lists on the board:

● Look at each picture in turn. Ask what room it is, and how you can tell (this reviews vocabulary of rooms and furniture). Expected answers:

small	big/large
dark	light
comfortable	uncomfortable
tidy	untidy
quiet	noisy
clean	dirty

> *Vocabulary option (good classes)*
> Add other adjectives for describing rooms, e.g. *sunny, bright, spacious, gloomy, messy, cosy.*

A *Bathroom:* shower, washbasin, toilet
B *Living room:* sofa, armchair
C *Office/study:* desk, computer

D *Kitchen:* cooker, fridge, sink
E *Hotel bedroom:* bed, TV, suitcase

2 Describing pictures: adjectives

● Ask what adjectives describe the room. Expected answers:

A small, dark, dirty B large, quiet, comfortable, tidy
C untidy, small D light, tidy, clean E clean, untidy, noisy

> *Optional extension*
> Ask students what adjectives describe rooms in their own house or flat.

3 Listening & speaking; describing a room

● ▭ Play the recording, pausing after each room. Ask students to say what room it was and what it was like. Expected answers:

1 a (hotel) bedroom 2 the speaker's living room 3 a doctor's (or dentist's) waiting room

> ▭ The tapescript is on page T37.

● Students describe a room they were in recently. Other students try to guess what kind of room it was.

3 Everything in its place

This exercise focuses on vocabulary for personal possessions in rooms (e.g. cushion, picture, plant). Students decide where things should go in a room.

➤ Workbook: Exercise C

> *New words:* rug, sound system, plant, poster, mirror, vase, cushion.
> *Recycled language:* everyday objects, furniture, place prepositions.

1 Introduction: vocabulary elicitation

● Look at the picture, and ask students to identify the objects and the furniture. Answers (left to right):

table, rug, bookshelves, cushions, magazines, plant, phone, books, sofa, photographs, sound system, mirror, vase, cupboard, picture, suitcase, poster

2 Activation: discussion

● Ask students to suggest where to put things in the room. Do this by asking about each object in turn, and getting a range of suggestions.

> *Presentation option*
> Present the modal verb *could* here:
> *He could put ...*
> *The rug could go ...*

3 Pairwork game: finding differences between pictures

● Give each student a letter, A or B. Ask students to turn to page 105 or 106, and look only at their own picture.

> *Alternative: pairwork*
> In pairs, students decide where to put the objects. Then ask different pairs what they decided.

● Students say where things are in their own picture. They try to find seven differences, and note them down, but without looking at each other's picture.

● Go through the answers together. Answers:

1 suitcase on cupboard/beside sofa
2 vase in window/on table
3 poster/mirror above sofa
4 photos on shelves/in window

5 plant on table/on shelf
6 phone by sofa/under table
7 magazines under table/by sofa

4 Two ghost stories

This combined reading and listening activity is about haunted houses and ghosts. The reading text is about a haunted house in England. The listening is a story of a child's encounter with a ghost.

> *New words (reading):* haunted, frighten, century, manor house, owner, servant, previous, farmer, hang, priest, visitor, hold, corridor, master, grew up, sailor, lock, scream, bang.
> *New words (listening):* cellar, coal, coloured, apron, upstairs.

1 Introduction: pre-reading vocabulary presentation

- Either let students use dictionaries to find out the meanings of the words, or present them, using examples of your own.

Option
Ask students to find out the meaning of the words at home before the lesson.

2 Reading & answering questions

- Give time for students to read through the first paragraph, and then discuss the answer to Question *a*. (Answer: It has four different ghosts.)
- Working alone or in pairs, students read the rest of the text and complete the table. Then go through the answers together. Answers:

Which ghost?	He killed ...	You can see/hear him in ...
1 priest	visitors	the bedrooms
2 servant	his master	the corridors
3 young man	a boy	a room at the back
4 previous owner	himself	the garden

- Look at the pictures, and ask students to find the four ghosts. Answers:
  - A the previous owner (a farmer)
  - B the young man (a sailor)
  - D the priest
  - G the servant

3 Listening; answering true/false questions

- Read through the questions and present any new words (e.g. *cellar, apron*).
- 🔲 Play the first part of the story. Students mark the sentences *T* (true) or *F* (false). Then go through the answers:

  a False *b* True *c* True *d* False *e* True *f* False *g* False *h* True

- Ask students to guess the ending of the story.
- 🔲 Play the end of the story.

Optional discussion
Ask students if they believe the story, and if they know anyone who has seen a ghost.

🔲 Tapescript for Exercise 2: *Rooms*

1 It was quite a small room. It had a bed – a single bed – a cupboard, a television, a very small table and a chair. Oh, and there was one picture on the wall. And there was a phone beside the bed.

2 It was a very comfortable room. It had a sofa and an armchair, and a thick carpet. There was a television and a music system, and some bookshelves with all my books on them.

3 It was quite a large room, and it had chairs round the walls. And in the middle of the room there was a low table with magazines on it. And there were posters on the walls, and a clock.

🔲 Tapescript for Exercise 4: *Two ghost stories*

This happened when I was about three years old. I don't actually remember it myself, but my parents told me about it later. Well, we had a cellar underneath the house where my mother did the washing, and I said I wanted to look in this little room at the side – we had a little room where we kept coal. And so we went inside, my mother and I, and it was empty and dark, and I said, 'Oh, look at that lady in the corner.' And I described an old lady in the corner – she had grey hair and she had a coloured apron, but I was the only person who could see this woman. And so we went upstairs very quickly, and my mother didn't want to go down to the cellar again for three weeks after that. And then later, my parents talked to the neighbours about it, and the neighbours said, 'Well, did you know that the woman who lived in the house before you was a rather strange old lady, and she had grey hair and she always wore a coloured apron. And she died in the cellar.'

4 Two ghost stories

Reading and listening activity

1 Before you read, find out what these expressions mean. Use a dictionary to help you.

ghost	servant	priest	owner	to scream
haunted house	master	sailor	farmer	to bang on the door

2 Read about Sandford Orcas Manor, and answer the questions.

Sandford Orcas Manor

THERE ARE many haunted houses in Britain. Most of them have one ghost. But the 16th century manor house in the village of Sandford Orcas, in south-west England, has four.

1 One is the ghost of an 18th century priest who used to kill visitors while they were asleep in their beds. He still sometimes frightens guests in the middle of the night by standing over their beds holding a knife.

2 The ghost of a servant sometimes walks along the dark corridors of the house at night. He killed his master at Sandford Orcas, but nobody knows why.

3 Another is the ghost of a young man who grew up in the house and then became a sailor. While he was at sea, he killed a boy. When he came home, they locked him in a room at the back of the house. He never left the room again, and died there several years later. On some nights when the moon is full, you can hear him screaming and banging on the door of the room.

4 The fourth is the ghost of a farmer. He often appears in the garden wearing old working clothes. He was a previous owner of the house, and he killed himself by hanging himself from a tree in the garden. Perhaps he was frightened of the ghosts.

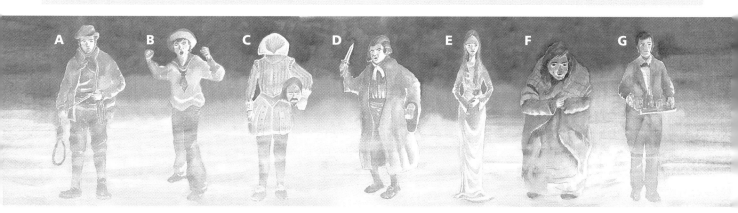

A   B   C   D   E   F   G

a How is Sandford Orcas Manor different from most other haunted houses?

b Complete the table about the ghosts.

c Find the four ghosts of Sandford Orcas Manor.

Which ghost?	He killed ...	You can see/hear him in ...
1	visitors	
2		the corridors
3		
4	previous owner	

3 🔲 A man talks about something that happened when he was a child.

Listen to the first part of the story, and write *T* (= True) or *F* (= False).

a ☐ The boy was six years old.

b ☐ He was with his mother.

c ☐ He saw an old woman in the cellar.

d ☐ She had black hair.

e ☐ She had a coloured apron.

f ☐ His mother saw her too.

g ☐ He stayed and talked to her.

h ☐ His parents told the neighbours about it.

What do you think the neighbours said? Listen to the end of the story. Were you right?

Focus on ... Both and neither

1 Look at these two houses.

How are they similar?

Both (of) the houses have got three floors.
Both of them have got balconies.

Neither of the houses has got a garage.
Neither of them has got a front garden.

How are they different?

One of the houses has got a blue door, but the other one has got a red door.

One of them has got six windows, but the other one has got eight windows.

2 🔲 Look at the picture on page 107. You will hear two people playing a game. Listen and complete the questions.

.... three floors?   .... trees?
.... a garage?   .... red doors?

Which two houses did the man choose?

Now you choose two houses and play the game.

3 Choose two people in the class and write some sentences about them. Can other students guess who you chose?

> Both of them have short hair.
> One of them is wearing a dress, and the other is wearing green trousers.
> Neither of them smokes.

Pronunciation: Small words (2)

1 🔲 Listen to the words in the box. They often have the sound /ə/ when they are not stressed.

are	My friends are here.
was	He was very hungry.
were	Where were you last night?
do	Where do you live?
does	What does that mean?
can	I can see them.

2 You will hear eight sentences. Each sentence contains one word from the box. Write the word you hear.

3 Practise saying the sentences.

Phrasebook: Finding a room

Fill the gaps in the conversation. Use these phrases.

£50 a night
a double room
any rooms free
two single rooms
with a shower

– Have you got .... ?
– Yes, we have. For how many people?
– Two.
– Do you want .... or .... ?
– Two single rooms, ...
– OK. Each room costs ....

🔲 Now listen and check. Do the people take the rooms?

Have similar conversations.

You want a double room with a shower.	You want a single room with a shower, a TV and a balcony.

Study pages D

Focus on ... *Both and neither*

This exercise focuses on the use of both, neither *and* one. *It also gives practice in describing houses and people.*

> *Key expressions:* both (of), neither of, one of.
> *Features of houses:* balcony, garage, floor, garden, tree, door, window.

1 Presentation of key expressions

● Look at the pictures, and read the examples. Make sure students understand the meaning of *both* (the two houses) and *neither* (= not one and not the other). If necessary give more examples, using the classroom and the students.

Point out that:
 – We can say *both of the houses* or *both the houses*, but we must say *both of them* (not 'both them').
 – We say *neither of the houses* and *one of the houses*.

2 Listening: introduction to the game

● Look at the houses on page 107. Tell the students they will hear people playing a game. One person has chosen *two* of the houses; the other person guesses which two houses they are.

● 🔲 Play the recording. Students listen and decide which houses the man chose. (Answer: A and E.)

● If necessary, demonstrate the game yourself by choosing two houses and getting students to ask you questions.

● Either let students play the game in pairs or groups, or play it with the whole class, with students taking it in turn to choose a pair of houses.

3 Extension: writing sentences

● Students write sentences about two people in the class, as in the example.

● They read out their sentences, and other students guess who the two people are.

> 🔲 Tapescript for Focus on ... *Both and neither*
>
> A Have the houses got three floors?
> B One of them has got three floors, yes.
> A And has one of the houses got a garage?
> B Yes, one of them has got a garage.
> A What about trees?
> B Both the houses have got trees.
> A Both of them, right. So both of them have got trees, one of them has got a garage, one of them has got three floors ... Have the houses got red doors?
> B Yes, both of them have got red doors.

Pronunciation: *Small words (2)*

> Common words which have the reduced sound /ə/ when unstressed.

1 Listening & practice

● 🔲 Play the recording and ask students to repeat the phrases. Focus on the /ə/ sound.

2 Recognition task

● Play the sentences. Students write the words they hear.

● Play the sentences again and check the answers:

 1 was 2 are 3 can 4 was 5 does 6 can 7 are
 8 was

3 Practice

● Practise saying the sentences round the class. Focus on the pronunciation of the 'small words'.

Phrasebook: *Finding a room*

This exercise practises language for enquiring about rooms. It picks up on language from Unit 8.

> *Key phrases:* a single room, a double room, Is there a room free?, (£50) a night, with a shower.

● Ask students to fill the gaps in the dialogue. As you do this, present any new expressions.

● 🔲 Play the dialogue to check.

● Look at the two situations with the class, and establish what the people will say. If you like, build dialogues up on the board.

● Either let students practise the dialogues in pairs, or ask two students to have each conversation in front of the class.

> 🔲 Tapescript for Pronunciation: *Small words (2)*
>
> 1 What was his name?
> 2 Where are you going?
> 3 You can get there by bus.
> 4 I was there a few days ago.
> 5 When does the train leave?
> 6 Where can I change money?
> 7 There are three bedrooms.
> 8 What was the film like?

> 🔲 Tapescript for Phrasebook: *Finding a room*
>
> A Have you got any rooms free?
> B Yes, we have. For how many people?
> A Two.
> B Do you want a double room or two single rooms?
> A Two single rooms, with a shower.
> B OK. Each room costs £50 a night.
> A £50? Oh, dear. Have you got anything cheaper?
> B No, sorry, that's all we've got.
> A OK, thanks. Bye.

Consolidation

Past time expressions

This exercise focuses on time expressions, used with the Past simple tense. It builds on language introduced in Exercises 7.2 and 7.3.

- Use the examples to make these points:
  - *yesterday* and *the day before yesterday* are fixed expressions – they have no preposition.
  - expressions with *this*, *last* and *ago* also have no preposition.
  - *this morning* = today; *this year* = the one we're in now.
- Do the exercise round the class, or give time for students to work through it themselves and then go through the answers together. Example answers (answers will of course vary):

When was the last time it rained? Three days ago. On Monday.
When did you start learning English? A year ago. Last September.
When did you have breakfast? At 7 o'clock this morning. A few hours ago.
When were you born? In March,1982. 18 years ago.
When did you last buy a pair of shoes? Last Saturday. Three days ago.

Very, quite …

This exercise focuses on the use of very, quite, fairly, rather and a bit, to modify adjectives. It builds on language introduced in Exercises 8.1 and 8.2.

- Look at the sentences, and ask students to match them with the desks. Expected answers:

A It's quite/rather untidy.
B It's very tidy.
C It's very untidy.
D It's quite/fairly tidy.

Point out that:
- *quite*, *fairly* and *rather* all mean 'not very'.
- we usually use *fairly* with a positive meaning and *rather* with a negative meaning (e.g. *fairly comfortable, rather uncomfortable, fairly quiet, rather noisy*).

If necessary, give other examples of your own.

- Either ask students to make sentences round the class or ask them to write two or three down and then read them out. Example answers:

My desk is fairly small and very untidy.
This classroom is not very big, and rather cold.
My neighbours are very friendly, but rather noisy.
Buses in my town are quite slow and very crowded.
My brother is quite clever but he isn't very friendly.

Review

Questions

Review of question forms from Units 1, 3 and 5.

1 Ask students to make *yes/no* questions from the sentences. Answers:

a Do kangaroos come from Peru?
b Does she speak Greek?
c Has the island got an airport?
d Is there a bank near here?
e Are there any good beaches?
f Is he working?

2 Ask students to make *Wh-* questions for each picture, and to suggest an answer. Answers:

A What are they playing? (They're playing chess.)
B What do pandas eat? (They eat bamboo.)
C What's the time? (It's a quarter to eleven.)
D How many legs have spiders got? (They've got eight legs.)
E Where does he come from? (He comes from Italy.)
F What is he playing? (He's playing a balalaika.)

Travelling

Review of language from Exercise 4.1.

1 Ask students to fill the gaps. Answers:

b go by plane   *c* go by bike   *d* walk   *e* by bus   *f* by train
g by boat

2 Ask a few questions round the class, based on the examples but substituting the items in brackets. Then get students to ask the same (or similar) questions in pairs.

Consolidation

Past time expressions

Here are some ways to talk about time in the past.

yesterday	I saw her	yesterday afternoon. the day before yesterday.
this …	I saw her	this morning. earlier this year.
last …	I saw her	last Saturday. last April.
in, on, at	I saw her	in January 2000. on Tuesday. at the weekend.
… ago	I saw her	a few days ago. two years ago.

Try to answer these questions in at least two ways.

When was the last time it rained?

When did you have breakfast?

When did you start learning English?

When were you born?

When did you last buy a pair of shoes?

Very, quite …

Look at these desks. Which sentences describe them best?

It's very tidy.

It's quite tidy.
    fairly

It's not very tidy.

It's a bit untidy.

It's quite untidy.
    rather

It's very untidy.

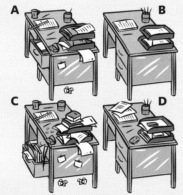

What are these things and people like?

– your desk
– this classroom
– your neighbours
– your house/flat
– buses in your town
– your brother/sister

My neighbours are quite rich, but they're not very friendly.

Review

Questions

1 Ask yes/no questions.

   a Kangaroos come from Peru – is that right?
   b I think she speaks Greek (but I'm not sure).
   c The island's got an airport (I think).
   d Maybe there's a bank near here (maybe not).
   e I hope there are some good beaches.
   f Maybe he's working. And maybe he isn't.

2 Ask *Wh-* questions. What are the answers?

A They're playing ? .

B Pandas eat ? .

D The time is ? .

C Spiders have got ? legs.

E He comes from ? .

F He's playing the ? .

Travelling

1 Here are some ways to travel. Fill the gaps.

   a You can | *drive*
             | go by car

   b You can | fly
             | ....

   c You can | cycle
             | ....

   d You can | ....
             | go on foot

   e You can go ....

   f You can go ....

   g You can go ....

2 Ask your partner questions.

How do you go to (the shops)?

When did you last go somewhere by (boat)?

9 I've done it!

1 It's just happened

Present perfect

1 Look at the pictures and read the bubbles.
What's the difference between the green verbs and the red verbs?

2 Now look at these pictures. Where is the man?
What is he saying? Match the bubbles with the pictures.

I've arrived at the station.

I've gone into the supermarket.

I've just got on the train.

I've just got off the train.

I've come out of the building.

Listen and check your answers.

3 Here are some more people with mobile phones. What do you think they're saying?

This unit introduces the Present perfect tense (positive, negative and questions).
It focuses on two main areas of use:
– talking about recent events (things that have just happened)
– talking and asking about preparations people have made.

9

1 It's just happened

This exercise introduces one of the basic uses of the Present perfect tense: for talking about things that have just happened, and which you can see the results of now. It shows the relationship between the Present perfect tense (what has happened) and the Present continuous tense (what is still going on).

➤ Focus on Form: Exercise 1
➤ Workbook: Exercise A

> *Key structure:* Present perfect tense. *Irregular past participles:* got, left, come, gone. *Verbs of motion:* arrive, leave, go into, come out of, get on, get off.

1 Introduction: presentation of Present perfect tense

● Explain that the pictures show scenes from the day of someone who likes using his mobile phone a lot. Look at the first set of pictures, and establish that:

– the green verbs are about what is happening *now* (at the moment of speaking). They are in the Present continuous tense (*I'm* + verb + *-ing*).
– the red verbs are about things that are already *finished* or *completed* now. They are in the Present perfect tense. (*I've* + past participle). Write these forms on the board:

Verb	Present perfect tense
finish	I've finished
leave	I've left
get	I've got
put	I've put

> *Presentation option*
> Give other examples to make the idea of the Present perfect clear, e.g. open the window and say *Look – I'm opening the window*; then say *Now I've opened the window*.

> *Language note*
> The Present perfect tense is formed with *have* + past participle. Often the past participle is the same as the Past tense (e.g. *open – opened – opened*; *leave – left – left*; *get – got – got*), but not always (e.g. *go – went – gone*). Past participles are shown in the table of irregular verbs on page 128.

2 Matching sentences with pictures; listening to check

● Look at Pictures A–F, and establish where the man is. Expected answers:

A He's in the street.   B He's at a railway station.   C He's on a train.
D He's coming out of the station.   E He's in a shop/supermarket.
F He's outside his house.

● Ask students to match the pictures with the bubbles. Answers:

A I've come out of the building.
B I've arrived at the station.
C I've just got on the train.
D I've just got off the train.
E I've gone into the supermarket.

As you go through the answers, write the verb forms on the board:

● 🔲 Play the recording.

Verb		Present perfect tense
come		come (out of)
arrive		arrived
get on	I've	got on
get off		got off
go		gone (into)

🔲 The tapescript is on page T42.

3 Activation: making sentences

● Look at the pictures and ask students to make sentences, using the verbs on the board. Expected answers:

I've just arrived at the airport. I've just got out of the taxi.
I've just got on the bus.
I've just come out of (the) school.
I've just arrived at the cinema.
I've just got into the bath.

> *Language note*
> We usually say *get on/off* a bus or a train, but *get into/out of* a car or a taxi.
>
> We also use *get* in other common expresions, e.g. *get into/out of the bath, get into/out of bed.*

2 What's new?

This exercise introduces the 3rd person forms of the Present perfect and more irregular past participles.

> **Key structures:** Present perfect tense (He's, She's, They've).
> **Irregular past participles:** had, got, lost, won, bought, sold, broken, cut.

1 Presentation of Present perfect tense & past participles

- Look at the table and establish what the basic verb forms are:

  have, get, lose, win, buy, sell, break, cut

2 Making sentences from pictures

- Look at the pictures. Ask students to make sentences. Answers:

  They've just got married.   He's just won the match.   They've just bought a new TV.
  He's just sold a clock.   She's just had a baby.   She's broken her leg.
  He's cut his face.   She's lost her keys.

3 Miming & guessing game

- Give each student (or pair of students) one of the sentences on page T103.
- In turn, students mime the situation. The others guess what has happened.

3 Have you …?

This exercise introduces Present perfect questions and negative forms.

> **Key structures:** Questions with have you + past participle; I haven't + past participle.   **Verbs:** pack, buy, clean, turn off, wash, close, buy.

1 Listening & gap-filling; presentation of questions and negatives

- Look at the picture and establish the situation: a couple in a car, they're going away for the weekend or for a holiday, they've packed everything.
- [cassette] Play the recording. Students listen and fill the gaps. Then check the answers:

  Have you turned the lights off? Have you closed all the windows? I haven't closed the front door.

- Show how questions and negatives are formed:

  > **Positive:**   *I've closed the windows.*
  > **Negative:**   *I haven't closed the windows.*
  > **Question:**   *Have you closed the windows?*

2 Practice: writing sentences

- Read through the list of 'Things to do', and present any new items.
- Look at one or two of the situations with the class, and discuss which things on the list you've done (e.g. *I'm going to a party: I've had a shower, I've cleaned my shoes, I've washed my hair, I've cleaned my teeth*).
- Students choose one of the other situations, and write a list of things they've done, using the Present perfect form *I've …*

3 Asking & answering questions

- To show what to do, choose a student and ask him/her questions (e.g. *Have you closed the windows?*). See if the class can guess which situation he/she chose.
- *Either* Students work in pairs, taking it in turn to ask questions and guess their partner's situation;
  Or Students come to the front of the class in turn. The others ask questions and try to guess their situation.

➤ Focus on Form: Exercise 2
➤ Workbook: Exercise B, Listening

> *Presentation option*
> Show the forms of the Present perfect on the board:
>
> > ***win – won***
> > ***I've won***
> > ***He's/She's won*** $1,000.
> > ***They've won***

> *Language note*
> These are all situations where we can see the result of something that has just happened. This is a typical use of the Present perfect tense. As always with the Present perfect, *when* it happened is not mentioned (and not important).

➤ Focus on Form: Exercise 3
➤ Workbook: Exercise C

[cassette] The tapescript is on page T42.

> *Language note*
> Most of these verbs are regular, and so add *-ed* to form the past participle: *pack – packed, clean – cleaned, turn – turned*, etc.
> *Buy – bought* and *have – had* are irregular.

> *Note*
> To answer the questions, students should give short answers: *Yes, I have* or *No, I haven't.*

2 What's new?

Past participles

1 The words in red are *past participles*.
What are the verbs?

	had
She's	got
	lost
	won
He's	bought
	sold
They've	broken
	cut

2 Look at the people in the pictures.
What have they just done?

3 The teacher will give you a sentence. Mime the situation.
Can other students guess what has happened?

3 Have you …?

Questions • negatives

1 🔲 Listen to the dialogue and fill the gaps.

A Right, off we go.
B .... ?
A Yes, I have.
B .... ?
A Yes, yes.
B OK. Let's go, then.
A Actually …
B What?
A Um, ...

2 Choose one of these situations.

You're going out with your
boy/girlfriend.

A friend is coming
to stay.

You're going to give a party.

You're going to a party.

You're going for an
interview for a job.

You're going to the theatre.

Look at the list of things to do. Which things have you done?
Write them down.

THINGS TO DO

pack some clothes
have a shower
buy a cake
clean your shoes
turn off the heating
buy tickets
turn off the lights
wash your hair
close all the windows
clean your flat
pack your toothbrush
buy some food
clean your teeth

3 *Student A*: Ask B questions about
things in the list. Can you guess
the situation?

Student B: Answer A's questions.

Have you closed
all the windows?

No, I
haven't.

Focus on Form

1 Past participles

	Infinitive	Past simple	Past participle
A	watch	watched	watched
	close	closed	....
	clean	cleaned	....
B	have	had	had
	leave	left	....
	buy	bought	....
C	take	took	taken
	write	wrote	....
	go	went	....

Write the missing past participles in the table. What are the differences between the three groups?

What are the Past simple and the past participle forms of these verbs? Which group do they belong in?

get   come   wash   put   arrive
turn   lose   open   break   sell

(There's a list of irregular verbs on page 128.)

2 Present perfect

> have or has + past participle

It's 8.00 in the morning, and Mike and Olivia are at home. Mike has had a shower, and Olivia has washed her hair. They've got dressed, and now they're having their breakfast.

Here are some other parts of their morning. What have they done? What are they doing? Put the verbs in the right tense.

It's 9.00. They (have) breakfast, and they (clean) their teeth. They (leave) the house, and they (walk) down the road.

It's 9.30. Mike (buy) a paper, and he (read) it in a café. Olivia (go) to the hairdresser.

It's 11.00. Mike and Olivia (come) back home. They (turn) on the TV, and they (watch) the news.

3 Questions & negatives

> Have you watched TV today?

> Yes, I have.

> No, I haven't.

Find out what your partner has done today. Use these ideas, and add one question of your own.

clean your teeth   watch TV   have a meal
write an email   buy a paper   wash your hair
have a cup of coffee   .... ? ....

Did you answer 'No' to any of the questions? Write sentences about you and your partner.

> I haven't bought a newspaper.
> She hasn't written an email.

How to say it

1 🔲 Listen to *I've*, *he's*, *she's* and *they've* in these sentences. Practise saying them.

I've done it!
He's just arrived.
She's bought some cheese.
They've cleaned the flat.

2 🔲 Listen to the intonation of these sentences. Practise saying them.

I've closed all the windows.
Have you closed all the windows?
They've just arrived.
Have they arrived yet?

Focus on Form

1 *Past participles*

- Complete the table with the class, getting them to guess the answers. Give examples to show how the past participle forms appear in a sentence (e.g. *I've closed the door, I've cleaned my shoes*). Answers:

  closed, cleaned, left, bought, written, gone.

- Establish the difference between the three groups:
  - *Group A:* regular verbs; past participle ends in *-ed*.
  - *Group B:* irregular verbs; past participle is the same as the Past tense (most irregular verbs are like this).
  - *Group C:* irregular verbs; past participle is different from the Past tense.

- Ask students to give all three forms of the verbs and say which group they belong to. If you like, ask them to look for the verbs in the list on page 128. Write them on the board in three groups:

A:	wash	washed	washed
	arrive	arrived	arrived
	turn	turned	turned
	open	opened	opened
B:	get	got	got
	put	put	put
	lose	lost	lost
	sell	sold	sold
C:	come	came	come
	break	broke	broken

2 *Present perfect*

- Give a few examples to focus on the difference between the Present continuous and Present perfect, e.g. *Look, I'm opening the book. Now I've opened the book, and I'm reading it.*

- Either go through the exercise with the class, or students do it in pairs and then go through it together. Answers:

  They've had … they've cleaned … they've left … they're walking …
  Mike has bought … he's reading … Olivia has gone
  Mike and Olivia have come … They've turned … they're watching …

3 *Questions & negatives*

- Look at the phrases and establish what the questions should be:

  Have you cleaned your teeth today?
  Have you watched TV today?
  Have you had a meal today?
  Have you written an email today?
  Have you bought a paper today?
  Have you washed your hair today?
  Have you had a cup of coffee today?

- Students ask and answer questions.

- Students write sentences. As a round-up, ask students to read out their sentences.

How to say it

1 *Pronunciation of contracted forms*

- 🔊 Play the recording, pausing after each sentence. Focus on the pronunciation of *I've*, *he's*, *she's* and *they've*, and especially on the reduced /ɪ/ in /hɪz/ and /ʃɪz/:

  /hɪz ˈdʒʌst əˈraɪvd/, /ʃɪz ˈbɔːt səm ˈtʃiːz/

- Practise saying the sentences.

2 *Intonation of sentences & yes/no questions*

- 🔊 Play the recording, pausing after each item. Point out that in the questions the voice rises higher and then falls more sharply.

🔊 Tapescript for Exercise 1: *It's just happened*

Hello. Yeah, I've just come out of the building, and I'm walking down the street to the station …
Hello. I've arrived at the station now, I'm just buying a ticket …
Hi. I've just got on the train – I'm having a cup of coffee …

Hello, it's me again. I've just got off the train, and I'm coming out of the station …
Hi. I've just gone into the supermarket – I'm buying some bread. Yeah, yeah, yeah, see you soon. Bye!

🔊 Tapescript for Exercise 3: *Have you … ?*

A Right, off we go.
B Have you turned the lights off?
A Yes, I have.
B Have you closed all the windows?
A Yes, yes.

B OK. Let's go then.
A Actually …
B What?
A I haven't closed the front door.

10

This unit deals with three areas of language connected with clothes:
– describing clothes
– buying clothes
– saying when and how often you wear particular clothes.
The reading and listening activity is about fashion and jewellery.

1 Things to wear

In this exercise students identify clothes people are wearing in a picture, then describe what they are wearing themselves. This is used to revise vocabulary that students may know already and also to introduce new items.

▶ Workbook: Exercise A

> *New vocabulary:* boots, sandals, trainers; scarf, uniform, sunglasses; cotton, leather, denim. *Recycled language:* basic clothes vocabulary, colours; Present continuous tense (Unit 5). (→ Beginner Unit 12.)

1 Brainstorming activity; review & presentation of clothes vocabulary

- Use the first part of the exercise to establish what words for clothes students already know. Give time for students to think about each category and write down three items. Then take each category in turn, and build up lists of words on the board. Possible answers:

  On your feet: shoes, boots, socks
  In cold weather: coat, hat, jumper/pullover, scarf, gloves
  In hot weather: T-shirt, shorts, (summer) dress, sun hat, swimming costume
  To a smart party: suit, tie, dress, shirt

> *Pairwork option*
> Each pair chooses one of the categories, and makes a list of words.

2 Identifying items in a picture; vocabulary presentation

- Read the sentences in turn and ask students to find each person in the picture. As you do so, present new vocabulary. Ask students to identify the people by saying what they are doing and what else they are wearing, e.g. *b: He's reading a magazine. He's wearing shorts and a shirt.*

> *Language note*
> *Trainers* are shoes used for sports and leisure activities.

3 Pairwork game: describing people in the picture

- To demonstrate the game, choose a person in the picture and say what he/she is wearing (e.g. *He's wearing blue jeans and red boots*). See if students can find the person.
- Pairwork. Students take it in turn to choose people and describe them.
- As a round-up, ask a few students to describe some of the people they chose.

> *Whole class option*
> One student chooses a person and describes him/her. The others listen and try to find the person. The first student to find him/her has the next turn, and so on.

4 Writing sentences; guessing game

- Students write one or two sentences on a piece of paper, describing what they are wearing.
- Collect all the papers. Read out the descriptions in turn, and see if students can identify the person who wrote them.

> *Alternative: magazine pictures*
> If most students are wearing similar clothes (e.g. a school uniform), bring magazine pictures into the class instead, and give a picture to each student (or pair of students). They write about the person in their picture. Then collect the pictures and give them out in a different order. Ask students to read out their sentences in turn, and ask who has the picture.

🖭 Tapescript for Exercise 2: *Can I try it on?*

A Excuse me. What size is this jacket?
B It's 46.
A Oh, good. Can I try it on?
B Yes, of course. Here you are.
A Thanks … How does it look?

B Mmm. It looks very good. It really suits you. Does it feel OK?
A Yes, it's fine. It fits very well – it's really comfortable. How much is it?
B £65.
A Oh, that's not too expensive. I think I'll buy it.

---

10 Clothes

1 Things to wear

1 What clothes do you know in English? Write down three things you wear ...

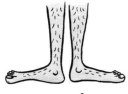 ... on your feet

 ... in cold weather

 ... in hot weather

... to a smart party

2 Look at the people in the picture.

Can you find

a a boy with sunglasses?

b a man wearing boots?

c a man wearing a uniform?

d a woman wearing a scarf?

e a girl wearing white trainers?

f a man wearing sandals?

g a woman in a yellow cotton dress?

h a woman in a denim jacket?

i a man in a leather jacket?

3 Choose one of the people in the picture. Say what he/she is wearing.

Can your partner find the person?

4 On a piece of paper, write down what you're wearing at the moment.

Give the paper to the teacher to read out. Can other students identify you?

I'm wearing a white shirt, a black denim jacket, black trousers, green socks and an old pair of trainers.

2 Can I try it on?

How much is it?

It fits very well.

I think I'll buy it.

Can I try it on?

It really suits you.

What size is this jacket?

1 Look at the sentences in bubbles. Where do you think they come in the conversation?

A Excuse me. .... ?
B It's 46.
A Oh, good. .... ?
B Yes, of course. Here you are.
A Thanks ... How does it look?
B Mmm. It looks very good. ....
   Does it feel OK?
A Yes, it's fine. .... – it's really
   comfortable. .... ?
B It's £65.
A OK. That's not too expensive. ....

🔲 Listen to the conversation and check your answers.

2 Imagine the woman doesn't like the jacket. What could she say?

3 *Student A*: You're in a clothes shop. Ask the shop assistant about one of these things.

Student B: You're a shop assistant. Help A.

3 When do you wear ...?

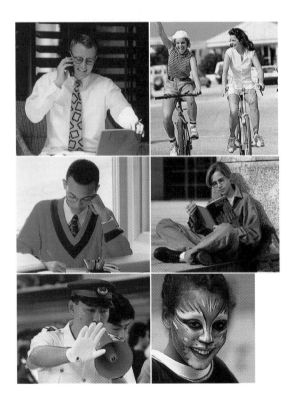

1 Read about these five people. Which words show how often they wear a tie?

John never wears a tie.

Alex doesn't wear a tie very often, but he sometimes wears one on special occasions.

Peter only wears a tie at weddings.

George always wears a tie at work, but he never wears one at home.

William usually wears a tie for business, and he often wears one when he goes out in the evenings.

🔲 Three of them say when they wear a tie. Who are they?

2 When do you wear ...

| ... a tie? | ... a hat? | ... gloves? | ... jeans? |
| ... make-up? | ... shorts? | ... trainers? | ... glasses? |

Tell your partner.

3 Choose something interesting that you heard about your partner. Write one or two sentences.

2 Can I try it on?

This exercise introduces expressions used for choosing and buying clothes.

> *Key phrases:* It fits, It suits you, try on, What size is …? How much is …?
> *Recycled language:* clothes vocabulary.

1 Vocabulary presentation; gap-filling task

- Look at the picture and establish the situation (*It's a clothes shop; there's a customer and a shop assistant; the customer is looking at a jacket*).
- Look at the remarks in the bubbles. Present the expressions *It fits, It suits you, What size …?* and *try something on*.
- Read through the dialogue, and ask students to suggest how to fill the gaps.
- ▭ Play the recording to check. (Answers: see tapescript.)

2 Eliciting alternative expressions; practice

- Go through the dialogue and discuss what the woman would say if she didn't like the jacket. Build up possible remarks on the board, e.g.
- Practise the dialogue, using some of the remarks.

> **It doesn't fit very well.**
> **It doesn't suit me.**
> **It isn't very comfortable.**
> **That's too expensive.**

3 Role-play

- To introduce this part, choose one of the situations and act out a conversation with one student.
- Students act out similar conversations in pairs. As a round-up, ask a few students what happened in their conversation.

➤ Workbook: Exercise B

> *Language notes*
> *It fits* = it's the right size.
> *It suits you* = it looks good on you.
>
> *Try on* is a phrasal verb: *on* can come before or after a noun, but after a pronoun. So we can say *I'd like to try on this jacket* or *I'd like to try this jacket on*, but only *I'd like to try it on* (not *I'd like to try on it*).

> ▭ The tapescript is on page T43.

> *Whole class option*
> Choose pairs of students to act out conversations in front of the class.

3 When do you wear …?

In this exercise, students say when they wear certain clothes, e.g. hats, gloves – clothes that reveal something of the speaker's lifestyle or personality.

> *Key vocabulary:* tie, hat, gloves, jeans, shorts, trainers, glasses; make-up.
> *Recycled language:* Present simple, frequency expressions (Unit 1).

1 Vocabulary & grammar focus; listening

- Look at the pictures and ask what the people are wearing. Use this to focus on the key vocabulary of the exercise.
- Read the sentences, and build up the frequency expressions on the board:
- ▭ Play the recording. Students match the people with the sentences. Answers:

  1 William   2 Alex   3 George

> always   never
> usually   not usually
> often   not (very) often
> sometimes
> only

2 Personalisation: speaking activity

- To introduce the activity, tell the class when you wear a tie, a hat, etc.
- Pairwork. Students say when they wear each of the items.
- Round-up. Find out how many students always, sometimes, never, etc. wear each item. Ask a few students to give you details about each one.

3 Extension: writing sentences

- Students write sentences about their partner.
- Students read out their sentences.

➤ Workbook: Exercise C, Listening

> ▭ The tapescript is on page T45.

> *Language note*
> *Only* has the meaning 'never except' (e.g. *I only get up late on Sundays*).

> *Optional extension*
> Play the recording again and establish what else each speaker says. You could also discuss what kind of person they seem to be.

4 The purple dress

This combined reading and listening activity is a story about a dress. In the reading part, students put paragraphs from the story in the correct sequence. They then guess the end of the story and listen to check.

> *New words (reading):* plastic, charity shop, throw away, borrow, match (v.), simply, cleaners. *New words (listening):* label.

1 Introduction: reading & sequencing task

- Begin by asking students to look at the pictures and say what they think the story will be about (e.g. *a woman, she buys a dress, she goes to a wedding*). Establish a few basic ideas, but do not go into too much detail.

- Read Paragraph 1 together. Then give time for students to read through the other paragraphs, either working alone or in pairs. They decide what order the paragraphs should be in, and number them.

- Read the first paragraph again, then ask students which paragraph they think should come next. (Answer: A week before the wedding, I met my cousin …) Read through it together, presenting any new words (e.g. *borrow*) as you go.

  Then ask students to identify the next paragraph, and so on, reading through each paragraph in turn. The correct order is:

Language note

Charity shops are common in towns in Britain. People give the shop things they do not need (e.g. clothes, books), and the shop sells them very cheaply. The money they make goes to a charity (e.g. Oxfam, the Red Cross).

2 A week before the wedding, …	6 So I got some big plastic bags, …
3 So after lunch I went round …	7 Later that week, I found …
4 The wedding was great. …	8 But I couldn't find the dress. …
5 The day after the wedding, …	9 So I went back to the charity shop …

2 Discussion: guessing the ending

- Ask students what the woman's problem is (Answer: She's probably sold her cousin's dress), and ask them to guess how the story ends.

3 Listening

- ▣ Play the recording and establish how the story ends. (Answer: see tapescript.)

- Ask students how the phrases from the story are used. If necessary, play the recording again to check. Answers:

  a I went round all the expensive shops.
  b By the bus stop there was another charity shop.
  c There was a purple dress in the window.
  d It had a label saying £5.
  e 'A woman brought this in this morning.'
  f 'She found it wasn't the right size.'
  g I took the dress to the cleaner's.
  h I gave it back to my cousin.

▣ Tapescript for Exercise 3: *When do you wear …?*

1 I usually wear a tie at work. I don't wear one at home usually – only if we have very important visitors or something. But I nearly always wear a tie if I go out for a meal, or to the theatre or cinema or something like that.

2 I don't usually wear a tie, but if I go out to a party or a meal or a wedding, some occasion like that, yes, then I do wear a tie.

3 Well, unfortunately I have to wear a tie at the office where I work, but I hate wearing ties, and usually I put on my tie just before I get to the office and I take it off again when I leave the office. I certainly don't wear a tie at home, no.

▣ Tapescript for Exercise 4: *The purple dress*

It was terrible. I thought, 'What am I going to do? I must buy her another one.' So I went round all the expensive shops in town, and of course I couldn't find the same dress. So I went to catch the bus home. And by the bus stop there was another charity shop. And it was amazing, there was a purple dress in the window just like my cousin's, and it had a label saying £5. So I went inside and bought it. And the shop assistant said 'Yes, a woman brought this in this morning. She said she only bought it yesterday, but when she got home, she found it wasn't the right size. So she gave it back to us.' So I took the dress to the cleaner's, and at the weekend I gave it back to my cousin. And she said, 'It's a funny thing. I was in town last week and I saw a dress just like this one. And do you know, it was in the window of a charity shop!'

4 The purple dress

Reading and listening activity

1 Here is the first part of a story. Can you put Parts 2–9 in the right order?

1 **When I was 20, a friend** invited me to her wedding. I had nothing nice to wear. I had a lot of clothes, but they were all very old, and I didn't have enough money to buy a new dress.

So I got some big plastic bags, and filled them up with old clothes. But I didn't throw them away – I took them into town and gave them to a charity shop in the High Street.

The day after the wedding, I looked in my cupboard and I thought 'I never wear a lot of these old clothes. It's time to throw some of them away.'

So after lunch I went round to her flat, and I borrowed a lovely, *very* expensive, purple dress, and some purple shoes and a purple handbag to match.

So I went back to the charity shop, and asked them about the dress. 'Oh yes, I remember it,' the woman said. 'But it's gone. We sold it yesterday afternoon.'

The wedding was great. I wore the purple dress, and everyone said how nice I looked. I danced all evening, and we all had a wonderful time.

But I couldn't find the dress. I looked all over my flat, but it simply wasn't there. And suddenly I thought 'Oh, no! I've given it to the charity shop!'

A week before the wedding, I met my cousin for lunch, and I told her I had nothing to wear. And she said 'Don't worry. You're about my size. You can borrow one of my dresses.'

Later that week, I found my cousin's purple shoes and handbag under the bed, and I thought 'Oh yes! I must take her dress to the cleaners and give it back to her.'

2 What is the woman's problem? What do you think will happen next?

3 [cassette icon] Now listen to the rest of the story. How does the speaker use these phrases?

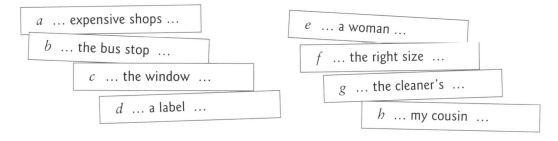

a … expensive shops …

b … the bus stop …

c … the window …

d … a label …

e … a woman …

f … the right size …

g … the cleaner's …

h … my cousin …

E Study pages

Focus on ... Mine, yours ...

1 📼 Listen and read the conversations. Then complete the table.

Is this coat yours?

No, I think it's hers.

I don't know – it isn't ours. Maybe it's theirs.

Is this coat John's?

Yes, it's mine.

Whose is this?

No, his is grey. That one's Sam's.

Whose coat is it?	Whose is it?
It's my coat.	It's mine.
It's your coat.	It's ....
It's his coat.	It's ....
It's her coat.	It's ....
It's John's coat.	It's ....
Whose umbrella is it?	*Whose is it?*
It's our umbrella.	It's ....
It's their umbrella.	It's ....

2 Use words from the table instead of the phrases in blue.

   a – These aren't my shoes. Are they your shoes?
   – No, they aren't my shoes. I think they're William's shoes.

   b – I don't like our flat much. I think their flat is much better.
   – Oh, I don't know. Our flat is bigger than their flat.

   c Richard and Helen have got two cars. The Fiat Uno is his car, and the Porsche is her car.

3 The teacher will point to some things in the class. Whose are they?

Pronunciation: Unusual words (2)

1 📼 Try saying these words, then listen to check.

vegetables	quiet
business	cushion
comfortable	sausage
sandwiches	sugar
cupboard	sunbathing

2 Write a sentence. Use at least two of the words from the box.

3 Read out your sentence.

Phrasebook: Paying for things

by cheque?   credit cards?   a receipt?

📼 Listen to the conversations. What are the three questions? What are the answers?

Have similar conversations.

You're buying some books. You want to pay by credit card and get a receipt.

You're paying for a cup of coffee. You can pay in cash, but you want a receipt.

You're buying a coat. You want to pay by cheque.

You're buying a CD. You haven't got any money with you – only a credit card.

46   *Study pages E*

Study pages E

Focus on ... *Mine, yours ...*

This exercise gives practice in using possessive pronouns.

> *Key language:* mine, yours, his, hers, ours, theirs, John's; whose?

1 Introduction: listening & gap-filling

- Look at the picture and establish the situation (people are leaving a party or a meeting, and they are trying to sort out their coats and umbrellas).
- 🔲 Play the recording and let students follow the conversations. Then students fill the gaps in the table. Answers:

  yours, his, hers, John's, ours, theirs

  Point out the difference between *my, your,* etc. and *mine, yours,* etc. If necessary, give other examples, using objects in the classroom (e.g. *Look – this is my book. It's mine*).

2 Practice

- Either go through the exercise with the class, or let students do it in pairs and then go through the answers together. Answers:

  a yours, mine, William's
  b theirs, ours, theirs
  c his, hers

3 Extension: answering questions

- Point to things in the class, and ask *Whose is this?* or *Whose are these?*. Try to elicit e.g. *It's mine, It's yours, It's (Maria's), They're ours, It's his, It's hers*, by asking different students.

> 🔲 Tapescript for Focus on ... *Mine, yours ...*
>
> 1 A Is this coat yours?
> B No, I think it's hers.
> C Yes, it's mine.
> 2 A Whose is this?
> B I don't know – it isn't ours. Maybe it's theirs.
> 3 A Is this coat John's?
> B No, his is grey. That one's Sam's, I think.

> 🔲 Tapescript for Phrasebook: *Paying for things*
>
> 1 A That'll be £6.50, please.
> B Can I pay by cheque?
> A Yes. Do you have a cheque card?
> B Yes, I do.
> A That's all right, then.
> 2 A So that's £2 altogether, then.
> B Do you take credit cards?
> A No, sorry, we don't.
> 3 A That's £25, then.
> B There you are. Could I have a receipt?
> A Yes, certainly. Just a minute.

Pronunciation: *Unusual words (2)*

> Words from previous units which may cause pronunciation problems.

1 Listening & practice

- 🔲 Ask students to try saying each word, then play the recording of it and get them to practise. Focus on:
  - the 'silent' vowels in /ˈvedʒtəbəlz/, /ˈbɪznɪs/, /ˈkʌmftəbəl/.
  - the silent 'p' in /ˈkʌbəd/.
  - the reduced /ə/ sound in /ˈvedʒtəbəlz/, /ˈkʌmftəbəl/, /ˈʃugə/, /ˈkuʃən/, /ˈkʌbəd/.
  - the reduced /ɪ/ sound in /ˈsɒsɪdʒ/, /ˈbɪznɪs/.
  - the pronunciation of /ˈsænwɪdʒɪz/, /ˈkwaɪət/ and /ˈsʌnbeɪðɪŋ/.

2 Writing sentences

- Students write a sentence using words from the box, and including any other words they like, e.g.

  I had sausage and vegetables for dinner.
  This cushion isn't very comfortable.

3 Reading sentences aloud

- Students read out their sentences in turn. Focus on the pronunciation of the key words.

  Alternative: Dictation. Students dictate their sentence to the person next to them. As a check, ask students to read out the sentence they wrote down.

Phrasebook: *Paying for things*

This exercise teaches expressions used when paying for things in shops or cafés.

> *Key phrases:* pay by cheque, credit card, a receipt.
> *Recycled language:* Could I have ...?

- Look at the pictures, and establish the meaning of *a cheque, a credit card* and *a receipt* (= a piece of paper showing how much you've paid).
- 🔲 Play the dialogue and ask what the questions and answers are:

  1 Can I pay by cheque?
   Yes. Do you have a cheque card?
  2 Do you take credit cards?
   No, sorry, we don't.
  3 Could I have a receipt?
   Yes, certainly.

  Point out that we use *by* in *pay by cheque, pay by credit card*.

- Look at the situations with the class, and establish what the people will say.
- Either let students practise the dialogues in pairs, or ask two students to have each conversation in front of the class.

Consolidation

Present perfect & Past simple

This exercise focuses on the contrast between Present perfect and Past simple tenses. It builds on language introduced in Units 7 and 9.

1 Look at the examples and ask students to complete the rule. Use it to make these points:
   – We use the Present perfect to talk about recent events. We can use it with the words *just* or *yet*, but not with past time expressions.
   – We use the Past simple to talk about events in the past. We often use it with past time expressions (e.g. *yesterday*, *at 3 o'clock*).

2 Do the exercise round the class, or give time for students to work through it themselves and then go through the answers together. Answers:
   a I've packed, I haven't put on
   b I saw, she was
   c I spoke
   d Have you had, I had

's

This exercise focuses on the different ways in which we use 's. Examples of these uses appear in various units, including Units 2, 3, 5 and 9.

- Read the examples. If necessary, give a few more examples of your own.
- Students write 1, 2 or 3 beside the sentences. Answers:
  a 2 (= John has arrived)
  b 3 (= the friends of Peter)
  c 2 (= he has just bought)
  d 1 (= Maria is my cousin)
  e 1 (= it is a bit small)
  f 2 (= it has got)
  g 1 (= where is my book?)

Review

Verbs in the past

Review of Past simple forms (positive and negative) from Unit 7.

- If you like, look at the verbs first and ask students to give you the Past tense forms, positive and negative (e.g. *came, didn't come; drank, didn't drink …*).
- Do the exercise with the class. Answers:
  a came, ate, drank, stayed, woke up, felt, didn't go
  b was, lived, had, were, moved, didn't like, wanted

Where?

Review of vocabulary from Study Pages B Focus and from Exercise 8.1.

- Ask students to suggest possible continuations. If you like, write them on the board. Possible answers:
  a in a village, in the country
  b in the suburbs
  c in the town centre, on a main road, on the ground floor, near the railway station
  d at the station, at the ticket office, on the bus, at a travel agency, on the platform
  e at a newsagent, at a kiosk, at the station, at the post office
  f at the reception (desk), in your room

Mixed-up words

Review of vocabulary from Units 6 and 8.

1 ● Look at the first red word together, and establish what it is (Answer: cinema).
   Working alone or in pairs, students work out the other words. Let them look back at Units 6 and 8 if they need help.
   ● Go through the answers together. Answers:
   Places to spend an evening: cinema, theatre, restaurant
   Containers for food: packet, bottle, carton
   Things in a living room: armchair, curtains, cushions

2 ● Students look through previous units to find a word. They write it in a jumbled form and add a clue.
   ● They give their word to another student to solve.

Consolidation

Present perfect and Past simple

1 Look at these examples.

Present perfect	Past simple
We've just arrived at the airport.	We arrived at the airport a few minutes ago.
Look – I've bought a new jacket.	I bought a new jacket last week.
She's had a baby.	She had a baby last Thursday.
Have you had a shower?	Did you have a shower yesterday?
Have you seen the new *Star Wars* film yet?	Did you see the new *Star Wars* film at the weekend?

Complete these rules.

We can use the .... tense with no time expression or with *just* or *yet*.

If we use a past time expression, we must use the .... tense.

2 Choose the Present perfect or Past simple.

a I'm nearly ready. I've packed/I packed my case, but I haven't put on/I didn't put on my coat yet.

b I've seen/I saw Jackie at the party last night. She's been/She was with her new boyfriend.

c I've spoken/I spoke to your friend John a few minutes ago.

d – Have you had/Did you have breakfast yet?
– Yes, I've had/I had it about an hour ago.

's

's is used in three ways:

1 = is: She's from Spain. (= She is from Spain)

2 = has: He's got a new jumper. (= He has got)

3 = possessive *'s*: Is this your friend's bike?
(= the bike of your friend)

What kind of *'s* is in these sentences?

Write *1*, *2* or *3*.

a I'm phoning to tell you that John's arrived.

b Peter's friends aren't here yet.

c He's just bought a new car.

d Maria's my cousin.

e I like my flat, but it's a bit small.

f It's got three bedrooms and a kitchen.

g Where's my book?

Review

Verbs in the past

These texts are about the past. Fill the gaps, using verbs from the boxes.

a Last night, some friends ☐ to my flat for a meal. We all ☐ a lot of food, and we ☐ quite a lot of wine. They ☐ until two o'clock in the morning. When I ☐ this morning, I ☐ very tired, so I ☐ *not* to work.

come
drink
eat
feel
go
stay
wake up

b When she ☐ a young child, Alice ☐ in an old house in Cambridge. It ☐ six bedrooms, and there ☐ lots of trees in the garden. Then her parents ☐ to a small flat in London. Alice *not* ☐ it at all. She ☐ to go back to Cambridge.

be
be
have
like
live
move
want

Where?

Complete these sentences. They're all about places.

a They don't live in a town. They live …

b I don't live in the town centre. I live …

c My flat's quite noisy, because it's …

d You buy your ticket …

e You can buy stamps …

f When you leave the hotel, leave your key …

Mixed-up words

1 Look at these mixed-up words. Can you make

– three places to spend an evening?

   A C E K P T   A C E I M N

– three containers for food and drink?

   A A C H I M R R   B E L O T T

– three things in a living room?

   A E E H R T T   A C I N R S T U

   C H I N O S S U

   A A E N R R S T T U   A C N O R T

How do you spell them?

2 Now you write a mixed-up word. Show it to your partner.

   G R O A N E (A kind of fruit)

Quantity

1 Find the differences

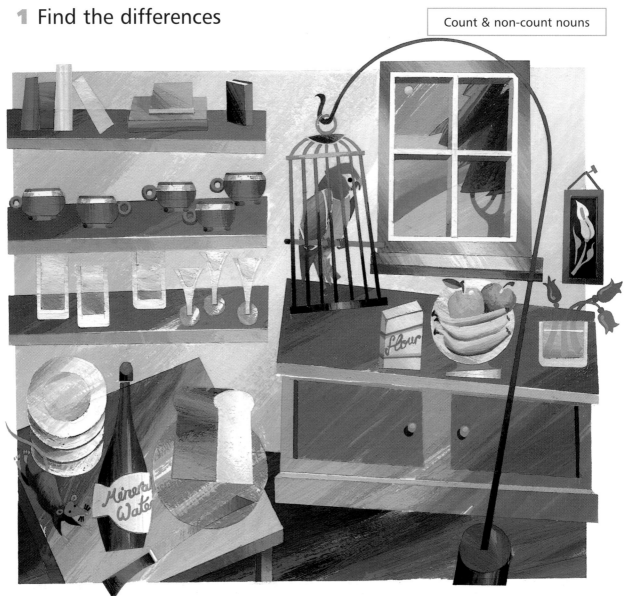

1 🔲 You will hear a man talking about a picture. How is it different from this picture?

Use these expressions.

There's a …

There are some …

There's some …

There isn't a …

There aren't any …

There isn't any …

2 Work in pairs.

Student A: Look at the picture on page 107.

Student B: Look at the picture on page 108.

Ask about your partner's picture, and talk about your own. Try to find eight differences.

Is there a mouse in your picture?

Yes. On the bottom shelf.

Is there any coffee on the cupboard in your picture?

No, there isn't any coffee, but there's some flour.

This unit teaches a range of structures used in expressing quantity:
– *some* and *any* with count and non-count nouns
– quantifiers (e.g. *a lot of, not much/many, little/few*)
– *too much/many* and *not enough.*

1 Find the differences

This exercise focuses on count and non-count nouns and the relationship between a, some and any. Students listen to two people talking about a picture, then look at two other pictures and discuss the differences between them.

▶ Focus on Form: Exercise 1

▶ Workbook: Exercise A

> *Key structures:* count and non-count nouns; a, some, any. *Vocabulary:* common objects in rooms, food.   (→ Beginner Units 5, 13.)

1 Listening; presentation of 'a', 'some' & 'any'

- Introduce the activity by asking students what they can see in the picture. Focus on any new items, e.g. *parrot, cage, plates, mouse,* and teach the phrases *top/middle/bottom shelf.*

- 🔲 Play the recording. Ask students to say how it is different from the picture on the page. Answer:

  In the picture, there isn't an orange / there aren't any oranges.
  There isn't any wine, but there's a bottle of mineral water.
  There isn't any cheese on the shelf, but there are some cups.
  There are six glasses.

- Show how we use *some* and *any* with count and non-count nouns:

<u>Count nouns</u>	<u>Non-count nouns</u>
There are some plates.	**There's some cheese.**
There aren't any plates.	**There isn't any cheese.**
Are there any plates?	**Is there any cheese?**

2 Pairwork activity: finding differences between pictures

- Divide the class into pairs, and give each student a letter, A or B. Students look only at their own picture, and try to find the differences between their pictures by talking and asking questions.

- Look at the pictures together and establish the differences. Answers:

  A
  There's a parrot on the cage.
  There are leaves on the tree.
  There isn't a picture on the wall.
  There's a plant on the top shelf.
  There isn't a mouse in the picture.
  There's some coffee on the cupboard.
  There isn't any bread on the table.
  There's a bottle of mineral water
      on the table.

  B
  There isn't a parrot in the picture.
  There aren't any leaves on the tree.
  There's a picture on the wall.
  There's a jug on the top shelf.
  There's a mouse on the bottom shelf.
  There's some flour on the cupboard.
  There's some bread on the table.
  There's a jug on the table.

Language note
The picture contains a mixture of count nouns (singular and plural: *a parrot, curtains, glasses*) and non-count nouns (*bread, water, flour*). We can also make non-count nouns countable by saying e.g. *a loaf of bread, a bottle of water, a bag of flour.*

Language note
Normally, we use *some* in positive sentences and *any* in negatives and questions. However, we use *some* in special types of question, e.g. requests and offers: *Can I have some cheese? Would you like some cheese?*

Whole class option
1 Ask one student to stand at the front of the class and look at one picture. The rest of the class all look at the other picture, and ask questions.
or
2 Divide the class into two halves or teams. Students in each team all look at the same picture, and they take it in turns to ask the other team questions.

🔲 Tapescript for Exercise 1: *Find the differences*

A Well, on the plate there are some bananas and an orange.
B What about grapes?
A No, there aren't any grapes.
B What's on the table?
A On the table there are some plates, and some bread, and a
   bottle of … wine, I think.

B Can you see any cheese in your picture?
A Yes. There's some cheese on the shelf.
B Are there any glasses?
A Glasses? Yes. Three glasses.
B Any cups?
A No, I can't see any cups.

2 I haven't got any money

This exercise introduces a range of expressions for talking about quantity.

> *Key expressions:* (quite) a lot of, lots of, plenty of; not many, not much; very few,
> very little; hardly any, not any. *Recycled language:* food, clothes.

➤ Focus on Form: Exercise 2
➤ Workbook: Exercise B, Listening

1 *Introduction: reading & presentation of quantity expressions*

- Begin by drawing these scales on the board:

> *I've got a lot of books.* ———————————— *I haven't got any books.*
> *I've got a lot of money.* ———————————— *I haven't got any money.*

Explain the aim of this exercise: to find
expressions that can go on this scale.

- Give time for students to read the text and find
quantity expressions to go in the table. Then go
through the answers together, and write them on
the board:
If you like, go through the table making
sentences, using *books* and *money* as examples.

Count	Non-count
a lot of	
lots of	
plenty of	
quite a lot of	
not many	not much
very few	very little
hardly any	
not any	

Language note
A *lot of*, *lots of* and *plenty of* are
alternatives: they mean the same.
Plenty of is usually used about
positive things (e.g. *He's got plenty
of money*, but not *He's got plenty
of problems*).

Note
Very few and *very little* are
practised further in Focus on Form
and Study Pages F Consolidation.

2 *Pairwork: making guesses*

- To introduce this stage, ask the class to look at the text and make guesses about
you (e.g. *You haven't got many cassettes and CDs; you've got lots of books;
you've got hardly any videos …*). Tell them whether they are right.
- Pairwork. Students make guesses about their partner. As a round-up, ask a few
students what they found out.

Practice option
Give prompts and ask students to
make sentences about themselves,
e.g. *Books – I've got lots of books;
ties – I haven't got many ties;
chocolate – I eat hardly any
chocolate.*

3 Complaints

This exercise is about things that are wrong with towns and cities. It introduces too
much/many *and* not enough.

> *Key structures:* too much/many + noun; not enough + noun.
> *New vocabulary:* traffic, noise, rubbish, crime.

➤ Focus on Form: Exercises 3 & 4
➤ Workbook: Exercise C

1 *Introduction: vocabulary focus*

- Look at the list of words, and present any new items (e.g. *traffic, noise, rubbish,
crime*). Ask students which they think are good, which are bad, and which
could be either good or bad.

2 *Grammar presentation; making sentences*

- Look at the examples in the corner of the picture. Point out that:
  – we use *too much* with non-count nouns (e.g. *traffic*), and *too many* with
  count nouns (e.g. *cars*); we can use *not enough* with either.
  – all these structures are followed directly by a noun (e.g. we don't say *too
  much of traffic, not enough of car parks*).
- Students make sentences using the words in the list, e.g. *There's too much
traffic, there aren't enough buses, there's too much noise.*
- 🖭 Play the recording to check what the people actually say. (Answers: see
tapescript.)

🖭 The tapescript is on page T50.

3 *Extension: writing sentences*

- Working alone or in pairs, students write three complaints about their own
town.
- Students read out their complaints. Find out which are the three most common
complaints.

Idea
To find out the most common
complaint, write complaints on the
board in note form (e.g. *too much
traffic*), and make a mark each
time they are mentioned.

2 I haven't got any money

1 Read the text. Can you find seven more quantity expressions? Write them in the table.

Paul, aged 19

Books, CDs, Cassettes and Videos

I've got lots of cassettes and CDs and quite a lot of books. But I've got very few videos.

Clothes and Jewellery

I haven't got many smart clothes, and I've got hardly any jewellery – just a gold ring.

Food

I eat a lot of fresh fruit. I love it. But I don't eat much chocolate – it's bad for you.

Sport and Exercise

I don't like sport. In fact I get very little exercise.

Free time and Money

I've got plenty of free time. My problem is – I haven't got any money!

Count	Non-count
	a lot of
	not much
very few	
	hardly any

2 Work in pairs.

Student A: Make guesses about your partner. Use the same topics.
Student B: How good are A's guesses?

> I think you eat hardly any fresh fruit, and you eat quite a lot of chocolate.

3 Complaints

1 Here are some things you find in towns and cities.

traffic	parks	nightclubs
buses	rubbish	clothes shops
noise	tourists	crime

Which do you think are good things? Which are bad? Which could be either?

2 Some people complain about the town where they live. What do you think they will say? Make sentences about the things in the list.

[cassette] Now listen and check.

3 Think about your own town. What don't you like about it? Write three complaints.

Read out your complaints. What are the three most common complaints in the class?

There are too many tourists.
There aren't enough cycle paths.
There aren't enough fast food restaurants.

There's too much traffic.
There are too many cars.
There aren't enough car parks.
There isn't enough fresh air.

Count & non-count nouns

Count nouns	Non-count nouns
We've got a lot of onions.	We've got a lot of sugar.
We've got some tomatoes.	We've got some bread.
We've got a lemon.	–
We haven't got many eggs.	We haven't got much rice.
We haven't got any beans.	We haven't got any wine.
How many apples have we got?	How much oil have we got?

Read the sentences. How can you say the same things using *there is/are* instead of *have got*?

> There are a lot of onions.   There's a lot of sugar.

Do you know how much food you've got at home? Make true sentences like those in the table.

very few & very little

There are hardly any sweets.	There's hardly any milk.
There are very few sweets.	There's very little milk.

Change *hardly any* to *very few* or *very little* in these sentences.

a They've got *hardly any* money.
b There are *hardly any* films on TV tonight.
c *Hardly any* people went to the concert.
d United have got *hardly any* good players.
e There's *hardly any* food in the fridge.

too much & too many

These two people have some bad habits. Make sentences about them from the table.

He	drinks	too much	chips.
	eats		coffee.
			ketchup.
She	reads	too many	magazines.
	watches		TV.

Do you have any bad habits?

not enough

I'd love to make a fire, but …
there isn't enough wood.
I'd love to invite you for coffee, but …
I haven't got enough cups.

Complete these sentences, using *not enough* …

a I'd love to come to the party, but … (*time*)
b I'd love an omelette, but … (*eggs*)
c I'd love to buy a new car, but …
d I'd love to invite you over for dinner, but …
e I want to make a cake, but …

How to say it

1 🔊 Listen to the word *some* in these sentences. Practise saying them.

I've bought some new clothes.
There are some apples in the cupboard.
I'd like some sugar, please.
Have some more coffee.

2 🔊 Listen to this sentence. Which parts are stressed? What happens when the speaker says it quickly?

I think there's some food in the fridge.

Practise saying these sentences quickly.

How much money have we got?
There aren't enough buses in the town.
He reads quite a lot of books.

Focus on Form

1 Count & non-count nouns

- Read through the sentences in the boxes. Point out that:
  - we use *much* with non-count nouns, *many* with count nouns.
  - we can use *a lot of*, *some* and *not any* with count or non-count nouns.
- Students say the sentences, using *There is* or *There are*. Answers:

There are a lot of onions.	There's a lot of sugar.
There are some tomatoes.	There's some bread.
There's a lemon.	–
There aren't many eggs.	There isn't much rice.
There aren't any beans.	There isn't any wine.
How many apples are there?	How much oil is there?

- Students make sentences about food they've got at home, using *I've got*, *We've got* or *There is/are*. They could either write sentences and then read them out, or you could do this round the class, giving prompts (e.g. *What about eggs? What about champagne?*).

2 very few & very little

- Look at the examples and point out that:
  - *hardly any* can be used with count or non-count nouns.
  - *few* is used with count nouns, *little* is used with non-count nouns.
- Do the exercise round the class. Answers:

  a They've got *very little* money.
  b There are *very few* films on TV tonight.
  c *Very few* people went to the concert.
  d United have got *very few* good players.
  e There's *very little* food in the fridge.

3 too much & too many

- Look at the picture and ask students to make sentences. Answers:

  He eats too many chips.
  He eats too much ketchup.
  He watches too much TV.
  She reads too many magazines.
  She drinks too much coffee.

- Students write one or two similar sentences about their own bad habits. Then ask them to read them out.

4 not enough

- Emphasise that after *enough* we use a noun without *of*.
- Either do the exercise round the class, or let students do it in pairs and then go through the answers. Possible answers:

  a ... I haven't got enough time.
  b ... there aren't enough eggs.
  c ... I haven't got enough money.
  d ... we haven't got enough food/plates/chairs.
  e ... there aren't enough eggs / there isn't enough flour / we haven't got enough sugar.

How to say it

1 Pronunciation of 'some' in sentences

- 🔲 Play the recording, pausing after each sentence. Focus on the pronunciation of *some*:

  /səm njuː kləʊðz/
  /ðɛər ə səm ˈæplz/
  /aɪd laɪk səm ˈʃʊgə/
  /hæf səm mɔː/

2 Rhythm of rapid speech

- 🔲 Play the sentence, and discuss what happens when it is said more quickly:
  - there is more difference between the stressed sounds (*think*, *food*, *fridge*) and the unstressed sounds (*I, there's some, in, the*).
  - the unstressed sounds become shorter, and some sounds are reduced (/ðɛəz/ → /ðəz/, /sʌm/ → /səm/).
- Play the other sentences and get students to repeat them quickly. Focus on the rhythm and reduced vowel sounds:

  /haʊ mʌtʃ mʌni əv wi gɒt/
  /ðər ɑːnt ɪnʌf bʌsɪz ɪn ðə taʊn/
  /hi riːdz kwaɪt ə lɒt əv bʊks/

🔲 Tapescript for Exercise 3: *Complaints*

1 Well, there's too much traffic, certainly, and too much noise from cars and lorries.
2 There aren't enough parks or trees, or green spaces generally.
3 Well, I think there are too many tourist buses, they make it very difficult to drive in the centre of town – in fact there are too many tourists in the summer, I think.
4 There's too much rubbish in the streets – they should clean the streets more often.
5 There aren't enough good clothes shops – I can never find anything I want to buy.

12

This unit deals with three areas of language connected with illness and injury:
– talking about aches and pains, and what caused them
– talking about remedies for illnesses
– describing what you do when you are ill (e.g. *go to the doctor*, *take medicine*).
The reading and listening activity is about how to have a healthy life.

1 Aches and pains

This exercise introduces expressions for talking about injuries and health problems, and also vocabulary for parts of the body.

➤ Workbook: Exercise A, Listening

> *Key vocabulary:* hurt, ache (v.), ache (n.), pain, headache, stomach ache.
> *Parts of the body:* head, wrist, knee, back, shoulder, chest, arm, stomach, foot.
> *Recycled language:* I've got, Past simple tense. (→ Beginner Units 20, 22).

1 Reading & vocabulary presentation

● Either give time for students to read the text using dictionaries, or read through the text yourself. Identify the words for parts of the body and match them with the numbered lines in the picture. Answers:

1 head 2 wrist 3 chest 4 stomach 5 knee 6 foot (*pl.* feet) 7 shoulder
8 arm 9 back

Practice option
As a check, point to parts of your own body, and ask students to say the words.

2 Presentation of key structures with 'ache', 'pain' & 'hurt'.

● Use the text to focus on the words *ache*, *pain* and *hurt*. Establish how they can be used to fill the gaps, and write the examples on the board:

| My wrist | hurts.
aches. | | I've got | a pain
an ache | in my wrist. |

Point out that:
– *pain* is a noun (*I've got a pain*).   – *hurt* is a verb (*It hurts*).
– *ache* is either a verb or a noun (*It aches, I've got an ache*). We can also talk about *a backache, a stomach ache, a headache*.

Language note
An *ache* is a continuous (and usually not very strong) pain.

3 Elicitation of activity verbs; practice: improvising conversations

● Read the conversation, and make sure students understand the question *What's the matter (with you)?* Ask them to identify the picture (Answer: F).

● Look at the other pictures. Establish what the person might say in each case (i.e. what they did, and what their problem is). Possible answers:

A I went walking. My feet hurt, my knee aches.
B I smoked too many cigarettes. I've got a headache, I've got a pain in my chest.
C I played the piano. My arms hurt, my wrists ache, my back aches.
D I ate too much ice-cream. I've got a stomach ache.
E I went to a disco, I went dancing. My feet hurt, I've got a headache.
F I moved a cupboard. My back hurts, I've got an ache in my shoulder.
G I painted my kitchen. My arm hurts, my shoulder aches.

● Demonstrate a conversation. Choose one of the situations, and get a student to ask you *What's the matter?*

● Pairwork. Students choose situations and improvise conversations.

Alternative: guessing game
Students secretly choose a situation, and say what their problem is (e.g. *My back aches*). Other students try to guess what they did (e.g. *Did you move a cupboard? Did you paint a wall?*).

🔊 Tapescript for Exercise 2: *Cures*

1 Well, I have very noisy neighbours in the flat above me, and they like dancing late at night. So I have a large cushion next to my bed, and I put the cushion over my head and I try to get to sleep. But if I still can't sleep, I take a broom and I bang on the ceiling. And then they always stop.

2 If you have hiccups, you should ask a friend to put his or her fingers in your ears, while you drink from a full glass of water.

3 This is my grandfather's cure for a cold. Get a bottle of brandy and a glass, and a hat. Then go to bed, and put the hat at the end of the bed. Drink a glass of brandy, then drink another glass, and keep drinking until you can see three hats at the end of the bed. Then go to sleep, and in the morning you'll be fine.

12 How do you feel?

1 Aches and pains

1 What parts of the body does the man mention? Match them with the numbers. Use a dictionary to help you.

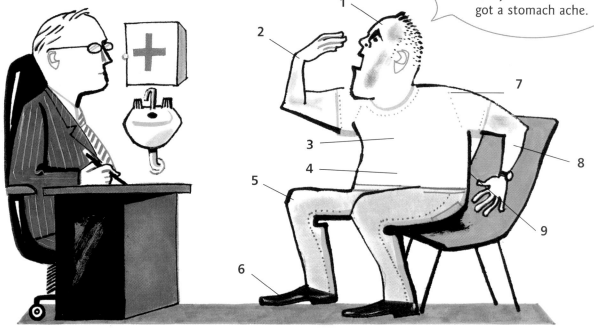

> I've got a headache, my wrist hurts, I've got a pain in my knee, I've got an ache in my back, my shoulder aches, my feet hurt, I've got a pain in my chest, my arm hurts and I've got a stomach ache.

2 Look at these sentences. What words can go in the gaps?

A My wrist ....s.
..................s.

B I've got a .... an .... in my wrist.

3 Read this conversation. Which photo does it go with?

> What's the matter?

> My back hurts.

> Oh dear. How did it happen?

> Well, yesterday I moved a very heavy cupboard.

Choose a photo and have another conversation.

2 Cures

1 **What do people do if ...**

   a they have a cold?   *d* they have 'flu?

   b they feel sick?   *e* they have toothache?

   c they can't get to sleep? *f* they have hiccups?

Choose answers from the box.

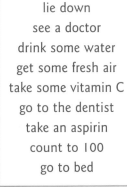

lie down
see a doctor
drink some water
get some fresh air
take some vitamin C
go to the dentist
take an aspirin
count to 100
go to bed

2 **You will hear three people talk about cures. How do you think they use these things? And for which problem?**

| a broom | a bottle of brandy | a cushion | a glass | a hat | a friend's fingers |

   Now listen and check.

3 **Choose one of the problems. What's your cure?**

3 Going to the doctor

1 **These pictures tell a story. Can you put them in the right order?**

Say what happens in each picture.
Use the expressions in the box.

write a prescription	take the medicine
feel better	feel ill
make an appointment	go to the chemist
examine	ask questions

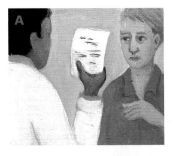

2   **A man tells a story about going to the doctor. Listen and answer the questions.**

   a Where did he work? What did he do in his job?

   b How did he feel?

   c What did the doctor do?

   d What did the doctor say?

   e What did the man have to do?

   f Did he feel better after three days?

   g What did he think about it?

3 **Try to tell the story yourself. Use the expressions in the box to help you.**

2 Cures

This exercise introduces a range of common expressions relating to everyday health problems and cures. In the second part, students listen to people describing unusual cures.

► Workbook: Exercise B

> *Key expressions:* have a cold, have 'flu, have a toothache, have hiccups, feel sick; take (an aspirin, vitamin C).   *Other new words:* broom, brandy.

1 Matching task; presentation of key expressions

- Look at the questions and ask students to suggest suitable remedies from the box. Possible answers:

  a take vitamin C *b* get some fresh air, lie down *c* count to 100 *d* go to bed, see a doctor *e* go to the dentist, take an aspirin *f* drink some water

- As you go through the items, focus on any new expressions. Point out that:
  – we use the verb *have* (or *have got*) for most illnesses: *have a cold, have 'flu*;
  – we use the verb *take* with medicines: *take an aspirin, take vitamin C.*

> *Language note*
> You feel *ill* = you don't feel well, there's something wrong with you.
> You feel *sick* = you want to be sick (e.g. you've eaten bad food).
> In US English, *sick* is used for both these meanings.

2 Listening: unusual cures

- Look at the pictures, and ask students to guess how they might use the items to cure any of the problems in Part 1, either alone or in combinations.
- ▭ Play the recording, pausing after each speaker. Students say which problem the person is talking about, and which items they use. Answers:

  1 *Can't get to sleep*: cushion, broom   2 *Hiccups*: glass, friend's fingers
  3 *Cold*: hat, bottle of brandy, glass

▭ The tapescript is on page T51.

3 Extension: speaking activity

- Go through the list with the class, and find out if students have unusual remedies for any of the problems.

3 Going to the doctor

This exercise introduces language for talking about being ill, seeing the doctor and getting medicine.

► Workbook: Exercise C

> *Key expressions:* feel ill, make an appointment, go to the doctor, ask questions, examine, write a prescription, go the chemist, take medicine, feel better.

1 Sequencing & describing pictures; presentation of key expressions

- Look at the pictures. Establish what order they should be in, and what happens in each one, using the expressions in the box. Expected answers:

  C He's at work. He *feels ill*.
  F He phones the doctor and *makes an appointment*.
  H He goes to see the doctor. The doctor *asks him questions*.
  E The doctor *examines him*.
  A The doctor *writes a prescription*.
  G He *goes to the chemist* and buys some medicine.
  B He *takes the medicine* and goes to bed.
  D He *feels better* and goes back to work.

2 Listening & answering questions

- ▭ Read the questions. Then play the recording and check the answers:

  a In an office. He used a computer.   *b* He had a temperature and a headache.
  c He examined him (looked at his eyes and ears).   *d* That he had 'flu.
  e Go to bed and take some medicine. *f* Yes. *g* He felt better just because he had three days away from his computer.

▭ The tapescript is on page T53.

> *Pairwork option*
> Students practise re-telling the story in pairs, telling half the story each.

3 Re-telling the story

- Ask students to re-tell the story, taking it in turns to say a sentence, and using the Past tense.

> *Optional extension*
> Role-play: students act out the scenes shown in the pictures.

4 A long and healthy life

This combined reading and listening activity looks at common beliefs about how to have a long and healthy life. In the reading, students consider eight ideas about how to live healthily, and in the listening they hear a doctor commenting on these ideas.

> *New words (reading):* healthy, vegetarian, energy, lose weight, partner, heart attack, afterwards, chance.
> *New words (listening):* calories, on average, dream (n. and v.), regularly.

1 Reading & discussion

- Give time for students to read quickly through the paragraphs and decide if they agree with each one or not.
- Read through each paragraph, and present any new words. After each one, ask the class whether they agree or not, and why.

> **Option**
> Take a class vote about each paragraph, and keep a record of the class's opinion on the board.

2 Listening & gap-filling

- [cassette] Play the recording, pausing after each section. Check whether the doctor thinks the idea is right or not, and ask students to complete the sentences.
  Expected answers:

  A Wrong. You can get energy from eggs, milk, fish and many vegetables.
  B Right. You need to sleep at least six hours.
  C Wrong. Bread, cheese and crisps have a lot of calories.
  D Partly right. On average, people with partners live longer.
  E Wrong. If you drink alcohol you sleep less well / you don't dream.
  F Partly right. A small amount of alcohol is good for your heart.
  G Wrong. If you do exercise you feel less hungry.
  H Right. If your parents and grandparents have long lives, you have a good chance of living long.

3 Extension: discussion

- Look at the paragraphs again, and use them as a basis for students to talk about themselves. Prompt them by asking questions, e.g. *Is anyone here a vegetarian? How many hours do you sleep? Does anyone sleep less than 7 hours a night? Does anyone have grandparents who are over 90?*

[cassette] Tapescript for Exercise 3: *Going to the doctor*

About a month ago I was at work as usual, I was at my desk working with my computer, and suddenly I felt really ill – I felt very hot and I had a headache and my eyes hurt a lot. So I phoned and made an appointment to see the doctor. And that evening I went to see the doctor, and he asked me a lot of questions, and he asked me to take my shirt off and he examined me. He looked at my eyes and my ears. And in the end he said, 'Well, you've got the 'flu'. And he wrote me a prescription for some medicine, and he told me to go to bed and take the medicine three times a day and stay in bed for a few days. So anyway, I went to the chemist's to get the medicine, and then I went home and went to bed, just as the doctor told me. And I stayed in bed for three days and slept. Well, sure enough, after that I felt better and I went back to work. But the funny thing is that I don't think I got better because of the medicine at all. I think I just needed three days away from my computer.

[cassette] Tapescript for Exercise 4: *A long and healthy life*

A This is quite wrong. You do get energy from meat, but also from eggs, milk, fish and many vegetables. You certainly don't need to eat meat to be healthy.
B Many people think you need eight hours' sleep. But in fact six hours is quite enough to be fit and healthy. And sleeping too long – nine hours or more – is actually bad for you.
C Bread, cheese, butter and crisps have a lot of calories, so they won't help you to lose weight. Maybe lunch in the restaurant was a better idea!
D It is true that, on average, people with partners live longer. But of course you have to be happy with your partner, and also have a healthy life.

E This is wrong. If you drink alcohol before you go to sleep, you sleep less well. You sleep very heavily for the first few hours, and you don't dream so much. And dreams are very important.
F It is true that if you have a heart problem, a small quantity of alcohol every day is good for you. But maybe your grandfather doesn't need half a bottle – just a glass or two would be better.
G In fact, that isn't true. If you do exercise regularly, you actually start to feel less hungry.
H Yes, it's true that if your parents and grandparents live long, then you have a good chance of living long – long life runs in families.

4 A long and healthy life

1 Look at what these people say. Do you think they are right? What would you say to them?

A My sister has just decided to become a vegetarian I don't think it's a very good idea, because you need meat to give you energy.

E I don't usually sleep very well, so I often have a glass or two of brandy before I go to bed. That makes me sleep better.

B I usually go to bed at midnight, and wake up at six. My husband is worried about me – he says I should sleep at least eight hours a night, but I feel fine – I don't need a lot of sleep.

F My grandfather had a heart attack a year ago. Now he has half a bottle of wine every evening. We all think it's bad for him to drink so much, but he says it's good for his heart.

C I'm trying to lose weight. I used to have lunch in the office restaurant, but now I just have a cheese sandwich and a packet of crisps.

G I'm trying to lose weight. My brother says I should do exercises or go running, but I don't think that would help. Exercise just makes you feel hungry, and then you eat more afterwards.

D I'm glad I'm married. I read that people with partners usually live longer than people who live alone!

H Three of my grandparents lived to be over 90, and both my parents are in their 70s and still very healthy. So I think I've got a good chance of having a long life, too.

2 🔲 A doctor comments on what the people say. Does she say they are right, wrong, or partly right? Listen and complete the sentences.

a You can get energy from ...

b You need to sleep at least ...

c Bread, cheese and crisps ...

d On average, people with partners ...

e If you drink alcohol, ...

f A small amount of alcohol ...

g If you do exercise, ...

h If your parents and grandparents have long lives, ...

3 Look again at what the people say, and the doctor's answers. Do you think you will have a long and healthy life?

Study pages

Focus on ... For and since

1 [cassette] Listen to the conversations and complete the sentences.

The man arrived at ....

He has been there for ....

The woman arrived at ....

She has been there since ....

2 **Add *for* or *since* in the gaps.**

  .... three years.
a He's lived here .... 1980.
  .... last June.

  .... two months.
b They've been married .... April.
  .... years.

  .... Monday.
c She's only had her computer .... a few days.
  .... a week.

3 **Look at these questions. What do you think the replies are?**

a – I hear you're engaged now.
  – Yes, ... September.

b – I see you've got a new car.
  – It isn't new. .... more than a year.

c – Are you new to this office?
  – Oh no, ... 1993.

d – Is that a new video recorder?
  – Fairly new. .... about three months.

4 **Write a true sentence about yourself. Choose one of these ways to begin.**

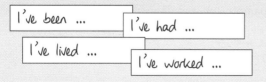

I've been ...   I've had ...
I've lived ...   I've worked ...

Pronunciation: Small words (3)

1 [cassette] Listen to the words in the box. They have a full sound when they are stressed, and the sound /ə/ when they are not stressed.

are	<u>Are</u> you <u>there</u>? <u>What</u> are you <u>doing</u>?
can	<u>Can</u> you <u>swim</u>? <u>Yes</u>, I <u>can</u>. I <u>think</u> I can <u>see</u> him.
was	He <u>wasn't</u> at <u>home</u>. <u>Yes</u>, he <u>was</u>. There was a <u>lot</u> of <u>food</u>.

2 You will hear six sentences. Does the word have a full sound or /ə/?

Practise saying the sentences.

Phrasebook: Making an appointment

Put this conversation in the correct order.

– How about 4.30?
– Fairly urgent, yes.
– Yes, that's fine.
– Yes. Is it urgent?
– Yes, I can.
– OK. Can you come this afternoon?
– I'd like to make an appointment to see the doctor.

[cassette] Now listen and check.

Have similar conversations.

Make an appointment to see the doctor for some time next week.

Make an appointment to see the dentist. It's urgent!

Make an appointment to go to the hair-dresser. You're only free at the weekend.

Study pages F

Focus on ... *For and since*

*This exercise focuses on the use of the Present perfect +
for/since to talk about things which started in the past and
are still going on. This exercise is limited to the stative
forms* have been, have had, have lived *and* have worked.

> *Key structures:* Present perfect tense; for, since.

1 Listening; presentation of key structures

- Look at the picture and establish the situation:

  It's a doctor's waiting room, some people are waiting to
  see the doctor, it's nearly twelve o'clock.

- ▢ Play the recording and complete the sentences:

  She arrived at 11 o'clock. She's been there for an hour.
  He arrived at 9 o'clock. He's been there since 9 o'clock.

- Show this time line to present the structure:

> **She <u>arrived</u> at 11.00.**   **She <u>is</u> still here now.**
>
> ┣━━━━━━━━━━━━━━━▶
>
> **She <u>has been</u> here** **<u>since</u> 11.00.**
>   **<u>for</u> an hour.**

Point out that:

- we can use the Present perfect to talk about things that
  started in the past and are still going on now.
- we use *for* + length of time: *for an hour, for 10 years.*
- we use *since* + the starting point: *since 11 o'clock,
  since Sunday.*

- If you like, give a few other examples to show how
  these structures work (e.g. *We came to the class at
  3.00. Now it's 3.30 and we're still here. So we've been
  here for half an hour / since 3.00*).

  Point out that this is a completely different use of the
  Present perfect from the one in Unit 9. This meaning is
  expressed in many languages by the present tense (*e.g.
  Je suis ici depuis 4 heures; ich bin seit Juni in London*).

2 Focus on 'for' & 'since': gap-filling exercise

- Students fill the gaps. Use this to check that they
  understand how *for* and *since* are used. Answers:

  a for three years, since 1980, since last June
  b for two months, since April, for years
  c since Monday, for a few days, for a week

3 Focus on Present perfect: gap-filling exercise

- Ask students to fill the gaps in the replies. Answers:

  a I've been engaged since September.
  b I've had it for more than a year.
  c I've worked here (been here) since 1993.
  d I've had it for about three months.

4 Freer practice: writing true sentences

- Students write sentences about themselves. As a round-
  up, ask students to read out their sentences.

Pronunciation: *Small words (3)*

> Common words which have the reduced sound /ə/ when
> unstressed.

1 Listening & practice

- ▢ Play the recording and ask students to repeat the
  sentences. Focus on the /ə/ sound.

2 Recognition task

- ▢ Play the sentences. Students listen for the words
  are, *can* or *was*, and decide if they have a full sound or
  a reduced /ə/ sound.

- Play the sentences again and check the answers:

  1 are: full 2 was: reduced /ə/ 3 can: reduced /ə/
  4 are: reduced /ə/ 5 can: full 6 are: full

- Practise saying the sentences round the class. Focus on
  the pronunciation of the 'small words'.

Phrasebook: *Making an appointment*

*This exercise practises language for making an appointment
to see a doctor, a dentist or a hairdresser. It picks up on
language from Exercise 12.3.*

> *Key phrases*: I'd like to ..., make an appointment, urgent,
> Can you come ...? How about ...?

- Ask students to put the dialogue in the correct order. As
  you do this, present any new expressions.
- ▢ Play the dialogue to check.
- Look at the three situations with the class, and establish
  what the people will say. If you like, build up one of the
  dialogues on the board.
- Either let students practise the dialogues in pairs, or
  ask two students to have each conversation in front of
  the class.

> ▢ Tapescript for Focus on ... *For and since*
>
> A How long have you been here?
> B Me? I've been here for about an hour.
> A How about you?
> C I've been here since 9 o'clock. I was one of the first
>   people here.

> ▢ Tapescript for Pronunciation: *Small words (3)*
>
> 1 Are you coming to the party?
> 2 What was his name again?
> 3 What can I do to help?
> 4 Where are we meeting them?
> 5 Can she swim? I think she can.
> 6 John! Where are you?

> ▢ The Phrasebook tapescript is on page T55.

Consolidation

a little, a few, very little, very few

This exercise focuses on the use of four common quantity expressions, and the differences between them. It builds on language introduced in Exercise 11.2.

- Read the examples, and if possible, give the equivalent of these expressions in the students' own language. If this is not possible, make these points:
  - *little* and *a little* are used with non-count nouns (e.g. *money*); *few* and *a few* are used with count nouns (e.g. *friends*).
  - *little* and *few* have a negative sense (= almost none at all; we usually say *very little* and *very few*).
  - *a little* and *a few* have a positive sense (= not much/many, but some).
- Students fill the gaps in the sentences. Either do this together, or let the students do the exercise alone or in pairs and then go through the answers. Answers:
  - *a* ... a piece of bread with *a little* butter ... (= some butter, not too much)
  - *b* *Very few* plants (= almost no plants at all) ... there's *very little* rain. (= it's very dry)
  - *c* ... Just *a little* (= some sugar, but not much)
  - *d* I've got *very little* time. (= almost no time, I'm very busy)
  - *e* He's got *very few* books ... (= almost no books at all)
  - *f* Bring *a few* CDs, ... (= some CDs)

well

This exercise focuses on the use of well *as an adjective and an adverb. It builds on language introduced in Unit 12.*

1 Look at the examples, and use them to show that *well* is used in two ways:
   - as an adverb from *good*:
     His English is good.
     He speaks English well.
   - as an adjective, meaning 'healthy, not ill':
     How are you?
     Very well, thank you.

2 Ask each question to one or two students, and get them to answer using 'well'. Possible answers:

How are you today?	Very well, thanks.
	Not very well – I've got a cold.
Do you speak English?	Yes, but not very well.
	Yes, I speak it very well.
How's your family?	They're very well.
	Not too bad, but my grandfather isn't very well.
Can you sing?	Yes, but not very well.
	Yes, I can sing fairly well.

If you like, ask students to ask and answer the questions in pairs.

Review

Irregular verbs

Review of Past simple and past participle verb forms (irregular verbs) from Units 7 and 9.

1 Ask students to give the forms of the verbs, and write them on the board:

get	got	got	have	had	had
come	came	come	go	went	gone
put	put	put	take	took	taken
buy	bought	bought	sell	sold	sold
lose	lost	lost	break	broke	broken
write	wrote	written	leave	left	left

Cover the board (or rub the verbs out). Students test each other, either in pairs or as a 'chain' round the class.

2 Students fill the gaps. Answers:

   a gone, left   *b* bought, sold
   c took, put (left), had, lost, taken

Words

Review of vocabulary from Units 2, 4, 6, 8, 10 & 12.

1 Give time for students to find the answers, working alone or in pairs. Then go through the answers together. Answers:

   a nephew, niece   *g* poster, mirror
   b chess, tennis   *h* table, sofa
   c coffee, beer   *i* boots, trainers
   d beef, chicken   *j* shorts, sunglasses
   e banana, apple   *k* coat, jumper
   f potato, onion

2 Ask students to add one more item to each category. Then go through the answers together.

   Note: You could also play this as a game:

   Students write one item for each category. They score one point for each correct answer, and two points if they wrote something that no one else thought of.

   Go through the answers, and find out who scored the most points.

🔊 Tapescript for Phrasebook: *Making an appointment*

A I'd like to make an appointment to see the doctor.
B Yes. Is it urgent?
A Fairly urgent, yes.
B OK. Can you come this afternoon?
A Yes, I can.
B OK. How about 4.30?
A Yes, that's fine.

Consolidation

a little, a few, very little, very few

Look at these examples:

> I don't know how she lives – she's got very little money.
> He's quite lonely – he has very few friends.
>
> I'll give you a little money, so you can buy a drink.
> I like being here – I've already made a few friends.

very little, very few = almost none

a little, a few = not a lot, but some

Fill the gaps with *a little*, *a few*, *very little* or *very few*.

a For lunch, I had a piece of bread with .... butter, and a tomato.

b .... plants grow here, because there's .... rain.

c – Do you want sugar in your coffee?
– Yes, please. Just ....

d Sorry, I can't talk to you now. I've got .... time.

e I don't think he likes reading. He's got .... books in his flat.

f Bring .... CDs, so that we can listen to some music.

well

1 Look at these examples.

She speaks English very well.

They're not playing well.

Are you feeling well today?

He's not very well.

What's the difference between well and well?

2 How could you answer these questions? Use *well*.

> How are you today?
>
> Do you speak English?
>
> How's your family?
>
> Can you sing?

Review

Irregular verbs

1 What are the Past simple and Past participle forms of these verbs? Test your partner.

get   come   put   buy   lose   write

have   go   take   sell   break   leave

2 Fill the gaps.

a – Hello. Can I speak to Tony, please?
– I'm sorry. He's .... to work. He .... the house about an hour ago.

b – Whose car is that?
– It's mine. I .... it yesterday. But I haven't .... my old one yet. Do you want to buy it?

c I can't find my watch. I .... it off and .... it on the table when I .... a shower, and now I've .... it. Do you think someone's .... it?

Words

C	O	A	T	M	C	H	E	S	S	Y	B
T	P	O	B	O	O	T	S	U	A	X	U
E	O	N	A	T	R	A	I	N	E	R	S
N	T	I	N	O	N	B	C	G	J	O	V
N	A	O	A	R	I	L	O	L	U	Z	M
I	T	N	N	B	E	E	F	A	M	A	I
S	O	F	A	I	C	Q	F	S	P	P	R
C	H	I	C	K	E	N	E	S	E	P	R
N	E	P	H	E	W	B	E	E	R	L	O
S	H	O	R	T	S	P	O	S	T	E	R

1 You can see two kinds of transport in the diagram. There are also

a two family members

b two games

c two drinks

d two kinds of meat

e two kinds of fruit

f two kinds of vegetable

g two things to put on the wall

h two pieces of furniture

i two things to wear on your feet

j two things to wear in hot weather

k two things to wear in cold weather

2 Add one more thing to each pair of answers.

13 What will happen?

1 Fortune telling

will, won't • questions with 'will'

1 What do you think the fortune teller says? Make sentences using *will* or *won't*.

> You'll meet a tall dark stranger. At first you won't like him ...

... meet a tall dark stranger ...

... like him ...

... fall in love ...

... be happy ...

... stay together ...

... leave him ...

... a long journey ...

... a foreign country ...

... a house ...

... married ...

... rich ...

... happy.

Listen and check your answers.

2 Imagine the fortune teller is telling your fortune. What questions could you ask?

Where?   How?

Who?   When?

How much?   What?

3 *Student A*: Tell B's fortune. Answer his/her questions.

Student B: A is telling your fortune. Find out more by asking questions.

> You'll meet someone special, and you'll go on a long journey. A tall stranger will give you some money, and you'll use it to buy something you need. Before the end of the year, a friend will tell you something important, and your life will suddenly change.

4 Write two predictions of your own, one with *will* and one with *won't*.

It won't rain tomorrow.

The world will end on Tuesday afternoon.

I won't pass my English exam.

The price of petrol will go up soon.

United will win the match on Sunday.

13

This is the first of two units concerned with future time (the other is Unit 21: *Future plans*). It covers language used in making predictions:
– *will* and *won't*
– expressing probability, using *will probably*, *probably won't* and *might*.

1 Fortune telling

This exercise focuses on the use of will *and* won't *for making predictions. The second part of the exercise practises questions with* will.

> *Key structures:* will, won't; questions with 'will'. *New words:* stranger, journey, foreign. *Recycled language:* meet, fall in love, get married (Unit 2).

1 Introduction; presentation of 'will' & 'won't'; making sentences

- Use the picture to introduce the expressions *fortune teller* and *tell someone's fortune* (= say what will happen to them).
- Look at the sentences in the speech bubble, and show these structures on the board:

> You'll + verb
>
> You won't + verb

  Point out that:
  – *you'll = you will; you won't = you will not.*
  – all the forms of *will* are the same: so we say *I'll, you'll, he'll, they'll*, etc.
- Look at the other phrases and ask students to make sentences using *you'll* or *you won't*. Introduce any new vocabulary (e.g. *stranger, journey, foreign*).
- ▢ Play the recording and check the answers. Answers:

  You'll fall in love ... You won't be happy ... You won't stay together ... You'll leave him ... You'll go on a long journey ... You'll live in a foreign country ... You'll buy a house ... You'll get married ... You won't be rich ... You'll be happy.

2 Presentation of questions with 'will'; elicitation of questions

- Show how to form *Wh-* questions with *will*:
- Read through what the fortune teller says. Then read it again, pausing and asking students to suggest questions:

> | Who | | I | |
> | Where | will | you | ...? |
> | How | | he/she | |

Who will I meet?	How much money will he/she give me?
Where will I go?	What will I buy?
How will I travel?	What will he/she tell me?
Who will the stranger be?	How will my life change?

3 Pairwork role-play: fortune telling

- If you like, demonstrate the activity with one student.
- Divide the class into pairs. They improvise conversations based on the text in the crystal ball: B tells A's fortune, A asks questions, and B makes up suitable replies, e.g.

  B *You'll meet someone special.*
  A *Who will I meet?*
  B *A young woman with dark hair ...*

4 Writing sentences

- Read through the sentences and make sure students understand them.
- Students write sentences of their own, using the sentences to give them ideas.
- As a round-up, ask students to read out their sentences.

> ▢ Tapescript for Exercise 1: *Fortune telling*
>
> Well, you'll meet a tall dark stranger. At first you won't like him, but after a time you'll fall in love with him. But you won't be happy together, and you won't stay together very long. After a few months you'll leave him, and then you'll go on a long journey, and you'll go to live in a foreign country. You'll buy a house there, a small house by the sea, and you'll get married. You won't be very rich, but you'll be happy.

➤ Focus on Form: Exercises 1 & 3
➤ Workbook: Exercises A & B, Listening

Optional lead-in
Ask the class what ways they know of telling someone's fortune, e.g. looking in a glass ball, with cards, with a cup of coffee or tea, with sticks, reading the lines on your hand. Ask if anyone has visited a fortune teller.

Language note
A *stranger* is someone you don't know. A *foreigner* is someone from a *foreign country* (i.e. not your own country).

2 It might rain

This exercise introduces the modal verb might *for talking about possibilities in the future.*

> *Key structures:* might + infinitive. *Other new expressions:* Don't forget …, take.

1 Presentation of 'might'

- Look at the picture and the examples, and establish the situation: a boy is going out for the day (perhaps on a school trip), his mother is telling him what to do. Focus on the meaning of *might*: = *Perhaps it will …*; *Perhaps you will …*.

  Point out that we say *it might rain*, etc., not ~~it might to rain~~.

2 Basic practice: adding continuations with 'might'

- Look at the other things the woman says. Ask students to suggest sentences with *might*, and write them on the board. Possible answers:

  Sandwiches: You might get/feel hungry. You might want to eat something.
  Jumper: You might get cold. It might be cold.
  Walkman: You might want to listen to music.

3 Freer practice: making suggestions

- Look at the first prompt (*swimsuit*), and ask students to make a suggestion using *might*, e.g.
  Don't forget your swimsuit. You might want to go swimming / The hotel might have a swimming pool.

- In pairs, students make suggestions for the other prompts. Then go through the answers together. Possible answers:

  Take some gloves. It might be cold.
  Have you got your sunglasses? It might be sunny.
  Don't forget your computer. You might want to send an email.
  Have you got your phone? You might want to phone me.
  Don't forget your camera. You might want to take some photos.

- Students think of one other item and make a sentence about it. Then ask for students' suggestions, e.g.

  Take some shampoo. You might want to wash your hair.
  Take a guide book. You might want to go sightseeing.

➤ Focus on Form: Exercise 1

> *Language note*
> *Might* is a modal verb (like *can*, *will*, *must*, *should*), so it is followed by the infinitive without *to*.

3 A bright future?

This exercise is in the form of a questionnaire which shows how optimistic you are about the future. It practises expressions for talking about probability.

> *Key expressions:* will, won't, might; probably. *New vocabulary:* optimist, pessimist, cancer, peace, discover, world war, disease, attack, the Earth, alien.

1 Vocabulary & grammar presentation; listening

- Look at the questionnaire heading, and establish the difference between an optimist and a pessimist. Tell the class the aim of the questionnaire: to find out if you are an optimist or a pessimist.

- Read through the questionnaire, presenting any new vocabulary. Then read the scores, and show how we use *probably*:

  | It | will probably / probably won't | happen. |

- 🔊 Play the recording, pausing when necessary. Students note down the person's score. Then discuss this together. Answer:

  24. He's quite pessimistic.

2 Answering the questionnaire; working out the score

- Pairwork. Students answer the questions and find out whether they or their partner have a higher score.
- Find out who has the highest and lowest score.

➤ Focus on Form: Exercise 4
➤ Workbook: Exercise C

> 🔊 The tapescript is on page T58.

> *Alternative*
> Do the listening as a whole class activity. Pause the tape after each response, and ask students what score to give the speaker. Write the scores on the board, and then work out the total together.

2 It might rain

might

1 Read what the boy's mother says.
What does *might* mean?

2 Here are some other things she says.
Add a sentence with *might*.

Take some
sandwiches …

Don't forget
your jumper …

Have you got your Walkman? …

3 This woman is going
on a business trip to Paris.
Make some suggestions.

swimsuit

gloves

sunglasses

computer

phone

camera

?

....

3 A bright future?

probably • might

I think
things will
get better.

Are you an
OPTIMIST or a PESSIMIST?

I think
things will
get worse.

1 ☐ Everyone will have enough food to eat.

2 ☐ People will live 100 years or more.

3 ☐ We'll find a cure for cancer.

4 ☐ There will be peace everywhere.

5 ☐ We'll discover a new kind of energy.

6 ☐ There will be another world war.

7 ☐ We'll run out of oil and gas.

8 ☐ All the fish in the sea will die.

9 ☐ New diseases will kill millions of people.

10 ☐ Unfriendly aliens will attack the Earth.

1 🔲 You will hear someone do this questionnaire. Listen and
write A, B, C, D or E by each sentence.

How optimistic is the speaker? Give him a score:

Green sentences A = 5, B = 4, C = 3, D = 2, E = 1
Red sentences   A = 1, B = 2, C = 3, D = 4, E = 5

A It will happen.
B It will probably happen.
C It might happen.
D It probably won't happen.
E It won't happen.

2 Do the questionnaire yourself with a partner. Who is more optimistic?

Who is the most optimistic person in the class? Who is the most pessimistic?

1 will, won't & might

It might rain tomorrow.	=	Perhaps it will rain, and perhaps it won't rain.
They might come.	=	Perhaps they'll come, and perhaps they won't come.

Look at the examples.

Explain these sentences in the same way.

a Careful – that dog might bite you!

b I might live to 100.

c He might pass his maths exam.

d One day, you might be rich.

e They might give you a birthday present.

Note: he'll = he will   he won't = he will not

2 There …

There will be lots of people. There won't be any rain.

Read about the summer camp, and say what there will/won't be.

3 Questions with 'will'

> Will we get to the camp by bus?

> How will we get to the camp?

Someone's thinking about the summer camp. What questions might they ask?

a I expect we'll get to the camp by bus.

b I expect we'll sleep in tents.

c I expect we'll go to bed late.

d I expect it'll cost a lot.

e I expect we'll wear shorts and T-shirts.

4 Probably

The price of petrol will probably go up.
He probably won't have a birthday party.

Can you unscramble these sentences?

a year probably married next get will they

b world win won't we next cup the probably

c won't stranger tall meet probably a dark you

d the rain day camp probably it every summer will at

COME TO OUR
SUMMER CAMP!

We won't have any electricity – so forget about TVs and computers! But we'll have bikes, boats, tennis classes, swimming competitions and lots of other activities. And every night (after your COLD shower!) we'll light a big camp fire and have a barbecue.
NOTE: No radios or mobile phones, please!

How to say it

1 ▭ Listen to the sound *'ll* in these sentences. Practise saying them.

You'll go on a long journey.
We'll probably get married in the summer.
I'm sure they'll write to us.
I'll phone you tomorrow.

2 ▭ Listen to the word *might* in this sentence. What happens when the speaker says it quickly?

You might get thirsty.

Practise saying these sentences quickly.

You might need some money.
We might stay at home tomorrow.
I might be a bit late.

Focus on Form

1 will, won't & might

- Read the examples. Then do the exercise with the class. Answers:

  a Perhaps it will bite you, and perhaps it won't bite you.

  b Perhaps I'll live to be 100, and perhaps I won't live to be 100.

  c Perhaps he'll pass his maths exam, and perhaps he won't pass his maths exam.

  d Perhaps you'll be rich, and perhaps you won't be rich.

  e Perhaps they'll give you a birthday present, and perhaps they won't give you a birthday present.

2 There ...

- Look at the examples, and show how these structures are related to *there is/are*:

Present	Future
There are lots of people.	**There will be lots of people.**
There isn't any rain.	**There won't be any rain.**

- Read the text, and ask students to say what there will and won't be at the summer camp. Possible answers:

  There will be bikes. There will be boats. There will be tennis classes. There will be swimming competitions. There will be camp fires. There will be barbecues. There will be cold showers.

  There won't be any electricity. There won't be any TVs. There won't be any computers. There won't be any radios. There won't be any mobile phones. There won't be any hot water.

3 Questions with 'will'

- Look at the examples.

- Students make questions, working alone or in pairs. They should make two questions for each item.

- Go through the answers:

  b Will we sleep in tents? Where will we sleep?

  c Will we go to bed late? When will we go to bed?

  d Will it cost a lot? How much will it cost?

  e Will we wear shorts and T-shirts? What will we wear?

4 Probably

- Look at the examples, and focus on the normal position of *probably*: after *will* but before *won't*.

- Working alone or in pairs, students write the sentences in the correct order. Then go through the answers:

  a They will probably get married next year.

  b We probably won't win the next World Cup.

  c You probably won't meet a tall dark stranger.

  d It will probably rain every day at the summer camp.

How to say it

1 Pronunciation of ''ll' in sentences

- ▭ Play the recording, pausing after each sentence. Focus on the pronunciation of *'ll*:

  /juːl gəʊ/, /wiːl prɒbəbli/, /ðeɪl raɪt/, /aɪl fəʊn yuː/

  If possible, get students to produce a 'dark' /l/ sound – pronounced with the back of the tongue touching the roof of the mouth.

2 Pronunciation of 'might' in rapid speech

- ▭ Play the sentence, and discuss what happens when it is said more quickly:
  – the /t/ in *might* links to the /g/ in *get*: /maɪt‿get/

- Play the other sentences and get students to repeat them quickly. Focus on the link between *might* and the following word:

  /yu maɪt‿niːd səm mʌni/
  /wi maɪt‿steɪ ət həʊm tə'mɒrəʊ/
  /aɪ maɪt‿biː ə bɪt leɪt/

▭ Tapescript for Exercise 3: *A bright future?*

OK, the first one: 'Everyone will have enough food to eat'. No, that won't happen – in fact I think people will probably have less food in the future.
'People will live 100 years or more' – maybe, it might happen. Rich people probably will live longer.
'We'll find a cure for cancer' – yes, I think we will, probably. I think it's happening already.
'There will be peace everywhere' – no, that certainly won't happen. I think there will always be wars.
'We'll discover a new kind of energy' – I'm not sure. That might happen – maybe some completely new way to travel. It's possible.

'There will be another world war' – yes, unfortunately, I think that will probably happen.
'We'll run out of oil and gas' – yes, certainly, that will happen.
'All the fish in the sea will die' – there are very few fish already, so I think it will probably happen.
'New diseases' – yes I think that will probably happen. It happens now, so why not in the future too?
'Unfriendly aliens will attack the Earth' – no, that won't happen.

14

This unit deals with three areas of language connected with towns:
– talking about public places and amenities
– talking about shops and shopping
– asking and giving street directions.
The reading and listening activity is about things to do in Los Angeles.

1 Places to go

This exercise introduces vocabulary for public places and amenities in towns, and activities associated with them.

➤ Workbook: Exercises A & B, Listening

> *Public places:* disco, nightclub, café, art gallery, museum, zoo, park, amusement park, sports centre, theatre, stadium, square, river, cathedral, castle.
> *Other expressions:* get some exercise, see the sights, souvenir, atmosphere.

1 Vocabulary presentation

- Read through what the people say, presenting any new words (e.g. *exercise, culture, night life, sights, souvenirs, relax, atmosphere*).

- Look at the pictures of places, and establish what they show.
  Answers (left to right):

  Top: bar/nightclub; art gallery; amusement park; river; castle
  Middle: café; museum; zoo; square; park/playground
  Bottom: theatre; sports centre; cathedral; disco; stadium

- Look at the first two people, and ask students to find places they would like to go to. Expected answers:

  sports centre, park, stadium, river

- Divide the class into pairs. They decide where the other people might want to go, and write lists of places.

- Discuss the answers together. Expected answers:

  Culture: art gallery, museum, cathedral, theatre
  Night life: disco, nightclub, theatre
  Sightseeing and souvenirs: square, cathedral, castle
  Children: river, castle, zoo, amusement park, park
  Relaxing: café, square, river, park

2 Preparation for the role-play: talking about your own town

- 'Brainstorm' places in your own town that tourists might want to visit, and build up a list on the board. As far as possible, use English words for this, and present any new items.

3 Role-play: giving information about your town

- To introduce the role-play, take the role of one of the six people, and ask the class questions about your town. Ask follow-up questions to get detailed information, e.g. *Where can I go running? Is there a swimming pool? When is it open?*

- Divide the class into pairs. One student takes the role of one of the tourists, and asks questions. The other student gives information about the town. Then they swap roles, with the other student taking the part of a tourist.

- As a round-up. Ask some of the 'tourists' what they wanted to do, and what they found out.

> *Language note*
> We can say *see the sights (of a town)* or *go sightseeing.* These mean the same.

> *Mixed nationality classes*
> Students could either talk about the town where they are now, or they could give information about the town they come from.

14 About town

1 Places to go

1 Read what the tourists say. Which of these places do you think they might want to go to? Make six lists.

2 Imagine the same tourists visit your town. What places do you think they might want to go to?

3 Role-play

Student A: Imagine you're one of the tourists. Think of some questions you might ask.

Student B: Answer A's questions.

> I want to sit somewhere quiet and write some postcards. Where do you suggest?

> Well, you could go and sit by the river. Or you could visit the Botanical Gardens ...

2 The best place in town

1 Think about shops in your town, and complete the table.

2 What's good about each place?
Choose from these reasons.

It's not too expensive.
They've got a good selection.
They sell things that are good quality.
The assistants are helpful.
The assistants are friendly.
It's convenient.
It's got a good atmosphere.
It's not too crowded.

Do other people agree with you?

3 Choose one of the shops you talked about
and write one or two sentences about it.

Which is the best place to ...

... buy books?   ....

... buy a jacket?   ....

... buy shoes?   ....

... buy CDs?   ....

... buy a camera?   ....

... get fast food?   ....

... get an ice-cream? ....

The best place to ...... is ...... because ...... and ......

3 How to get there

1 Look at these directions. What words go in the gaps?

Go ..... this road.   Go .... the square.   Go .... the bridge.   Go .... the bank.   You'll see the house .... your left

2 Two people give
directions from the
station. Follow the
directions – where
do they take you?

Choose one of the
places and give
directions back to
the station.

3 Work in pairs.

Student A: Choose a
place on the map.
Give B directions to
it from the station.

Student B: Follow the
directions – where do
they take you?

2 The best place in town

This exercise is about shops and shopping, and introduces a range of vocabulary for talking about good and bad features of shops.

> *Key words and expressions:* expensive, friendly, helpful, convenient, crowded; a good selection, a good atmosphere, good quality.

1 Introduction: listing shops in a table

- Read through the items in the table. Then give time for students to write names of places that they know (they should of course write names of particular shops, cafés, etc., e.g. *DL's Bookshop* rather than *bookshop*).

2 Vocabulary presentation; activation

- Read through the reasons, presenting new vocabulary as you go. Focus especially on the meaning of *a good selection* (= there are lots of things to choose from) and *it's convenient* (= you can get there easily).
- To show how the activity works, choose a shop yourself, and give a few reasons why you think it is the best of its kind (e.g. *I think DL's Bookshop is the best place to buy books, because the assistants are friendly and helpful, and they've got a very good selection of books* ...).
- Divide the class into pairs. Students show their list to their partner, and give reasons for their choice, using the expressions in the list.

3 Extension: writing sentences

- Students write sentences about one of the shops.
- Students read out their sentences. Ask other students if they agree.

3 How to get there

This exercise gives practice in following and giving simple street directions.

> *Key phrases:* Turn right/left, on your right/left, carry on.
> *Direction prepositions:* along, across, over, past.
> *Vocabulary:* places in towns.   (→ Beginner Units 10, 18.)

1 Introduction: presentation of prepositions

- Look at the drawings, and ask students to fill the gaps. Answers:

  Go *along* (*up*, *down*) this road. Go *across* the square. Go *over* (*across*) the bridge. Go *past* the bank. You'll see the house *on* your left.

2 Listening & following directions

- Look at the map and check that students can see the station.
- 🔲 Play each set of directions, and see if students can find the destination. If necessary, play them again, pausing and checking where they lead to. Answers:

  1 The hospital   2 The restaurant

- Ask students to give directions back to the station from the two destinations. Do this with the whole class, prompting and building up key expressions on the board:

> **Go (straight) on ...**
> **Turn left/right at the ...**
> **Go on**
> **Carry on** | **until you get to ...**

3 Practice: pairwork activity

- To introduce the activity, establish how you ask for street directions:

> **Excuse me,** | **can you tell me the way to ...?**
> **how can I get to ...?**

- Pairwork. In turn, students choose a place on the map and give their partner directions to it. The other student follows and says where the place is.

Mixed nationality classes
If students are fairly new to the place where they are studying, this is an opportunity to give them advice about where to go.

Optional extension
Take a vote on the places the class thinks are the best, and write them on the board.

➤ Workbook: Exercise C

🔲 The tapescript is on page T61.

4 Los Angeles

This combined reading and listening activity is about things to do and see around Los Angeles. The reading texts are taken from a travel guide, and recommend various places to visit. In the listening, someone describes a visit to Los Angeles.

> *New vocabulary (reading):* lazy, director, surfing, champion, magnificent, surrounded, lawn, guided tour, film set, face to face, shark, wax figure, best-known, collection, tropical, jungle, spaceship, monorail.
> *New vocabulary (listening):* enormous, wonderful.

Optional lead-in
Find out what students already know about Los Angeles and Hollywood. Prompt them by asking questions, e.g. *Where is it? Is it on the coast? Is it a nice place to live? What about Hollywood? What kind of people live there?*

1 Reading & matching

- Working alone or in pairs, students read the texts and match them with the pictures.
- Go through the answers together. Ask students why they chose the answers they did. Answers:

  A Disneyland   B Beverly Hills / Belair   C Malibu Lagoon   D Universal Studios
  E Movieland Wax Museum   F Sunset Boulevard

Vocabulary option
As you go through the answers, read each paragraph with the class, and present new vocabulary.

2 Reading for implied meaning

- Read the sentences in the bubbles, and discuss the answers with the class. Ask students to say why they think the places they chose would be suitable for each person. Possible answers:

  Children: Disneyland, Movieland Wax Museum
  Movie stars: Malibu Lagoon, Beverly Hills Hotel
  To relax: Malibu Lagoon, Sunset Boulevard
  Hollywood movies: Movieland Wax Museum, Universal Studios

3 Listening

- 🔲 Play the recording and discuss the answers to Question 1. Answers:

  – She visited Belair, Universal Studios and Disneyland.
  – She also went to Santa Barbara.

- Play the recording again, and focus on the adjectives the woman uses. Answers:

  Hollywood is *untidy* and *dirty*.　　　　Santa Barbara is a *beautiful* resort.
  Belair is an *expensive* area.　　　　　　People were *polite* and *friendly*.
  The houses in Belair were *enormous*.　　She had a *wonderful* time.

🔲 Tapescript for Exercise 3: *How to get there*

1 Well, you go out of the station, and you come to a main road. Turn left there, go along that road to the end. Then turn left again, go under a railway bridge, and a bit further on you'll come to a garage. Turn left there, go down that road, and you'll see it on your left – it's a big building.

2 OK. Well, when you come out of the station you'll see a main road, all right? Turn right, go along that road, and carry straight on till you come to the main square – it's a big square, you'll see it. Then turn left, go past a church, and you'll come to the river, OK? Now just before the river, there's a small road to the left. So go down that road, and it's about 100 metres down that road.

🔲 Tapescript for Exercise 4: *Los Angeles*

Last year I went to Hollywood for two weeks. My friend picked me up at the airport and we drove in her car back to Hollywood. At first I was a bit disappointed, because it all looked rather untidy and dirty. But later on she showed me some of the sights. She drove me through all the very expensive areas like Belair, where the houses are absolutely enormous. And she took me to Universal Studios, where they make the great Hollywood films.

We went to Disneyland, which is a little way outside Los Angeles, and we spent a whole day there – I really enjoyed it. And on another day she took me to see a place about 50 miles from Los Angeles, called Santa Barbara, which is a beautiful resort on the beach, and I swam in the Pacific Ocean. The people there were so polite and friendly, which I liked a lot. I had a wonderful time.

4 Los Angeles

1 Here are descriptions of six places in the Los Angeles area. Match them with the photos.

Spend a lazy afternoon down at Malibu Lagoon. Many of Hollywood's younger film stars and directors come here to relax, and some have homes by the sea. Malibu is also a great place for surfing, and champion surfers come here from all over the world.

Go on a tour of the suburbs of Beverly Hills and Belair. Here you can see the homes of the rich and famous – magnificent houses surrounded by green lawns, swimming pools and very high walls. There are Rolls Royces everywhere you look.

Have a look round Universal Studios, where some of Hollywood's greatest films were made. You can take a guided tour which will take you through the film sets, and will bring you face to face with King Kong and the shark from *Jaws*.

Drive down Sunset Boulevard, probably the most famous street in Los Angeles. Here you can see cheap nightclubs side by side with smart shops and expensive restaurants, as well as the Beverly Hills Hotel, where you'll see lots of famous faces.

Visit the Movieland Wax Museum, and see the wax figures of famous stars such as Jack Nicholson, Clint Eastwood and Marilyn Monroe – all in scenes from their best-known films. The museum also has a great collection of old movie cameras.

Spend a day at Disneyland, a place for children of all ages. You can go on a boat journey through a tropical jungle; take a train through the American Wild West; travel in a spaceship to the stars; take a trip on a monorail ... or just sit in the sun and eat ice-cream.

2 Which places would you recommend to these people?

Are there any good places for children?

I just want to relax and have a good time.

I've never met a famous movie star face to face.

I'd love to know how they made all those Hollywood movies.

3 A woman talks about a holiday in Los Angeles. Listen and answer the questions.

a Which of the six places did she visit? Where else did she go?

b She uses these adjectives. Who or what is she talking about?

untidy and dirty   beautiful

expensive   polite and friendly

enormous   wonderful

Focus on ... If and when

1 🔲 Listen and read the conversation.

Who do you think the people are? Where is the younger one going?

Don't forget to phone me.

OK, I'll phone when I get to the airport.

And send me a postcard. Don't forget.

Yes, when I get to the hotel I'll send you a postcard.

And be careful.

Don't worry. I'll phone you if anything happens.

Well, if you don't phone, I'll phone the hotel – just to be sure ...

When do the people use
– *will*?
– the Present simple?

2 **Match the phrases together, and make sentences beginning *If* ... or *When* ...**

If	I win the lottery	I'll buy her a car
	my daughter is 18	I'll buy you some socks
	you don't leave now	she'll be very pleased
When	I go to the shops	I'll call the police
	you send her a card	I'll go round the world
	we get home	I'll cook a meal

3 **Think of ways to continue these sentences.**

   a We'll probably catch the train if ...
   b That meat will go bad if ...
   c I'll write to you when ...
   d She'll never make any new friends if ...
   e He'll be very disappointed if ...
   f I'll start looking for a job when ...

Pronunciation: Unusual words (3)

1 🔲 Try saying these words, then listen to check.

furniture	it suits you
receipt	delicious
jewellery	a foreign country
handkerchief	probably
stomach ache	building

2 Write two sentences. Use one word from the box in each.

3 Read out your sentences.

Phrasebook Buying a ticket (2)

Put this conversation in the correct order.

– At 7.30.
– Both adults?
– That's £13, please.
– No, one adult and one child.
– What time does the film start?
– Two tickets for *Star Wars*, please.

 Now listen and check.

Have similar conversations.

A You're going to the theatre this evening. You want two adult tickets for *Romeo and Juliet*.

B Tickets cost £30 or £15. The play starts at 9.00.

A You want three tickets for the football match this afternoon.

B Tickets cost £12. The match starts at 2.30.

Study pages G

Focus on ... *When & if*

This exercise focuses on the use of If *and* When + *Present simple, to talk about the future. It also gives practice in using* will *(introduced in Unit 13).*

> *Key structures:* If + Present simple ... will (first conditional); When + Present simple ... will.
> *New vocabulary:* lottery, go bad, pleased, disappointed.

1 Presentation of key structures

- ▣ Play the recording and let students follow the conversation. Then establish these points:
  - the girl uses *will* to talk about the future (*I'll phone you, I'll send you a postcard*).
  - she uses the Present simple after *When ...* and *If ...*
  - we use *when* for things we know will happen, *if* for things that may or may not happen.

  Show this structure on the board:

  > **When** | **+ Present simple ... will ...**
  > **If** |
  >
  > **When I get to the airport** | **I'll phone you.**
  > **If anything happens** |

  (We can, of course, use the same structure the other way round: *I'll phone you when/if anything happens.*)

2 Controlled practice: matching sentences

- Give time for students to match the phrases, working either alone or in pairs, then go through the answers together. Expected answers:

  If I win the lottery, I'll go round the world.
  When my daughter is 18, I'll buy her a car.
  If you don't leave now, I'll call the police.
  If/When I go to the shops, I'll buy you some socks.
  If you send her a card, she'll be very pleased.
  When we get home, I'll cook a meal.

3 Open-ended practice: continuing sentences

- Either get ideas from the whole class, or let students do the exercise in pairs and then go through the answers. Possible answers:

  a ... we walk fast; ... we leave now; ... we take a taxi.
  b ... we don't eat it today; ... you don't put it in the fridge; ... you leave it in the sun.
  c ... I arrive; ... I have time; ... I know where I'm staying.
  d ... she stays at home every evening; ... she doesn't go out.
  e ... he doesn't pass the exam; ... you leave him; ... you don't invite him to the party.
  f ... I leave university; ... I come back from holiday; ... I need some money.

Pronunciation: *Unusual words (3)*

> Words from previous units which may cause pronunciation problems.

1 Listening & practice

- ▣ Ask students to try saying each word, then play the recording and get them to practise. Focus on:
  - the reduced /ə/ sounds in /ˈfɜːnɪtʃə/, /ˈdʒuəlri/, /ˈstʌmək/, /dəˈlɪʃəs/ (or /dɪˈlɪʃəs/), /ˈfɒrən/, /ˈprɒbəbli/.
  - the silent *p* in /rəˈsiːt/, and silent *d* in /ˈhæŋkətʃiːf/.
  - the pronunciation of /eɪk/, /ˈbɪldɪŋ/, /suːts/ (or /sjuːts/), /ˈkʌntri/.

2 Writing sentences

- Students write a sentence using words from the box, and including any other words they like, e.g.
  They probably live in that building.
  I like your jewellery – it suits you.

3 Reading sentences aloud

- Students read out their sentences in turn. Focus on the pronunciation of the key words.
  Alternative: Dictation. Students dictate their sentence to the person next to them. As a check, ask students to read out the sentence they wrote down.

Phrasebook: *Buying a ticket (2)*

This exercise practises language used when buying tickets for a show or an event (e.g. cinema, theatre, concert, football match). It links with topics covered in Unit 14.

> *Key phrases:* ticket, adult, child; What time does (it) start?

- Ask students to put the dialogue in the correct order. As you do this, present any new expressions.
- ▣ Play the dialogue to check.
- Look at the two situations with the class, and establish what the people will say. If you like, build up possible dialogues on the board.
- Either let students practise the dialogues in pairs, or ask two students to have each conversation in front of the class.

> ▣ Tapescript for Phrasebook: *Buying a ticket (2)*
>
> A Two tickets for *Star Wars*, please.
> B Both adults?
> A No, one adult and one child.
> B That's £13, please.
> A What time does the film start?
> B At 7.30.

Consolidation

Short answers

This exercise focuses on yes/no questions and short answers. It practises verb tenses introduced in Units 1, 5, 7, 9 and 13.

1 ● Read the questions and ask students to complete the missing answers:

> No, I don't.
> Yes, they are.
> Yes, she did; No, she didn't.
> Yes, I have; No, I haven't.
> Yes, she will; No, she won't.

● Establish that:
  – to make short answers, we repeat the auxiliary verb (*do*, *did*, *is*, *have*, *will*, etc.) in the question.
  – we don't repeat the whole verb. If you like, show this on the board:

> **Do you like Japanese food? Yes, I do. ✔**
> **Yes, I like. ✗**
> **Yes, I do like. ✗**

2 ● Look at the questions, and establish what the possible answers are:

> *Did you go out last night?* Yes, I did; No, I didn't.
> *Will you be at home this evening?* Yes, I will; No, I won't.
> *Have you had lunch yet?* Yes, I have; No, I haven't.
> *Have you got a dictionary?* Yes, I have; No, I haven't.
> *Is the teacher wearing glasses?* Yes, (s)he is; No, (s)he isn't.
> *Is there a computer here?* Yes, there is; No, there isn't.

● Pairwork. Students ask the questions and give true answers.

Two-word verbs

This exercise focuses on two-word verbs that have appeared in the book so far.

1 Look at the verbs and check that students know what they mean. If necessary, give simple examples of each verb. Ask students the Past and Present perfect forms:

go, went, has gone out	put, put, has put on
go, went, has gone away	take, took, has taken off
wake, woke, has woken up	try, tried, has tried on
get, got, has got up	turn, turned, has turned on
stand, stood, has stood up	turn, turned, has turned off
sit, sat, has sat down	

2 Students fill the gaps in the sentences. Answers:

a woke up, turned on
b go out
c has gone away (went away)
d took off, turned off
e Sit down
f try on
g stood up (got up), put on

Review

Verbs

Review of verb forms from Units 1, 3, 5, 7, and 9.

● Do the exercise with the class. Use any problems to pinpoint areas that you need to practise. Answers:

a I work ... my brother works ... he doesn't like ... I quite like ...
b There are plenty of eggs ... there isn't much milk.
c ... have got cars ... my parents have got ...
d ... usually sit ... watch television ... are staying ... are going out ...
e ... Ian woke up ... made ... has just arrived ... is sitting.

Words

Review of vocabulary from Exercises 6.3, 10.1, and 12.1.

1 Ask students to identify the containers. Answers:

a jar *b* can *c* packet/bag *d* packet *e* bottle

2 Elicit things that you can have pairs of, and write them on the board. Possible answers:

> trousers, jeans, shorts, pyjamas
> shoes, boots, trainers, sandals
> socks, (tights, stockings)
> gloves
> glasses, sunglasses
> earrings

3 Look at the picture and ask what part of the body the numbers point to. Answers:

1 shoulder 2 arm 3 hand 4 wrist 5 finger 6 knee
7 leg 8 foot

Consolidation

Short answers

1 Look at these questions and answers.
What are the missing answers?

Do you like Japanese food?   Yes, I do.
                             No, ...

Are they staying here?   Yes, ...
                             No, they aren't.

Did she speak to you?   Yes, ...
                             No, ...

Have you closed the window? Yes, ...
                             No, ...

Will Diana be there?   Yes, ...
                             No, ...

2 Give true answers to these questions.

| Did you go out last night? | Will you be at home this evening? | Have you had lunch yet? |

| Have you got a dictionary? | Is the teacher wearing glasses? | Is there a computer here? |

Two-word verbs

1 These are all two-word verbs. Check that you
know what they mean.

go out   wake up   stand up   put on   turn on
go away   get up   sit down   take off turn off
                               try on

What are the Past and Present perfect forms?

2 Fill the gaps with verbs from the box.

a I .... suddenly at 2 o'clock in the
  morning. The room was dark, so I ....
  the light.

b I think I'll .... and buy some bread.

c John isn't here. He .... for the weekend.

d I .... my clothes, went to bed, ...
  the light and went to sleep.

e '.................. in that chair,' said the police
  officer. 'We want to ask you some questions.'

f 'Could I .... this jacket?' I asked the
  shop assistant.

g She finished her coffee, then .... and
  .... her coat. 'It's time to go,' she said.

Review

Verbs

Choose the correct form of the verbs.

a I work/works in a supermarket, and my brother
  work/works in a bank. He don't like/doesn't like
  his job very much, but I quite like/likes mine.

b There's/There are plenty of eggs in the fridge,
  but there isn't/there aren't much milk.

c Most people in our street have got/has got cars,
  but my parents have got/has got motorbikes.

d We usually sit/are sitting at home in the
  evening and watch/are watching television, but
  some friends stay/are staying with us at the
  moment, so we go out/are going out quite a lot.

e Yesterday morning, Ian woke up/has woken up
  with a terrible toothache, so he made/has
  made an appointment to see
  the dentist at 10.00 the next
  day. It's 9.55 now, and Ian
  just arrived/has just arrived
  at the dentist's. He sits/
  is sitting in the waiting
  room, reading a magazine.

Words

1 Look at the pictures. What are the containers?

a a .... of olives
b a .... of beans
c a .... of sugar
d a .... of biscuits
e a .... of oil

2 You're probably wearing a pair of shoes now.
Think of other things to wear that come
in pairs.

A pair of ....

3 What parts of the body do the diagrams show?

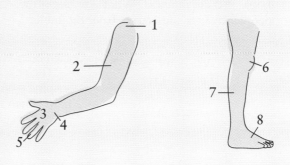

15 Comparing things

1 It's much better

Comparative adjectives • than

A Do you think so? Why?

The Regal Hotel's not bad, but the Metropole's much better.

B I really like my new job. It's much better than my old one.

Is it? How?

C Really? Why's that?

I'm glad I moved into the city centre. It's much better than living out in the suburbs.

1 Read the three conversations. What do you think the people might say next? Mark the sentences *A*, *B* or *C*.

☐ 'It's livelier at the weekends.'	☐ 'It more convenient for the shops.'
☐ 'The hours are shorter.'	☐ 'It's nearer my office.'
☐ 'The rooms are more comfortable.'	☐ 'It's cheaper.'
☐ 'The staff are more helpful.'	☐ 'The work's much more interesting.'
☐ 'Everyone's friendlier.'	☐ 'It's much quieter at night.'

🔲 Now listen to the conversations. What do the people say?

2 Read the sentences again, and add adjectives to the table.

Now write these adjectives in the table:

fast   attractive   reliable
clean   relaxing   big

adjective + -er	more + adjective
livelier	more comfortable
shorter	

3 Look at these remarks. What else might the people say? Use adjectives from the table.

I don't go to work by bus. I always go by train.

We don't go to the Star Disco any more. The Oasis is much better.

The new hospital's much better than the old one.

I don't go to work by car now. I've bought a motorbike.

We live in the country now. It's much better than the city.

This unit covers some of the common uses of comparison: expressing preferences, talking about dimensions, talking about the outstanding features of places and comparing yourself to other people. It focuses on the comparative and superlative forms of adjectives.

1 It's much better

This exercise introduces comparative forms of adjectives, and practises the use of comparative structures for expressing preferences.

➤ Focus on Form: Exercises 1 & 2
➤ Workbook: Exercises A & B

> **Key structures:** Comparative forms: adjective + -er, more + adjective; better.
> *Adjectives:* lively, short, comfortable, helpful, friendly, convenient, near, cheap, interesting, fast, attractive, quiet, reliable, clean, relaxing, big.
> (→ Beginner Unit 21.)

1 Presentation of adjectives; grammar presentation; listening

- Look at the examples, and ask what the people are talking about. Answers:
  A two hotels   B her new job and her old one   C living in the town and living in the country.

  Use the examples to present the idea of comparison:

  > **My new job is <u>good</u>.**
  > **It's <u>better than</u> my old job.**

- Read the sentences, and ask students which conversation they might go with. As you do this, present any new adjectives (e.g. *lively, helpful*), giving simple examples of your own to make the meaning clear.
- 🔲 Play the recording and check the answers:
  A: It's much quieter at night. The rooms are more comfortable. The staff are more helpful. It's cheaper.
  B: The work's much more interesting. Everyone's friendlier. The hours are shorter.
  C: It's nearer my office. It's more convenient for the shops. It's livelier at the weekends.

🔲 The tapescript is on page T66.

Presentation option: much
Some of the sentences use the word *much* before the comparative form (*much better, much quieter, much more interesting*). If you like, present this on the board, and then get students to use this form in Stage 3.

2 Presentation of comparative forms; completing a table

- Present the two comparative forms on the board:

  > **The Metropole is** | cheaper / more comfortable | **than the Regal.**

- Write the table on the board, and ask students to suggest adjectives for each column. Then look at the new adjectives, and add them in the appropriate column:

adjective + -er	more + adjective
livelier	more comfortable
shorter	more helpful
friendlier	more convenient
nearer	more interesting
cheaper	more attractive
quieter	more reliable
faster	more relaxing
cleaner	
bigger	

Language note
Adjectives with one syllable add -er.
Two-syllable adjectives ending in -y change to -ier.
Most other two-syllable adjectives add *more*.
Adjectives with three or more syllables add *more*.
Good/better is an irregular form.

3 Activation: making sentences

- Look at each remark in turn, and ask students to add sentences. Possible answers:

  Going by train: It's more comfortable, it's faster, it's more relaxing, it's more reliable.
  The Oasis: It's livelier, the people are friendlier, the music's better.
  The new hospital: It's quieter, it's bigger, it's cleaner, the staff are friendlier.
  Motorbike: It's faster, it's cheaper, it's more convenient.
  The country: It's more relaxing, it's quieter, people are friendlier.

Optional extension: role-play
Pairwork. Students use the sentences in short conversations like those in the recording.

2 General knowledge

This exercise introduces comparison questions with Which?

> *Key structures: Which is … -er? Comparative adjectives:* bigger, further, more, longer, heavier, hotter, deeper, longer, higher, older. *Other vocabulary:* Jupiter, Saturn, calories, spider, fly (n.), temperature, human being, crocodile, was built.

➤ Workbook: Exercises A & B

1 *Answering questions; grammar & vocabulary presentation*

- Ask the questions round the class, and present any new vocabulary. Answers:

  1 An African elephant
  2 Saturn (1400 million km from the Sun; Jupiter is 780 million km from the Sun)
  3 100 grams of chocolate (= 500 calories; sugar has 400 calories)
  4 The Nile (= 6670 km; the Amazon is 6440 km)
  5 A spider (8 legs; a fly has 6 legs)
  6 A litre of beer (about 50 grams more)

Show the structure of *Which?* questions on the board:

Which	is bigger / has bigger ears	X or Y?

> *Language note: irregular forms*
> *Further* is the comparative of *far*. *More* is the comparative of *much* or *many.*

2 *Writing 'Which?' questions; asking & answering questions*

- Divide the class into pairs, and give each pair a letter, A or B. Students in each pair look only at their own facts on pages 105 or 106. They work out their questions and write them down. Go round the class giving help.
- Students form new pairs, and ask each other their questions. As a round-up, check the questions and go through the answers.

  A 1 Which is hotter, Rio de Janeiro or Hong Kong? (Rio)
    2 Which has more teeth, a crocodile or a human being? (A crocodile)
    3 Which is higher, Mont Blanc or Mount Kilimanjaro? (Mount Kilimanjaro)
    4 Which is older, the Kremlin or Buckingham Palace? (The Kremlin)

  B 1 Which is bigger, the USA or Canada? (Canada)
    2 Which has more letters, the Greek alphabet or the Russian alphabet?
      (The Russian alphabet)
    3 Which is longer, the Suez Canal or the Panama Canal? (The Suez Canal)
    4 Which is deeper, the Atlantic Ocean or the Pacific Ocean? (The Pacific Ocean)

> *Presentation option*
> Before you divide the class into pairs, present the adjectives they will need for their questions: *hot/hotter, many/more, high/higher, old/older, big/bigger, long/longer, deep/deeper.*

> *Whole class option*
> Divide the class into two teams to prepare and ask their questions.

> *Background notes*
> *Mont Blanc* (the highest mountain in the Alps) is in France; *Mount Kilimanjaro* (the highest mountain in Africa) is in Tanzania. *The Kremlin* in Moscow is the centre of the Russian government; *Buckingham Palace* in London is the home of the British royal family.

3 Outstanding features

This exercise gives facts about Britain. It introduces superlative adjectives.

> *Key structures:* the + adjective + -est, the most + adjective. *Superlative forms:* largest, furthest, smallest, highest, longest, deepest, wettest, warmest, oldest, greatest, most famous, most important, most popular. (→ Beginner Unit 21.)

➤ Focus on Form: Exercise 3
➤ Workbook: Exercise C, Listening

1 *Reading; presentation of superlative forms*

- Read the text, and build up a list of superlative adjectives:
  largest, furthest, smallest, most popular, most famous.
- Present superlative structures:

London is the	largest / most important	city in Britain.

> *Language note*
> We say *the largest city in Britain* (not 'the largest city of Britain').

2 *Vocabulary presentation; reading & gap-filling*

- Turn to page 104, and look at the words in the box. Then ask students to complete the texts. Answers (clockwise from top):

  the deepest lake … the most famous; the largest wild animal; Scotland's most famous poet; the greatest / most famous English writer … his greatest / most important play; the oldest university; the warmest place; the oldest castle; the longest river; Britain's longest place name; the wettest place; Britain's largest football stadium; the highest mountain

> *Note*
> *Llanfair…goch* is Welsh. It means: St Mary's Church in the hollow of the white hazel tree near the rapid whirlpool of St Tisillio's Church by the red cave.

3 *Extension: writing sentences*

- Students think of similar facts about their own country, and write them down.
- As a round-up, ask students to read out their sentences.

> *Homework option*
> Students draw a rough map of their own country and add sentences like those in the exercise.

2 General knowledge

Comparative adjectives • Which ...?

1 Which has bigger ears, an African elephant or an Asian elephant?

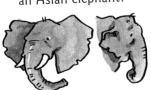

2 Which is further from the Sun, Jupiter or Saturn?

3 Which has more calories, 100 grams of sugar or 100 grams of chocolate?

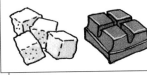

4 Which is longer, the River Nile or the River Amazon?

5 Which has more legs, a spider or a fly?

6 Which is heavier, a litre of water or a litre of beer?

1 Can you answer these questions?

2 What questions can you ask?

   Student A: Look at your facts on page 105.
   Student B: Look at your facts on page 106.

3 Outstanding features

Superlative forms

1 Read the two texts. How many superlative forms can you find?

BRITAIN

Britain consists of three countries: England, Scotland and Wales. England is the largest of the three, and has the biggest population. Scotland is the furthest north. Wales is the smallest, with a population of about three million.

LONDON

London is the largest city in Britain, and is also one of the most popular places for tourists to visit. Its most famous buildings are Buckingham Palace and the Houses of Parliament.

2 Look at the map of Britain on page 104.

   Fill the gaps with superlative forms. Use words from the box.

3 Think about your own country. What are its outstanding features?

   Write sentences using superlative forms.

Focus on Form

1 Rules

Here are some rules for making comparative and superlative forms. Add examples from the unit.

One-syllable adjectives		
old	older	the oldest
....	....	....
....	....	....
Two-syllable adjectives ending in -y		
happy	happier	the happiest
....	....	....
....	....	....
Most other two-syllable adjectives		
boring	more boring	the most boring
....	....	....
....	....	....
Three or more syllables		
reliable	more reliable	the most reliable
....	....	....
....	....	....
Irregular forms		
bad	worse	the worst
....	....	....

2 Comparing

> I'm taller than my mother.
> My sister's younger than me.
> I'm more intelligent than my brother.

How are you different from other people in your family? Make two or three sentences. Choose from these adjectives:

> tall   short   old   young
> nice   friendly   happy
> lazy   intelligent   interesting   serious

3 Superlatives

> *Japanese*
> ~~British~~ cooking is the best in the world.
> *most dangerous*
> The ~~safest~~ way to travel is by motorbike.

Do you agree with these opinions? If not, change them so that they are true for you.

> British cooking is the best in the world.

> The safest way to travel is by motorbike.

> The news is the most interesting programme on TV.

> Football is the most boring game in the world.

> Money is the most important thing in life.

> Computers are the greatest invention of all time.

How to say it

1 🔲 Listen to these *-er* and *-ier* endings.

cheaper	friendlier
younger	happier
quieter	lazier

Practise saying these sentences.

This room's much quieter.
Are you feeling happier now?
Everyone's friendlier here.

2 🔲 Listen to this sentence. What happens when the speaker says it quickly?

She's much younger than my brother.

Practise saying these sentences quickly.

It's the fastest car in the world.
I'm a bit taller than my father.
Living in the country is much better than living in the city.

Focus on Form

1 Rules

● Ask students to find examples in the unit, and add them to the table. There are of course many possibilities. An example answer:

One-syllable adjectives:

big	bigger	the biggest
fast	faster	the fastest

Two-syllable adjectives ending in -y:

friendly	friendlier	the friendliest
lively	livelier	the liveliest

Most other two-syllable adjectives:

helpful	more helpful	the most helpful
famous	more famous	the most famous

Three or more syllables:

important	more important	the most important
relaxing	more relaxing	the most relaxing
interesting	more interesting	the most interesting

Irregular forms:

good	better	the best
much/many	more	the most

2 Comparing

● Look at the examples. Then ask students to write a few sentences about themselves. Example answers:

My mother is older than my father.
My brother's taller than me.
I think I'm more interesting than my sister.

3 Superlatives

● Look at the examples, which show how students might change the statements.

If you like, introduce the word *least* as the opposite of *most* before you do the exercise (e.g. *Money is the least important thing in life*).

● Give time for students to read the sentences alone or in pairs, and make changes. Then ask students what changes they made. Example answers:

French cooking is the best in the world.
The most dangerous way to travel is by motorbike.
Films are the most interesting programmes on TV.
Chess is the most boring game in the world.
Happiness is the most important thing in life.
Clocks are the greatest invention of all time.

How to say it

1 Pronunciation of '-er' and '-ier' endings

● 🔊 Play the words and focus on the endings:
/ˈtʃiːpə/, /ˈjʌŋɡə/, /ˈkwaɪətə/
/ˈfrendlɪə/, /ˈhæpɪə/, /ˈleɪzɪə/

● Play the sentences, and get students to repeat them.

2 Rhythm of rapid speech

● 🔊 Play the sentence, and discuss what happens when it is said more quickly:
– there is more difference between the stressed sounds (<u>young</u>er, <u>broth</u>er) and the unstressed sounds (she's, than, my);
– the unstressed sounds become shorter, and some sounds are reduced (/ʃiːz/ → /ʃɪz/, /ðæn/ → /ðən/).

● Play the other sentences and get students to repeat them quickly. Focus on the rhythm and reduced vowel sounds:
/ɪts ðə <u>faː</u>stɪst <u>kaː</u>r ɪn ðə <u>wɜː</u>ld/
/aɪm ə <u>bɪt</u> <u>tɔː</u>lə ðən maɪ <u>faː</u>ðə/
/<u>lɪ</u>vɪŋ ɪn ðə <u>kʌn</u>tri ɪz <u>mʌtʃ</u> <u>be</u>tə ðən <u>lɪ</u>vɪŋ ɪn ðə <u>sɪ</u>ti/

🔊 Tapescript for Exercise 1: *It's much better*

a A The Regal Hotel's not bad, but the Metropole's much better.
   B Do you think so? Why?
   A Well, for one thing it's much quieter at night, the rooms are more comfortable as well – and I think the staff are more helpful. And it's cheaper.
b A I really like my new job. It's much better than my old one.
   B Is it? How?

A Well, the work's more interesting, everyone's friendlier, and the hours are shorter, too.
c A I'm glad I moved into the city centre. It's much better than living out in the suburbs.
   B Really? Why's that?
   A Well, it's nearer my office, that's the main thing. But it's also more convenient for the shops and things, you know? It's livelier too, especially at the weekends.

16

This unit covers three areas of language connected with leisure activities:
– saying what leisure activities you do
– talking about enjoyment and ability
– talking about sport.
The reading and listening activity is a sports quiz.

1 Leisure activities

This exercise introduces ways of talking in general about leisure activities. It focuses on names of outdoor and indoor activities, and the verbs go *and* play.

➤ Workbook: Exercise A

> *Outdoor activities:* swimming, running, cycling, playing (golf), sailing, skateboarding, going to (the theatre). *Indoor activities:* cooking, playing (the piano), playing (chess), collecting (stamps), painting, knitting, reading (novels), writing (poetry), listening to (music), learning (languages). (→ Beginner Unit 22.)

1 Presentation of vocabulary; guessing; listening to check

- Look at the activities, and present any that are unfamiliar. Then ask students to try to guess which activities each of the people does. As you do this, establish how the expressions can be used in sentences:
  - using a verb: *she knits, she listens to jazz, she plays the piano.*
  - using *like/enjoy* + *-ing*: *she likes knitting, he likes collecting shells.*
  - using *go* + *-ing* for activities involving movement (*he goes swimming, she goes running, she goes cycling*).

- 🔲 Play the recording and establish what else each person does. Answers:

  Louisa: Plays the piano, collects shells, goes swimming, goes cycling. Plays the violin.
  Carsten: Goes running, listens to jazz, cooks. Watches motor racing.
  Josephine: Goes swimming, knits, reads novels, writes poetry. Goes for walks.
  Patrick: Goes to the theatre, reads books, plays golf. Looks after his house.

2 Dictionary task; vocabulary presentation

- Either ask students to look up the leisure activities in their dictionaries, or try to elicit them, and present any that students do not know. Answers (left to right):

  sailing, collecting coins and stamps, learning languages, playing the guitar, painting, playing computer games, reading science fiction, skateboarding, listening to classical music, rock climbing (mountaineering)

3 Personalisation: pairwork interviews

- To introduce the activity, ask the class to find out what you do in your free time by asking questions. Then get them to tell you what they have found out.
- Pairwork. Students take it in turns to interview their partner. If you like, ask them to make brief notes on a piece of paper.
- As a round-up, ask students what they found out about their partner.

> *Blackboard option*
> Write the class's guesses on the board.

> *Language note*
> With musical instruments, we use *play* + *the*: *play the piano, play the guitar.* With sports or games, we use *play* without *the*: *play chess, play golf.*

> *Language note*
> We say *go skateboarding* and *go sailing.* The other activities can all be used with a direct verb, e.g. *I collect stamps, I learn languages.*

> *Homework option*
> Students write a short paragraph about their own or their partner's leisure activities.

🔲 Tapescript for Exercise 1: *Leisure activities*

Louisa
I enjoy practising the piano, and doing the piano. I have a very good teacher called Miss Rowe. And I learn the violin, and I enjoy that a lot. I collect shells and rocks, and I've got quite a lot of them. And I go swimming now and again, and I like bike riding.

Carsten
Well, I go running a lot – I live near a forest, so I go running in the forest. I listen to music, especially jazz. And I also cook – I like cooking for other people, especially. Oh, and I also watch Formula 1 motor racing – that's a hobby of mine, too.

Josephine
I live very near the sea. All through the year I go for walks along the shore, and in the summer I go swimming every day. In the winter I like knitting – I make jumpers for my children and my grandchildren, and I enjoy doing different patterns. I spend a lot of time reading, mostly novels, and I'm very fond of poetry – I also write poetry now and then.

Patrick
I go to the theatre a lot, to see plays. I read a lot, I read a lot of books. I play golf sometimes, when I can. And I have an old house, which needs a lot of work, so I spend a lot of time at home painting the walls, mending things – looking after the house, really. I enjoy that.

16 Free time

1 Leisure activities

1 Look at these four people. What do you think they do in their spare time? Choose from these activities:

swimming

going to the theatre

cooking

collecting shells

knitting

cycling

running

writing poetry

reading books

playing the piano

listening to jazz

playing golf

Louisa, age 10, school pupil

Carsten, age 20, musician

Josephine, age 76, retired teacher

Patrick, age 39, radio producer

Now listen to them talking about their leisure activities. Were you right? What other activities do they mention?

2 What leisure activities can you see? Use a dictionary to help you.

3 Find out about your partner. Make some notes.

Does he/she ...

... play a musical instrument?

... play any sports?

... play any games?

... cook?

... listen to music?

... collect anything?

... read a lot?

... have any other hobbies?

Tell other students one or two things about your partner.

Do you play a musical instrument?

Yes, I do.

What do you play?

2 Would you enjoy …?

parachute jumping

bird watching

water-skiing

horse-riding

hunting

playing in a band

1 Have you ever done any of these activities? Which ones? What was it like?

2 *a* Talk about each activity where you said *Yes*. What was it like?

> I found it
> interesting   boring
> exciting   frightening
> easy   difficult

> I was
> I wasn't   (very) good at it.

b Talk about each activity where you said *No*. Would you enjoy it?

> I'd find it
> interesting   boring
> exciting   frightening
> easy   difficult

> I'd be
> I wouldn't be   (very) good at it.

3 Think of another activity, and find out the English word for it.

Find out if other people would enjoy doing it.

3 Spectator sports

1 Look at the photos.

What sports can you see?

2 What happens in each sport?
Talk about each one.
Use these phrases to help you.

drive round a track
ride round a track
run round a track

hit the ball
throw the ball
kick the ball

with a racket
with a club

over the net
into the hole
into the basket
into the goal

score a goal
score points

win the game
win the race

3 *Student A*: Turn to page 107. Describe your pictures to B.
Student B: Turn to page 108. Describe your pictures to A.

What differences can you find?

2 Would you enjoy ...?

In this exercise students consider unusual leisure activities. This introduces adjectives for describing reactions, the phrase good at, *and the structure* I'd ...

> Key phrases: I found it ..., I'd find it ..., good at. *Adjectives:* interesting, boring, exciting, frightening, easy, difficult. *Other vocabulary:* names of activities.

1 Introduction; vocabulary presentation

● Check that students understand what the activities are. Ask them to mark them *Yes* or *No* (or ✓ or ✗), to show whether they have tried them or not.

2 Presentation of key expressions; speaking activity

● Look at the expressions in *a*. Present the adjectives (*interesting, boring,* etc.), and the phrase *be good at* (= you can do it well).

● Look at the expressions in *b*. Point out that *I'd* means *I would* – we use it if we're just imagining something.

● Pairwork. Students talk about the activities. They say what they were like, or if they think they would enjoy them.

● As a round-up, go through the activities. Find out who has done them and what students think about them.

3 Extension: vocabulary expansion & speaking activity

● Ask students to suggest activities, and tell them what they are in English.

● Pairwork. Students find out if their partner has done each activity, and whether they enjoyed it or would enjoy it.

3 Spectator sports

This exercise introduces vocabulary for talking about spectator sports.

> Names of sports: athletics (running), football, basketball, golf, motor racing, horse racing, tennis. *Verbs:* run, ride, drive, hit, throw, kick, score, win. *Other vocabulary:* net, hole, basket, goal; racket, club; point, track, race.

1 Elicitation & presentation of vocabulary

● Look at the pictures. Establish what sports are shown:

athletics (running); horse racing; motor racing; basketball; football; golf; tennis

2 Presentation of key phrases; making sentences

● Help students to match the phrases with the sports, presenting new words as you do this. Then get students to put the phrases together to build up a simple description of each sport. Possible answers:

Athletics: You *run round a track*. The fastest runner *wins the race*.
Football: You try to *kick the ball into the goal*. If you do this, you *score a goal*.
Basketball: You try to *throw the ball into the basket*.
Golf: You *hit the ball with a club*. You try to hit it *into the hole*.
Motor racing: You *drive round a track*. The fastest car *wins the race*.
Horse racing: You *ride round a track*. The fastest horse *wins the race*.
Tennis: You *hit the ball with a racket*. You try to hit it *over the net*.

3 Activation: pairwork game

● Pairwork. Students describe their pictures and find the differences.

● Go through the answers together. Answers:

1 In A the player has scored a goal, in B he hasn't.
2 In A the brown horse is winning, in B the white horse is winning.
3 In A a woman has hit the ball, in B a man has hit it.
4 In A the player is throwing the ball, in B the player has already thrown the ball and it's going into the basket.

➤ Workbook: Listening

> *Option*
> Quickly find out at this stage how many students have tried each activity (*Who has tried parachute jumping?*, etc.).

> *Language note*
> This is the conditional form of the verb: I *would/wouldn't* + infinitive. In this exercise it can be treated simply as a set phrase; there is no need to go into a detailed grammar explanation.

> *Alternative: dictionary task*
> Students think of an activity and look it up in a dictionary. They then go round the class, finding out how many students have done the activity and whether they would enjoy it or not.

➤ Workbook: Exercise B

> *Pairwork option*
> Students find suitable phrases in pairs. Then go through the answers together.

4 A question of sport

This combined reading and listening activity is in the form of a sports quiz. In the listening part, students hear excerpts from sports commentaries and identify the sports.

> *New words (reading):* boxing, gymnastics, title, captain, team, medal, car crash, Olympic Games, judo, rugby, snowboarding, baseball, volleyball. *New words (listening):* on the far side, in second place, shot, save, in the lead, lose control.

Alternative
If some students do not know very much about sport, divide the class into groups of four or five to do the quiz, so that they can help each other.

1 Doing the quiz; going through the answers

- Give time for students to do the quiz, working alone or in pairs. Give help if they do not understand any of the questions or items.

- Go through the quiz together, presenting any new vocabulary as you do so, and tell the class the answers. Let students keep their own score. Answers:

  1 Carl Lewis; athletics; USA; won nine gold medals at four Olympic Games.
    Steffi Graf; tennis; Germany; won 22 Grand Slam titles.
    David Beckham; football; England; married one of the Spice Girls.
    Ayrton Senna; motor racing; Brazil; died in a car crash in 1994.
    Olga Korbut; gymnastics; Russia; won three gold medals in 1972.
    Muhammed Ali; boxing; USA; said 'I am the greatest'.
    Diego Maradona; football; Argentina; captain of the team that won the
    World Cup in 1986.

  2 *a* Athens, 1896 *b* 40 km *c* men *d* rugby and skateboarding *e* jumping
    f 2.5 *g* 7

  3 baseball: 9 rugby: 15 football: 11 basketball: 5 volleyball: 6

  4 *a* Manchester United, Inter Milan, Spartak Moscow, Real Madrid, Bayern Munich
    b Most times: Brazil Only once: France, England 1930: Uruguay 1998: France

- 🔲 Play the commentaries. Pause after each one, so that students can note down their answers.

- Play the commentaries again and go through the answers. Students keep their own score. Answers:

  1 Horse racing. Primo Valentino wins the race.
  2 Golf. Woods hits the ball, but it doesn't go in the hole.
  3 Football. Owen tries to score, but Seaman saves the ball.
  4 Athletics. Maurice Green wins the race in 9.79 seconds (it's a new world record).
  5 Motor racing. Mika Hakkinen's car goes off the track.

- Give time for students to add up their score. Then find out who had the highest score.

> *Note*
> The names aren't important here. To score a point, students should just be able to say simply what happens (e.g. *A horse wins the race; the ball doesn't go in the hole; he doesn't score a goal; someone wins the race; a car goes off the track*).

> 🔲 Tapescript for Exercise 4: *A question of sport*
>
> 1 Just three hundred metres to go now, and it's Comistar, then London Lady, and then coming up fast is Primo Valentino on the far side, and Primo Valentino is now in second place. Comistar, then Primo Valentino, and here comes Primo Valentino, he's going to win, just a few metres to go and it's Primo Valentino first, Comistar is second, and London Lady in third place …
>
> 2 And this is Woods at the fifteenth, just off the green. This is a difficult shot, about six and a half, seven metres from the hole. And he hits it. And it's looking good, looking very good, and oh, it's stopped just short of the hole. And he'll be disappointed with that …
>
> 3 Murphy … to Berger … lovely little run up the right side, and now Owen, and it's still Owen, he's in the box, he's going to score, and – oh, what a save! A fantastic save
>
> from Seaman! The ball goes behind the goal, and it's a corner for Liverpool …
>
> 4 And they're away, and Green has made a very good start in lane 2, and so has Boldon in lane 5, and this is going to be a very fast time, and Green is way ahead of the rest of the field, and it's a very fast time indeed. And Maurice Green has won the gold in the men's hundred metres – oh, and it's a new world record – an incredible time of 9.79 seconds …
>
> 5 … So, 29 laps gone, 25 laps still to go, and it's still Mika Hakkinen in the lead, and Frentzen just behind in second place. And Hakkinen's lost control! He's taken the corner too fast, and he's left the track. Incredible! Mika Hakkinen is out of the race, so now it's Heinz Harald Frentzen in the lead and quite surprised to be so …

4 A question of sport

Sports quiz

If you're interested in sport, you should do well in this quiz. If not, have a try anyway – you might be surprised at how much you know!

1 People in sport (21 points)

Look at the photos. Can you match the people with the sports, countries and facts?

Carl Lewis   Steffi Graf   David Beckham   Ayrton Senna   Olga Korbut   Muhammed Ali   Diego Maradona

athletics	Argentina	said 'I am the greatest'
boxing	Brazil	won 22 Grand Slam titles, including seven at Wimbledon
football	England	was captain of the team that won the World Cup in 1986
football	Germany	won three gold medals at the 1972 Olympic Games
gymnastics	Russia	won nine gold medals at four Olympic Games
motor racing	USA	married one of the Spice Girls
tennis	USA	died in a car crash in 1994

2 The Olympic Games (9 points)

Can you choose the correct answers?

a The first modern Olympic Games were held in Athens / Berlin / London / Paris / Rome in 1876 / 1896 / 1916.

b The marathon race is just over 20 km / 30 km / 40 km long.

c The Decathlon is just for men / just for women / for both men and women.

d Which two are *not* Olympic sports? football / judo / rugby / snowboarding / skateboarding / tennis / table tennis

e Which is *not* part of the triathlon? cycling / jumping / running / swimming

f The world record for the men's high jump is about 1.5 / 2 / 2.5 metres.

g The world record for the men's long jump is about 7 / 9 / 11 metres.

3 How many players in a team? (5 points)

Match the sports with the numbers.

5   6   9   11   15

☐ baseball   ☐ rugby   ☐ football

☐ basketball   ☐ volleyball

4 Football (10 points)

a Can you make five European football clubs?

United   Inter   Spartak   Real   Bayern
Moscow   Munich   Madrid   Manchester   Milan

b Here are all the countries who won the World Cup in the 20th century:

> Argentina   Brazil   England   France   Germany   Italy   Uruguay

– Which country won the Cup the most times?
– Which two countries won only once?
– Which country won the first ever World Cup, in 1930?
– Which country won the last World Cup of the century, in 1998?

5 Sports commentaries (15 points)

🔊 You will hear commentaries on five sports.

a Match the recordings with the pictures.
b Say what happens in each recording.

Do the quiz in teams. Which team won?

Focus on ... Ability

1 Look at these examples.

I can swim very well.
I'm very good at swimming.

I can play chess quite well.
I'm quite good at chess.

I can't mend things at all.
I'm no good at mending things.

Complete this sentence.

After good at, we can use .... or ....

2 Make true sentences about yourself. Talk about:

English	swimming	getting up early
singing	dancing	organising your time
music	saving money	remembering names

3 Look at this opinion. Do you agree with it?

> I think men and women are good at different things. Women are better at some things, and men are better at other things.

Do this test. Think about your own family. Who is the best at the things below: a *female* in your family (e.g. your mother, your sister, your daughter) or a *male* (e.g. your father, your brother, your son)? Write M or F in the spaces.

'Male' activities	M or F
1 driving	
2 mending things in the home	
3 football	
4 computer games	
5 organising money	
'Female' activities	
1 cooking	
2 mending clothes	
3 writing letters	
4 foreign languages	
5 listening to people's problems	

Now compare your results with other students.

Pronunciation: Clusters (2)

1 🔲 These words and phrases have an *-r* sound after another consonant.
Try saying them, then listen to check.

Australia	toothbrush
hairdresser	prescription
front garden	credit card
children	throw
umbrella	musical instrument

2 Write a sentence. Use at least two of the words or phrases from the box.

3 Read out your sentence.

Phrasebook Asking where

Look at these questions. How could the person reply?

Excuse me. Is there anywhere near here where we can play football?

Excuse me. Is there a park near here?

🔲 Listen to the conversations. Where is the nearest park?

What questions could you ask about these things?

Study pages H

Focus on ... *Ability*

This exercise focuses on the use of good at + noun or -ing to talk about ability. It builds on language introduced in Study pages C Focus Exercise 16.2.

> *Key structures:* good at / better at / best at + noun or -ing.
> *New verbs:* mend, save, organise, remember.

1 Presentation of key structures

- Remind students of the way we use *like* with a noun or an *-ing* form:

| I like | chess. |
| | playing chess. |

  Look at the examples and show how we use *good at* in the same way:

| I 'm good at | chess. |
| | playing chess. |

- Ask students to complete the sentence:

  After good at, we can use a *noun* or a *verb* + *-ing*.

2 Practice: making true sentences

- Say the prompts, and get different responses from several students (e.g. *English – I'm quite good at English, I'm no good at English, I'm very good at English*).

  Alternative: Let students look at the prompts in pairs and make true sentences about themselves. Then go through this part of the exercise together.

3 Activity: personality test

- Read the opinion, and ask how many students agree with it.

  Give examples to show how we can use *better at* and *best at* in the same way as *good at*, e.g. *I'm good at singing. My brother's better at singing. My sister's the best at singing in our family.*

- Read through the instructions and the test. Present any new vocabulary (e.g. *mend, organise*).

- Give time for students to do the test alone. Then ask them to tell their partner what answers they gave.

- As a round-up, find out which students have 'typical' families and which don't.

> Tapescript for Phrasebook: *Asking where*
>
> 1 A Excuse me, is there anywhere near here where we can play football?
>   B Well, there's quite a big park just down that road. You can play football there.
> 2 A Excuse me, is there a park near here?
>   B There isn't one very near here, but there's one down by the river. That's about 15 minutes away.

Pronunciation: *Clusters (2)*

> Consonant clusters with /r/ in words from previous units.

1 Listening & practice

- Play the words and ask students to repeat them. Focus on the clusters with /r/ in each word (underlined below):

/ɒsˈtreɪlɪə/	/ˈtuːθbrʌʃ/
/ˈhɛədresə/	/prəˈskrɪpʃən/
/frʌnt ˈgɑːdən/	/ˈkredɪt kɑːd/
/ˈtʃɪldrən/	/θrəʊ/
/ʌmˈbrelə/	/ˈmjuːzɪkəl ˈɪnstrʊmənt/

2 Writing sentences

- Students write a sentence using words from the box, and including any other words they like, e.g.
  The children are in the front garden.
  Can I use a credit card at the hairdresser's?

3 Reading sentences aloud

- Students read out their sentences in turn. Focus on the pronunciation of the consonant clusters.

  Alternative: Dictation. Students dictate their sentence to the person next to them. As a check, ask students to read out the sentence they wrote down.

Phrasebook: *Asking where*

This exercise practises ways of asking where things are in towns, or asking the way to places. It picks up on language from Units 3 and 14.

> *Key expressions:* Excuse me, is there a ...?, Is there anywhere ...?, near here.

- Ask students to suggest possible replies (e.g. *Yes, there's a park over there. Sorry, I don't know. I don't live here*).

- Play the dialogue and establish what the people actually reply. Answers:

  1 Well, there's a big park just down that road. You can play football there.
  2 There isn't one very near here, but there's one down by the river. That's about 15 minutes away.

- Look at the pictures. Ask students to suggest suitable questions, e.g.

  Excuse me, ...
  ... is there anywhere near here where I can go swimming?
  ... is there a river/lake near here?
  ... is there a souvenir shop near here?
  ... is there anywhere near here where I can buy souvenirs?
  ... is there a camp site near here?
  ... is there anywhere near here where we can camp?
  ... is there anywhere near here where I can get a drink?

- Either let students practise dialogues in pairs, or ask students to have conversations in front of the class.

Consolidation

more, less and fewer

This exercise focuses on the comparative forms more, less *and* fewer. *It builds on language introduced in Units 13 and 15.*

1 Look at the examples. Point out that *more* has two opposites:
   – *less* with non-count nouns (*more grass – less grass*; *more money – less money*).
   – *fewer* with count nouns (*more teeth – fewer teeth*; *more people – fewer people*).

2 Do the exercise round the class, or give time for students to work through it themselves and then go through the answers together. Answers:
   a Men have more blood than women. Women have less blood than men.
   b Saturn has more moons than Jupiter. Jupiter has fewer moons than Saturn.
   c Families in Indonesia have more children than families in the USA. Families in the USA have fewer children than families in Indonesia.
   d A BMW 520 uses more petrol than a VW Golf. A VW Golf uses less petrol than a BMW 520.

go and play

This exercise focuses on the use of the verbs go *and* play *to talk about leisure activities. It builds on language introduced in Exercise 16.1.*

1 ● Look at the remarks, and show these structures:

go + -ing	go swimming
go for + noun	go for a walk
play + noun	play football

   ● Students make sentences using the words in the box. Answers:
   Shall we play golf?
   Yesterday we went climbing.
   Shall we play chess?
   Let's go for a walk.
   Let's go for a picnic.
   Yesterday we went sailing.

2 Ask students to suggest other continuations, e.g.

   Yesterday we went swimming, skateboarding, climbing, walking, running.
   Let's go for a drive, a meal, a drink.
   Shall we play cards? football? baseball? volleyball? tennis?

Review

Prepositions

Review of prepositions from Units 1, 4, 5, 7, 8, and 13.
Ask students to fill the gaps. Answers:
   a … listens *to* music *at* home, … goes out *to* concerts … goes *to* bed … *at* the weekend.
   b … *at* 6.30 *in* the morning …
   c … *by* bus or *by* taxi.
   d … *on* time, *at* 11.00.
   e … *on* the grass.
   f … go out *for* a drink …
   g … *in* the country … *in* a lovely position, right *on* the edge *of* a small lake.
   h … *on* Tuesday afternoon.
   i … millions *of* people.

Making predictions

Review of language from Unit 13.

● Read through the topics, and remind students of these structures for talking about the future:

● Ask students to write one prediction about each topic, using the structures on the board.

will
will probably
might
probably won't
won't

● Take each topic in turn, and ask students to read out their predictions.

Words

Review of vocabulary from Units 6 and 14.

1 'Brainstorm' places for each activity, and build up lists of words on the board. Possible answers:
   a stadium, football ground, park, sports centre, swimming pool
   b cinema, theatre, concert hall, disco, (night)club, restaurant
   c hotel, castle, cathedral, river, souvenir shop, museum, art gallery
   d park, cinema, zoo, amusement park, swimming pool

2 Students unscramble the ingredients. Then go through the answers and write them on the board. Answers:

Moussaka: aubergines, onions, tomato, lamb, beef, cheese
Noodles: prawns, pork, chicken, peppers, garlic, mushrooms, spices

Consolidation

more, less and fewer

1 Look at these examples.

Crocodiles have 64 teeth. Humans have 32 teeth.

> Crocodiles have *more* teeth than humans.
> Humans have *fewer* teeth than crocodiles.

Cows eat about 60 kilos of grass in a day.

Sheep eat about 20 kilos of grass in a day.

> Cows eat *more* grass than sheep.
> Sheep eat *less* grass than cows.

When do we use *fewer*? When do we use *less*?

2 Make comparisons, using *more*, *fewer* and *less*.

a On average, men have about 6 litres of blood. Women have about 5 litres.

b The planet Jupiter has 7 moons. The planet Saturn has 21.

c In the USA, the average family has 1.8 children. In Indonesia, the average family has 3.3 children.

d A Volkswagen Golf uses about 45 litres of fuel to get from London to Edinburgh. On the same journey, a BMW 520 uses about 60 litres.

go and play

1 Look at the remarks in the bubbles. How might they continue? Choose endings from the box.

| golf |
| climbing |
| chess |
| a walk |
| a picnic |
| sailing |

Yesterday we went …

Shall we play …?   Let's go for …

2 What other activities could go in the three bubbles?

Review

Prepositions

| at | by | for | in | of | on | to |

Here are some sentences from earlier units. Fill the gaps with prepositions from the box.

a He listens .... music .... home, and he often goes out .... concerts and clubs. He goes .... bed late and sleeps a lot .... the weekend.

b If I leave home .... 6.30 .... the morning, I can catch the 7.30 flight.

c You can get there .... bus or .... taxi.

d My sister arrived exactly .... time, ... 11.00.

e There are some people lying .... the grass.

f When did you last go out .... a drink or a meal?

g They've got a little cottage .... the country. It's .... a lovely position, right .... the edge .... a small lake.

h The world will end .... Tuesday afternoon.

i New diseases will kill millions .... people.

Making predictions

Choose one of these topics and make predictions.

> Do you watch any TV serials? What do you think will happen in the next programme?

> Think of someone you know very well. How do you think he/she will spend the evening?

> Think of some of the news in today's paper. What do you think will happen next?

Words

1 Think of places where

a people watch and play sport.

b people go out for the evening.

c tourists go.

d parents take their children.

2 Can you unscramble the ingredients?

Moussaka. This dish has abeeginrsu, innoos and amoott in it, with ablm or eebf, and there's also ceeehs in it.

Singapore Stir-fried Noodles. The noodles are cooked with anprsw, pieces of okpr or ccehikn, eeppprs, acgilr, hmmoorssu and ceipss.

Rules and advice

1 Renting a room

can • have to

1 Someone is asking about a room to rent. Look at the questions.
Which ones begin with *Can I …*? Which begin with *Do I have to …*?

… share a room
with other people?

… have visitors?

… keep pets?

… pay in advance?

📼 Now listen to the conversation and complete these sentences.

He can …   He can't …   He has to …   He doesn't have to …

2 What other questions might the man ask? Use these ideas.

food?   parties?   clean?   electricity?

                                                           pictures?
smoke?   sheets?   late at night?   music?

3 Role-play

Student A: You want to rent a room. Ask the owner questions, and decide if you want to rent
the room.
Student B: You are one of the three people below. Answer A's questions about the room.

4 Are you going to rent the room? Tell other students.

This unit deals with two related areas of language, both of which involve modal verbs:
– talking about obligation and lack of obligation, using *must*, *have to* and *can*
– giving advice, using *should* and *ought to*.

1 Renting a room

This exercise focuses on the use of can, can't, have to *and* don't have to *for talking about renting a room.*

> **Key structures:** can, can't, have to, don't have to; Can I …? Do I have to …?
> **New words:** rent, share, pets, in advance, sheets, electricity.   (→ Beginner Unit 19.)

➤ Focus on Form: Exercise 1
➤ Workbook: Exercise A

1 Introduction; presentation of key structures; listening

• Look at the picture and establish what questions the person might ask. Write these on the board:

Can I	have visitors? keep pets?	Do I have to	share a room? pay in advance?

If necessary, explain that we ask *Can I …?* about things we want to do, *Do I have to …?* about things that may be necessary. If you like, give other examples of your own to make this clear (e.g. *Can I use your dictionary? Do I have to do my homework?*).

• Establish what the answers to the questions might be (e.g. *Yes, you can have visitors, No, you can't have visitors; Yes, you have to share a room, No, you don't have to share a room*).

• ▱ Play the recording and check the answers:

He can have visitors, but they have to leave by 9 o'clock.
He can't keep pets.
He has to pay one month's rent in advance.
He doesn't have to share a room.

Vocabulary option
Teach these vocabulary items: *rent a room, to pay rent, owner, (landlord/landlady), tenant.*

Language note
To *rent a room* can mean either to pay for a room or to let someone use a room. Compare:
I was in London for a month, so I *rented* a room.
She needed money, so she *rented* (*out*) rooms in her house to students.
Rent is also a noun:
How much *rent* do you pay?

▱ The tapescript is on page T74.

2 Activation & preparation for the role-play: making questions

• Ask students to suggest questions. If you like, write them on the board under two headings: *Can I …?* and *Do I have to …?* Possible questions:

Can I cook food in the room?	Do I have to cook my own food?
Can I have parties?	Do I have to clean the room (myself)?
Can I smoke in the room?	Do I have to pay for electricity?
Can I come back late at night?	Do I have to be quiet late at night?
Can I play/listen to music?	Do I have to wash my sheets?
Can I put pictures on the wall?	Do I have to bring my own sheets?

3 Pairwork role-play: renting a room

• If you like, demonstrate the activity with one student. Take the role of one of the people, and get the student to ask you questions.

• Divide the class into pairs. Each pair chooses one of the house owners in the pictures. One student takes the role of this owner, the other the role of a person who wants to rent a room. They improvise conversations, and then Student A decides if he/she wants to take the room.

4 Reporting back

• In turn, ask the A students to say what they found out, and whether they want to rent the room. Then ask the B students what they think.

Optional lead-in
Look at the people in the pictures. Discuss what they might be like and what kind of room they might have.

Alternative
Divide the class into 'owners' and 'tenants'. The tenants visit two or three owners and ask about their rooms. As a feedback stage, find out how many tenants managed to rent rooms.

2 Rules

This exercise gives further practice in language from Exercise 1, and also introduces the modal verbs must *and* mustn't.

> ➤ Focus on Form: Exercises 2 & 3
> ➤ Workbook: Exercise B

> *Key structures:* can, can't, have to, don't have to, must, mustn't.

1 Gap-filling; presentation of key structures

- Ask where you might see the signs, and ask students to fill the gaps. Answers:

  In a library. You *must* (*have to*) be quiet. You *mustn't* make a noise.
  In a shop window. You *can* pay by credit card. You *don't have to* pay in cash.
  By the side of a road or in a car park. You *can* park here, but you *can't* (*mustn't*) stay more than half an hour.

  Use these examples to show that:
  – *must* and *have to* mean more or less the same.
  – *mustn't* means 'don't do it, it's forbidden'.
  – *don't have to* means 'it isn't necessary' (but you can do it if you like).

> **Language note**
> There is a slight difference between the use of *must* and *have to*:
> – *must* is more usual when we *tell* people what to do (e.g. teacher to student: *You must do your homework*).
> – *have to* is more usual when we *talk about* obligations (e.g. one student to another: *We have to do homework every day*).

2 Recognition exercise; making sentences

- Discuss the other signs. Possible answers (left to right):

  On a train. You mustn't throw bottles out of the window.
  At the entrance of a cinema, zoo, park, etc. Adults have to pay $5. Children don't have to pay – they can go in free.
  At a camping-site, by a road, in a forest. You mustn't light fires.
  In the street (traffic lights). You mustn't cross the road – you must wait.
  On an envelope. You don't have to use a stamp.
  By a church. Men can't wear shorts. Women must cover their shoulders.

> **Pairwork option**
> Students decide together in pairs what they think the signs mean. Then go through the answers together.

3 Writing sentences; guessing game

- Look at the sentences, and ask students which place it is. (Answer: a nightclub.)
- Pairwork. Students choose one of the places and a write a few rules for it.
- Students read out their rules. Other students guess which place it is.

> **Optional extension/Homework**
> Students write a list of rules for the school they are in.

3 Personal problems

This exercise introduces the modal verbs should *and* ought to, *used for advising on a problem.*

> ➤ Focus on Form: Exercise 4
> ➤ Workbook: Exercise C, Listening

> *Key structures:* should, shouldn't.   (→ Beginner Units 19, 22.)

1 Reading & discussion; presentation of key structures

- Read the problem letter, and check comprehension by asking questions, e.g. *What does her son do? When did it start? Does he have his own money? What happens when she catches him? Does she know why he steals?*
- Look at the pieces of advice, and use them to present *should* and *shouldn't*:

  | She | should / shouldn't | punish him. |

- Ask students which advice they agree and disagree with, and what else they think the woman should do. Then read the reply on page 109.

> **Presentation option**
> Teach *ought to* as well as *should*:
> – She *ought to* punish him.
> – She *ought not to* punish him.
> *Should* and *ought to* mean more or less the same.

2 Activation: giving advice

- Look at the problems, and ask students to make sentences with *should* or *shouldn't*. Possible answers:

  New friends: You should invite your neighbours for a drink. You should join a club.
  Can't sleep: You shouldn't work so hard. You should relax in the evenings.
  I'm 15: You should try to talk to them. You shouldn't argue so much.

> **Optional extension: writing**
> In pairs, students write a problem letter of their own.
> Collect the letters and give them to another pair. They write replies, giving advice.

2 Rules

must & mustn't

1 Where would you find these signs? What do they mean? Fill the gaps with verbs from the box.

must	mustn't
have to	don't have to
can	can't

You .... be quiet.
You .... make a noise.

You .... pay by credit card. You .... pay by cash.

You .... park here, but you .... stay more than half an hour.

2 What about these signs? Where would you see them? What do they mean?

3 Choose one of these places, and write two or three rules.

a cinema   a football stadium   a bus   a swimming pool
a hotel   a school   a nightclub   a beach   a hospital

Read out your rules. Can other students guess the place?

You mustn't wear jeans.
You don't have to be a member.
You have to pay to go in.

3 Personal problems

should

1 Here's a problem from a magazine. Do you agree with any of the advice in the bubbles?

She should punish him every time he steals from her.

She should ask the boy's doctor for help.

She should tell the police.

My son steals

We're a married couple with two children, an 11-year-old boy and a 4-year-old girl. Two years ago, my son started to steal money from me. If I catch him, he cries a lot and says he will never do it again. I don't think he's unhappy: we get on well as a family, and we all do things together in the evenings and at weekends. We give him plenty of pocket money, too. I just can't understand why he keeps on stealing.

She shouldn't leave money lying around the house.

She shouldn't give him any more pocket money.

She shouldn't punish him – she should try to find out why he steals.

The magazine's reply is on page 109. Do you agree with it?

2 Look at these problems. What's your advice? Make sentences with *should* and *shouldn't.*

We moved house recently, and I'm finding it very difficult to make new friends.

I get up early and work hard all day, and I go to bed around 12 – but I just can't get to sleep.

I'm 15, but my parents think I'm still a child. They don't understand me, and we argue all the time.

Focus on Form

1 Questions with 'can' & 'have to'

This man is just starting a new job. He wants to know the rules.

"Can I listen to music while I'm working?"

"Do I have to wear a suit and tie to work?"

Now complete these questions.

a .... smoke in the office?
b .... work on Saturdays?
c .... make private phone calls?
d .... wear shorts?
e .... pay for my coffee?
f .... stay after 4 o'clock?
g .... use the Directors' car park?
h .... type my own letters?

2 mustn't & don't have to

You mustn't / can't go = Don't go!

You don't have to go = Don't go if you don't want to.

Look at Exercise 1 again. The answer to all the questions is 'No'. Tell the man the rules.

"You mustn't listen to music while you're working."

"You don't have to wear a suit and tie to work."

3 They mean the same

| You mustn't go. | ↔ | You must stay.
 You have to stay. |
| You don't have to go. | ↔ | You can stay. |

Student A: Make sentences with *mustn't* or *don't have to*.

Student B: Make sentences that mean the same. Use the words in brackets.

a get up (stay in bed)
b be quiet (make a noise)
c do it now (leave it till later)
d come back early (come back late)
e take your shoes off (keep them on)

4 should & shouldn't

"I want to live to 100, just like you. What should I do?"

"You should go for a run before breakfast every morning. And you shouldn't listen to doctors."

Give the boy some more advice. Tell him what he should and shouldn't do. You can use these ideas, or you can use your own.

drive carefully   smoke   work hard
eat fruit   eat meat   get angry

How to say it

1 🔊 Listen to the sound *n't* in these sentences. Practise saying them.

You mustn't make a noise.
You mustn't get up yet.
She shouldn't listen to him.
You shouldn't smoke.

2 🔊 Listen to the word *should* in this sentence. What happens when the speaker says it quickly?

I think you should tell the police.

Practise saying these sentences quickly.

He should have more to eat for breakfast.
Do you think I should phone the doctor?
What should I buy him for his birthday?

Focus on Form

1 Questions with 'can' & 'have to'

- Look at the questions, and make sure students understand the meaning of *Do I have to?* (= Is it necessary?).

- Ask students to complete the questions. (Obviously, the man will ask *Can I ...?* for things he wants to do and *Do I have to ...?* for things that he doesn't want to do.) Answers:

  a Can I smoke in the office?
  b Do I have to work on Saturdays?
  c Can I make private phone calls?
  d Can I wear shorts?
  e Do I have to pay for my coffee?
  f Do I have to stay after 4 o'clock?
  g Can I use the Directors' car park?
  h Do I have to type my own letters?

2 mustn't & don't have to

- Look at the examples and make sure students understand the difference between *mustn't* (or *can't*) and *don't have to*.

- Ask the man's questions again, and ask students to give sentences in reply, using *mustn't* or *don't have to*. Answers:

  a You mustn't/can't smoke in the office.
  b You don't have to work on Saturdays.
  c You mustn't/can't make private phone calls.
  d You mustn't/can't wear shorts.
  e You don't have to pay for my coffee.
  f You don't have to stay after 4 o'clock.
  g You mustn't/can't use the Directors' car park.
  h You don't have to type your own letters.

3 They mean the same

- Look at the examples, and point out that *You must/have to stay* and *You mustn't go* are two ways of saying the same thing; similarly, *You can stay* means the same as *You don't have to go.*

- Make a sentence from one of the prompts, and ask students to make a sentence with the same meaning, using the prompt in brackets. There is more than one combination you could make each time. Possible answers:

  a You can get up – you don't have to stay in bed.
  You mustn't get up – you must stay in bed.
  b You must be quiet – you mustn't make a noise.
  You don't have to be quiet – you can make a noise.
  c You don't have to do it now – you can leave it till later.
  You must do it now – you mustn't leave it till later.
  d You don't have to come back early – you can come back late.
  You must come back early – you mustn't come back late.
  e You can take your shoes off – you don't have to keep them on.
  You don't have to take your shoes off – you can keep them on.

4 should & shouldn't

- Look at the examples. Then ask students to make sentences from the prompts, using *should* or *shouldn't.* Expected answers:

  You should drive carefully.
  You should eat fruit.
  You shouldn't smoke.
  You should (or shouldn't) eat meat.
  You should work hard.
  You shouldn't get angry.

How to say it

1 Pronunciation of 'n't' in sentences

- 🔲 Play the recording, pausing after each sentence. Focus on the pronunciation of /mʌsnt/ and /ʃʊdnt/, and the way the /t/ links with the following word: /mʌsnt‿meɪk/, /mʌstnt‿get/, /ʃʊdnt‿lɪsən/, /ʃʊdnt‿sməʊk/

- Students practise saying the sentences.

2 Pronunciation of 'should' in rapid speech

- 🔲 Play the sentence, and discuss what happens when it is said more quickly:

– there is more difference between the stressed sounds (*think, tell, police*) and the unstressed sounds (*you, should, the*).
– /ʃʊd/ is reduced to /ʃəd/.

- Play the other sentences and get students to repeat them quickly. Focus on the rhythm and the reduced sound of *should*:

/hi ʃəd hæv mɔː tu iːt fə brekfəst/
/də ju θɪŋk aɪ ʃəd fəʊn ðə dɒktə/
/wɒt ʃəd aɪ baɪ hɪm fə hɪz bɜːθdeɪ/

🔲 Tapescript for Exercise 1: *Renting a room*

A Hello. 764 293.
B Oh, hello. I'm phoning about the rooms you have to rent. Is there still one free?
A Yes, there is, yes.
B Could you tell me a few things about it? Do I have to share the room with other people?
A No, you don't. They're all single rooms.
B I see. And what about visitors? Can I have visitors?

A Yes, you can, but only till 9 in the evening. They have to be out by 9.
B OK. Do I have to pay in advance?
A Yes. You have to pay one month in advance.
B I see. One other thing – can I keep pets in the room? I've got a small cat.
A No. You can't have pets, sorry.
B Oh, that's a pity. Well, I think I'll leave it, then. Thanks.
A All right, then. Goodbye.

18

This unit is concerned with three language areas connected with work:
– describing jobs
– talking about the good and bad points of jobs
– describing events connected with work (e.g. applying for a job, being promoted, leaving a job).
The reading and listening activity is about job applications and interviews.

1 Occupations

This exercise introduces names of jobs and other occupations. It also focuses on language used in describing jobs (e.g. work in/for, look after, deal with*).*

➤ Workbook: Exercise A

> *Jobs:* hairdresser, dentist, accountant, mechanic, disc jockey, musician, window-cleaner, plumber, nurse, housewife, receptionist, manager. *Recycled language:* taxi driver, lorry driver, shop assistant, doctor, waiter, singer, painter, police officer. *Verbs:* work in, work for, deal with, look after.   (→ Beginner Unit 12.)

1 Vocabulary presentation: identifying jobs

- Look at the words in the list, and ask students to find the jobs in the picture. Present new items, using examples, gestures, students' own language and the picture itself.

  Then ask students to find the other eight jobs in the picture (most of which should be known; shown in italics below). Answers (left to right):

  Top floor: painter, singer, musician, dentist, window-cleaner
  Middle floor: plumber, disc jockey, nurse, *doctor,* accountant
  Ground floor: shop assistant, receptionist, hairdresser
  Street: lorry driver, waiter, police officer, housewife, *taxi driver,* (hotel) manager, mechanic

2 Reading & matching; presentation of key expressions.

- Read the sentences in the bubbles, and ask students to match them with the jobs. Answers (left to right):

  receptionist   accountant   plumber

- As you read the sentences, present any new words and phrases (e.g. *enquiries, reservations, company, pipe, tap*). Focus especially on key verbs for talking about jobs, and write these on the board:

work in	**look after**
work for	**deal with**

  If you like, quickly practise these verbs by asking questions, e.g. *What does a nurse do? (She looks after people in hospital.) Where does a secretary work? What does a housewife do?*

3 Writing sentences; guessing game

- Students choose one of the people in the picture and write a few sentences describing what they do.
- Students read out their sentences. Other students try to identify the person.

> *Pairwork option*
> Students work in pairs and identify the jobs they think they know. Then go through the answers together.

> *Language note*
> Common endings of nouns which are names of jobs:
> *-er*: singer, painter, driver, officer, plumber, hairdresser, manager
> *-or*: doctor
> *-ist*: receptionist, dentist.

> *Alternative*
> Students choose a person and say what he/she is doing in the picture (e.g. *She's sitting in an office, and she's typing a letter*). Other students identify the person.

📼 Tapescript for Exercise 3: *A working life*

Well, I studied economics at university, and then I got a job as an accountant in a local department store. It wasn't exactly what I wanted, but you know, it was a first job. Then after three years they promoted me to accounts manager, and I stayed in that job for a year, but then I got really bored, so I decided to leave, and I applied for other jobs in the area. But I couldn't find anything at all. So in the end I had to work as a waitress in a restaurant. Well, I wasn't very good at it, I was too slow and I kept breaking things, so after a few weeks they gave me the sack. And then just by chance I met an old friend who I knew at university, and he had a job in television. And he got me a job as a researcher for a TV programme called 'Business Today'. And then after a few months they decided they wanted younger presenters on the programme, so I got the job – and I love it.

18 A day's work

1 Occupations

1 Look at the picture. Can you find these occupations?

hairdresser	accountant	disc jockey	window-cleaner	nurse	receptionist
dentist	mechanic	musician	plumber	housewife	manager

There are eight more occupations in the picture. What are they?

2 Look at the bubbles. Who are the speakers?

> I work in a hotel. I sit at the desk by the entrance. I deal with enquiries and reservations.

> I work for a large company. I have my own office and a secretary. I look after the company's money.

> I work in other people's houses. I put pipes and taps in their kitchens and bathrooms.

3 Choose an occupation. Write two or three sentences about where you work and what you do. Other students will guess who you are.

2 A good job?

1 Imagine you could have any of these jobs.

nurse   journalist   hairdresser   teacher   police officer   gardener

Which job do you think you would like most? Which would you like least? Put them in order.

2 Show your answer to another student. Say what you would like and dislike about each job. Use these ideas to help you.

difficult?

long holidays?

interesting?   useful?   good salary?

long hours?

travel?   hard work?   meet people?

3 Imagine you're asking someone about their job. What questions could you ask?

4 Now work in pairs.

Student A: Imagine you have one of the six jobs. Answer B's questions.
Student B: Ask A about his/her job.

3 A working life

1 Look at these sentences. What do you think the red words mean?

When I left school, I applied for a job in a hotel. But I didn't get it.	He worked in a café. But he was always late for work, and after a few weeks he got the sack.	She started as a shop assistant, but she was very good, and they soon promoted her to sales manager.

2 You will hear a woman talking about her career. Here are some of the things that happened to her. What order do you think they should be in?

- [ ] She got the sack.
- [ ] She became a researcher for a TV programme.
- [ ] They promoted her to accounts manager.
- [ ] She applied for a lot of jobs.
- [ ] She studied economics at university.
- [ ] She became a TV presenter.
- [ ] She left her job.
- [ ] She worked in a restaurant.
- [ ] She got a job in a department store.

🔲 Listen and check your answers.

3 Listen again and answer these questions.

a How long did she stay in her first job?
b Why did she leave?
c Why did she get the sack?

d How did she get a job in television?
e What job does she have now? Does she like it?

2 A good job?

This exercise practises ways of talking about the good and bad points of a job.

> **Key expressions:** long holidays, long hours, salary, hard work, meet people; interesting, useful, difficult. *New names of jobs:* journalist, gardener.

➤ Workbook: Exercise B, Listening

1 *Introduction; ranking jobs in order of preference*

- Look at the jobs, and make sure students understand *journalist* and *gardener*. Students write the jobs in a list, starting with the one they'd like most.

2 *Activation of key expressions; discussion*

- To introduce the activity, choose one of the jobs, and ask students to say what they think it is like (e.g. nurse: probably interesting, the salary isn't very good, it's very hard work, you have to work long hours).
- Divide the class into pairs. Students show their lists to each other, and explain what they would like and dislike about each job.

> *Language note*
> *Salary* is the money you earn. We usually say *salary* for professional jobs and *wages* for simple manual jobs.

3 *Preparation for the role-play: establishing questions*

- Look at the ideas, and ask students to make them into questions, e.g.

  Is it an interesting job? Do you travel much? Is it useful? Do you have to work hard? Do you get a good salary? Do you meet many people in your work? Do you have long holidays? Is it a difficult job? Do you have to work long hours?

> *Whole class option*
> Ask different students what their 'best' and 'worst' jobs were, and get them to say what they think are the good and bad things about them.

4 *Role-play: asking & answering questions about a job*

- Divide the class into pairs. One student in each pair chooses one of the jobs, and pretends that it is his/her job. The other student asks questions about it.

3 A working life

This exercise introduces a range of expressions for talking about things that happen in jobs. The main focus of this exercise is on comprehension.

➤ Workbook: Exercise C

> **New vocabulary:** apply for (a job), get the sack, promote; accounts manager, researcher, presenter, department store.

1 *Presentation of key expressions*

- Read through the sentences and check that students understand the expressions. Encourage them to say what they mean in simple English, e.g.
  – You want a job, so you *apply for* it; maybe you send a letter.
  – You *get the sack* = the boss tells you 'Sorry, you have to leave'.
  – You have a job, then you get a better one in the same company: they *promote* you.

2 *Reading & sequencing task; listening to check*

- Read through the events in the list, presenting any new vocabulary (e.g. *accounts manager, department store, researcher, presenter*).
- Working in pairs, students put the events in the order they think most likely. Then get students to tell you their version of the woman's career.
- 🔲 Play the recording, pausing from time to time to check the answers. Answers:

  1 She studied economics at university.   2 She got a job in a department store. 3 They promoted her to accounts manager.   4 She left her job.   5 She applied for a lot of jobs.   6 She worked in a restaurant.   7 She got the sack.   8 She became a researcher for a TV programme.   9 She became a TV presenter.

> 🔲 The tapescript is on page T75.

3 *Detailed listening & answering questions*

- 🔲 Play the recording again, and discuss the questions. Answers:

  a Four years.   *b* It was boring.   *c* She was too slow and kept breaking things. *d* A friend told her about it.   *e* TV presenter. Yes, she loves it.

4 Applying for a job

In this combined reading and listening activity, students read a woman's letter of application for a job, and then listen to part of her job interview.

> *New words (reading):* general, applicant, outgoing, experience, application, secretarial college, including, enclose, curriculum vitae.
> *New words (listening):* generally, present (adj.).

Vocabulary option
Show the different words connected with *apply*, all of which are used here: *apply for* (verb), *applicant* (noun: person who applies), *application* (noun: the letter the applicant writes).

1 *Reading & discussion*

- Read through the advertisement, presenting any new words, e.g. *outgoing, experience, application, CV* (= curriculum vitae).

- Ask students what they think a receptionist/general assistant has to do. Possible answers:

  sit at the desk, talk to guests, deal with problems, take money from people, talk on the phone, use the computer.

- Discuss what sort of person the hotel is looking for. Possible answers:

  someone who is friendly and outgoing, someone who will work hard, a reliable person, able to speak foreign languages, able to use a computer.

Language note
A *curriculum vitae* is a list of a person's education and work experience (Latin = course of life). It is often shortened to *CV*.

2 *Reading & discussion*

- Read the questions. Then give time for students to find answers in the letter.
- Go through answers *a–c* together. Possible answers:

  a Office work: 4 years   *Receptionist:* 10 months   *Hotel work:* 6 months
  b At the Sands Hotel, Brighton. She's a receptionist.
  c She wants to work abroad.

- Discuss Question *d*. Bring out these points: she's the right age, she hasn't got much experience of hotel work, her letter sounds good.

3 *Listening & answering questions; discussion*

- ▣ Play the recording, pausing after each section. Students listen and mark the sentences. Then go through the answers, playing the recording again to check. Answers:

  a False *b* True *c* True *d* False *e* True *f* False

- Discuss how well the woman answered the questions. Bring out these points: she's very nervous, she arrives late, she doesn't really say what her job involves, she doesn't have a clear idea why she wants the job. Possible score:

  3–4. She probably won't get the job.

▣ Tapescript for Exercise 4: *Applying for a job*

Part 1
A I'm so sorry I'm late. I couldn't find your office.
B That's all right. Sit down. Now. You're working at a hotel in Brighton.
A That's right.
B What kind of work do you do?
A Well, I'm a receptionist, so I answer the phone, and sit at the reception desk, obviously, and give people their keys and … generally work as a receptionist.

Part 2
B Now at this hotel we do everything on computers, of course, so you'll have a computer at the reception desk. Do you have experience of computers?
A Well, I don't use a computer in my job at the moment, no – it's just a small family hotel – but we learned about computers at college, and I used a computer when I worked in an office, so I don't think that would be a problem.

Part 3
B Now, why do you want to leave your present job and come here?
A Well, as I said, the hotel where I am now is a very small hotel, and I really want to work somewhere bigger. Also the hours are very long.
B The hours are long. So you don't want to work long hours, then?
A Oh yes, I don't mind working hard. I just mean that the job's a bit boring, you know. There isn't really enough to do.
B I see.

4 Applying for a job

1 Read the advertisement.

– What do you think a Receptionist/ General Assistant has to do?

– What sort of person is the hotel owner looking for?

Receptionist/ General Assistant

for a 3-star hotel in a popular tourist resort. Applicants must be at least 21 years old. They should be friendly and outgoing, and have at least one year's experience. Excellent salary.

Please send your application, with a photograph and CV to
Alan Chalmers
White Rocks Hotel, Barbados
Tel: 0534 199388

2 Read the letter and answer the questions.

a How much experience does Penny Wright have
  – of office work?
  – of work as a receptionist?
  – of hotel work?

b Where is she now? What is her job?

c Why does she want to leave her job?

d Do you think she is suitable for the job?

3 🔊 You will hear parts of Penny Wright's job interview. Listen and write *T* (= true) or *F* (= false).

a She arrives on time.

b She's quite nervous.

c She knows how to use a computer.

d She uses a computer in her present job.

e She works long hours in her present job.

f She enjoys her present job.

Do you think she answered the questions well? Give her a score out of 10.

Do you think she will get the job?

6 Arundel Place
Brighton
England

14 April

Dear Mr Chalmers,

I am writing to apply for the job of Receptionist/General Assistant.

I am 25 years old. I left school at 18 and studied for one year at Pitmans Secretarial College, where I got a Diploma. I worked as a secretary in London for four years, including four months as a receptionist for a large company.

At the moment I am working as a receptionist at the Sands Hotel, Brighton. I have been there for the past six months.

I would like to work as a receptionist in your hotel because I enjoy hotel work and I would like the experience of working abroad.

I enclose a photograph and my curriculum vitae, and I look forward to hearing from you.

Yours sincerely,

Penny Wright

Penny Wright

Study pages

Focus on ... Someone, anyone

1 Look at these examples.

John?
A neighbour?
My uncle?
...

A bird?
A plane?
A UFO?
...

On the desk?
Behind the chair?
In my pocket?
...

He looks like someone I know.

I can see something.

I know my glasses are somewhere.

2 Change these sentences using *someone*, *something* or *somewhere*.

  a There's a man/a woman at the door.
  b I need some lemonade/some water to drink.
  c Why don't you sit down on a chair/on the sofa?
  d I want to buy flowers/chocolates for my wife.
  e Put those flowers on the table/by the window.

3 Read the letters and complete the table.

Dear Paula

How was your holiday? Did you do anything exciting? Did you go out anywhere? Did you meet anyone? Did you buy any souvenirs? Tell me about it!

Love,

Anna

Dear Anna

It was a really boring holiday. It rained all the time, so we didn't go anywhere. We didn't do anything interesting. I went out once, but I didn't meet anyone. The only good thing about it – I didn't spend any money.

Love,

Paula

some	any
someone	....
something	....
somewhere	....

When do we use forms with *any* ... ?

4 Find out what your partner did last weekend. Think of questions with *any*, *anyone*, *anything* and *anywhere*.

Pronunciation: Words with *-ion*

1 🔊 These words all have *-ion* in them.

Try saying them, then listen to check.

station	invention
television	population
receptionist	position
information	application
directions	question

2 Write two sentences. Use one word from the box in each.

3 Read out your sentences.

Phrasebook Renting things

Fill the gaps in the conversation. Use these phrases.

a £10 deposit

How much does it cost

pay in advance

£5 an hour

for the whole day

– .... to rent a bike?
– It's .... , or £30 ....
– Do I have to .... ?
– No. You just give me ....
– OK.

🔊 Now listen and check. What does the man rent, and for how long?

Have similar conversations.

| You want to rent a boat. Boats cost £4 an hour for each person. There's no deposit. | You want to rent a video. It costs £2 for 24 hours. There's a £15 deposit. |

Study pages I

Focus on ... *Someone, anyone*

This exercise focuses on the use of something, someone, somewhere *and* anyone, anything, anywhere. *It also gives further practice in talking about the past.*

> *Key words:* something, someone, somewhere; anyone, anything, anywhere. *Recycled language:* some, any.

1 *Presentation of 'someone', 'something', 'somewhere'*

- Look at the pictures, and use them to present the meaning of *someone*, *something* and *somewhere*:
  – *someone* = he isn't sure who the picture looks like.
  – *something* = she doesn't know what it is.
  – *somewhere* = he doesn't know where his glasses are.

2 *Practice*

- Do the exercise with the class, or let them do it in pairs and then go through the answers. Answers:

  a There's *someone* at the door.
  b I need *something* to drink.
  c Why don't you sit down *somewhere*?
  d I want to buy *something* for my wife.
  e Put those flowers *somewhere*.

3 *Presentation of 'anyone', 'anything', 'anywhere'*

- Read the letters and ask students to help you complete the table on the board:

some	any
someone	anyone
something	anything
somewhere	anywhere

  Make these points:
  – we usually use *some* in statements, and *any* in negatives and questions.
  – in the same way, we use *someone, something, somewhere* in sentences and *anyone, anything, anywhere* in negatives and questions.

- If necessary, give examples to show these differences, e.g.
  I went somewhere interesting yesterday.
  I didn't go anywhere interesting.
  Did you go anywhere interesting?
  I can see something.
  I can't see anything.
  Can you see anything?

4 *Extension: asking & answering questions*

- To introduce the activity, get students to suggest questions, e.g. *Did you go anywhere interesting? Did you do anything exciting? Did you spend any money? Did you buy any clothes?* (If you like, include other questions, e.g. *Did you see a film? Did you get up late?*)
- Pairwork. Students ask each other questions. As a round-up, ask a few students what they found out.

Pronunciation: *Words with -ion*

> Words from previous units ending in *-ion*.

1 *Listening & practice*

- 🔲 Play the words and ask students to repeat them. Focus on the sound of the *-tion* and *-sion* endings:

/'steɪʃən/	/ɪn'venʃən/
/'teləvɪʒən/	/pɒpjʊ'leɪʃən/
/rɪ'sepʃənɪst/	/pə'zɪʃən/
/ɪnfə'meɪʃən/	/aplɪ'keɪʃən/
/də'rekʃənz/	/'kwestʃən/

2 *Writing sentences*

- Students write a sentence using words from the box, and including any other words they like, e.g.
  Is there an information desk in the station?
  Give your application to the receptionist.

3 *Reading sentences aloud*

- Students read out their sentences in turn. Focus on the pronunciation of the consonant clusters
  Alternative: Dictation. Students dictate their sentence to the person next to them. As a check, ask students to read out the sentence they wrote down.

Phrasebook: *Renting things*

This exercise practises expressions used for renting bicycles, boats, videos, etc.

> *Key expressions:* rent (v.), pay in advance, a deposit.

- Ask students to fill the gaps in the dialogue. As you do this, present any new expressions.
- 🔲 Play the dialogue to check.
- Look at the two situations with the class, and establish what the people will say. If you like, build up dialogues on the board.
- Either let students practise dialogues in pairs, or ask students to have conversations in front of the class.

> 🔲 Tapescript for Phrasebook: *Renting things*
>
> A How much does it cost to rent a bike?
> B It's £5 an hour, or £30 for the whole day.
> A Do I have to pay in advance?
> B No. No, you just give me a £10 deposit.
> A OK.

Consolidation

Verbs with prepositions

This exercise focuses on common verb + preposition pairs. This recycles verbs which have appeared in earlier units.

- Look at the pictures and present any expressions that students are not familiar with. Emphasise that we must say e.g. *listen to music*, *pay for a meal* (not ~~listen music~~, ~~pay a meal~~).

   If you like, point out the past forms *pay – paid*, *deal – dealt* (though they are not needed for the exercise).

- Ask students to complete the sentences.
- Go through the answers. Expected answers:

   a looked for *b* pay for *c* deal with *d* waited for *e* look after *f* apply for *g* works for *h* looked at *i* listen to

do

This exercise focuses on common questions with do. *It builds on language introduced in Study Pages A Phrasebook and Units 5 and 18.*

1 • Ask students to match the questions, replies and pictures. Answers:

   A What are you doing? I'm writing a letter.
   B What do you do? I'm an electrician.
   C How do you do? How do you do?

   • Make these points:
      – *What do you do?* means 'What work do you do?'
      – *What are you doing?* means either 'just at this moment' or 'these days'.
      – *How do you do?* is a polite formula meaning 'Hello'. The expected answer is not e.g. *Fine, thanks* but *How do you do?*

2 • Ask students the questions. Expected replies are:

   What are you doing? I'm listening to you/I'm learning English.
   What do you do? I'm a student (I'm a businessman, I work in a bank, etc.).
   How do you do? How do you do?

   • Students ask and answer in pairs.

Review

One's right, the other's wrong

Review of language from Study Pages A Consolidation, Study Pages D Focus, Study Pages E Focus, Unit 11 and Study Pages F Consolidation.

1 Ask students to choose the correct answers Answers:

   a ... the teachers' room, ... the Head Teacher's office.
   b Maria's French ... mine ... my English ... hers.
   c ... both of them ... neither of them ...
   d ... some nice people ... any bad weather ... much money ... a few beautiful places ... very few people ... too many people ...
   e ... since 1996, ... for two years.

What's in the middle?

Review of comparative structures from Unit 15.

- Ask students to suggest comparative adjectives that could go in the gaps. Possible answers:

   Dogs are *friendlier / nicer / more interesting / dirtier / bigger* than cats.

   Living in the city centre is more *interesting / more dangerous / livelier / more expensive / better / more convenient / noisier* than living in the suburbs.

   My country is *warmer / richer / poorer / more beautiful / more dangerous / more crowded* than Britain.

   My country has *more mountains / better food / hotter weather / worse roads* than Britain.

- Students write their own gapped sentence, as in the example. Then ask students in turn to write their sentence on the board. Other students suggest ways of completing it.

Words

Review of vocabulary from Units 10, 14 and 16.

1 Ask students to suggest possible continuations for the sentences, and build up lists of words on the board. Possible answers:

   a the piano, the guitar, the violin ...
   b football, tennis, basketball, baseball ..., cards, chess ...
   c running, swimming, walking ... to the sports centre, to the swimming pool, to the mountains ...
   d stamps, coins, shells, old bottles, clocks, toy cars ...

2 Ask students to make sentences about each topic. If you like, build up ideas on the board. Possible answers:

   The clothes: They're not too expensive, there's a good selection, they're good quality, they look nice.
   Shop assistants: They're friendly, they're helpful, there are plenty of shop assistants.
   The shop: It has a good atmosphere, it isn't too crowded, it's near the city centre.

Consolidation

Verbs with prepositions

apply for a job

pay for a meal

wait for a bus

look for a pen

look at a notice

listen to music

look after a baby

deal with a customer

work for a company

Fill the gaps. Use infinitive, present or past forms of the verbs in red.

a I .... my keys everywhere, but I couldn't find them.

b I haven't got any money. Could you .... the drinks?

c Give that letter to the secretary. She'll .... it.

d We .... you for an hour, then we left.

e Go and have a good time. I'll .... the children.

f When I leave school, I might .... a job in a bank.

g This is Mr Tanaka. He .... the Sony Corporation.

h I .... my watch. It was nearly 3 o'clock.

i Don't .... him. He's talking nonsense.

do

1 Match two bubbles with each picture.

How do you do?

What do you do?

What are you doing?

I'm writing a letter.

I'm an electrician.

How do you do?

A   **B**   **C**

2 Ask your partner the questions.

Review

One's right, the other's wrong

Choose the correct answers.

a The teachers have coffee together in the teacher's/teachers' room, but Mr Brown has his coffee alone in the Head Teacher's/Head Teachers' office.

b Maria's/Marias' French is better than my/mine, but my/mine English is better than her/hers.

c – Where's Mike? And where's Bob?
 – Well, I invited both/neither of them, but both/neither of them could come.

d It was a great holiday. We met some/any nice people, and there wasn't some/any bad weather. We didn't spend much/many money, and we visited a few/a little beautiful places. There were very few/very little people in our hotel, but there were too much/too many people on the beach.

e Jack has worked for this company for/since 1996, and he's been Managing Director for/since two years.

What's in the middle?

Make comparisons.

Dogs are .... than cats.

Living in the city centre is .... than living in the suburbs.

My country is/has .... than Britain.

Now you write a sentence. Can other students complete it?

French is .... than English.

Words

1 How might these sentences continue?

 a She's very musical. She plays ...

 b He enjoys sports and games. He plays ...

 c We like keeping fit. We often go ...

 d I like collecting things. I collect ...

2 **What might the person say about**

 – the clothes?

 – the shop assistants?

 – the shop itself?

I think The Clothes Store is an absolutely wonderful shop ...

19 Telling stories

1 How did it happen?

Past continuous • Past simple

1 Three people talk about accidents they had. Can you find them in the picture?

I was playing with my baby son on the floor. Suddenly the phone rang, and I jumped up and hit my head on the table.

I was cutting some onions in the kitchen when the knife slipped and I cut my thumb.

I was walking along quietly by the river when a boy went past on his skateboard and pushed me in.

Say what happened to each person. Say what they were doing at the time.

2 What do you think happened to the other people in the picture?
Continue these sentences, using verbs from the box.

I was walking under a ladder …

I was running for a bus …

I was going down some steps …

I was walking through the park …

bite
break
hit
hurt
cut
slip
fall
trip

Now listen. What really happened?

3 Talk about one of these people.
What happened to them? What were they doing at the time?

80   *Unit 19* Telling stories

This unit covers the use of the Past continuous and Past simple in narration. It focuses particularly on two main areas:
– talking about past events and things going on at the time
– describing scenes in the past.

19

1 How did it happen?

This exercise introduces the Past continuous tense, and focuses on the relationship between events (what happened) and things that were going on at the time (what was happening). The unit also practises ways of talking about accidents.

> Focus on Form: Exercises 1 & 3
> Workbook: Exercise A

Key structures: Past continuous, Past simple. 'Accident' verbs: bite, break, hit, hurt, cut, slip, trip, fall. Other new words: skateboard, thumb, push, paint (n.).

Optional lead-in
Ask students to say what they think happened to each of the people. Use this to introduce verbs and other vocabulary needed for Part 2 of the exercise, e.g. *He broke his arm; he bumped his head; she's covered in paint.*

1 Reading & matching task; presentation of Past continuous tense

- Look at the picture, and establish what it shows: people at a doctor's or a hospital; they all had accidents.
- Read the three texts, and present new vocabulary (e.g. *hit, slip, thumb, skateboard, push*). Ask students to identify the people. Answers:

back row left; front row right; back row second from right

- Use the texts to present the two key verb tenses:
  - Past simple for talking about events in the past (saying what happened):
  - Past continuous for saying what was going on at the time:

The phone rang.
I hit my head.

I was playing with my son.

Show the structure of the Past continuous:

I
He/She | was + -ing

They were + -ing

As a check, ask students to say what happened and what was happening in each situation.

2 Presentation of verbs; making sentences; listening to check

- Look at the verbs in the box. Check that students understand what they mean, and show the Past simple forms on the board:
- Ask students to continue the sentences.

bite	bit	hurt	hurt	slip	slipped
break	broke	cut	cut	trip	tripped
hit	hit	fall	fell		

- Play the recording to check. (Answers: see tapescript.)

3 Activation: making sentences

- Pairwork. Students decide what happened to the people and what they were doing at the time.
- Discuss the answers together. Example answers:

He was climbing in the mountains. He fell and cut his head.
She was getting on a bus. She slipped and cut her arm.
He was shaving. He slipped and cut his face.
She was walking along the road. Something fell from the window and hit her head.

Alternative: guessing game
Each pair or group chooses one of the people and writes sentences. They read out their sentences and other students identify the person.

Tapescript for Exercise 1: *How did it happen?*

1 I was on my way home from work. I was walking under a ladder, and someone was painting a window. And he slipped, and a can of green paint fell on my head.
2 I was going down some steps, and it was raining, and I slipped and went down about ten steps, and I broke my leg.
3 I was late for work and I was running for a bus when I tripped and I hurt my arm.
4 I was walking through the park when suddenly a huge dog came up to me and bit me on the leg.

2 Very short stories

This exercise focuses on ways of joining sentences together using when, while *and* so. *It also gives practice in telling stories using the Past simple and continuous.*

> ➤ Focus on Form: Exercise 2
> ➤ Workbook: Exercise B, Listening

> *Key structures:* when, while, so; Past simple and continuous.
> *New words:* pick up, century, antique shop, broke down, knock, miss (v.).

1 Reading; presentation of 'when', 'while' and 'so'

● Read the two stories, and establish these two ways to join sentences:

> **Past continuous + when + Past simple**
> **While + Past continuous, Past simple**

2 Joining sentences

● Give time for students to read the sentences. Then build them up on the board as complete stories. Possible answers:

We were driving to the theatre when the car broke down, so we missed the beginning of the play.
While I was having supper at home one evening, a policeman knocked at the door. He told me my car lights were on, so I went out and turned them off.
I was doing some shopping yesterday morning when I met my old friend Alex. So we decided to have lunch together.

3 Completing a short story

● Pairwork. Students make up stories around the sentences given. Encourage them to develop the stories beyond just three sentences. Possible answers:

a He was just falling asleep when he heard a noise outside the window. So he got up and looked out. It was just a cat.
b I was driving along an empty road when an old woman ran out and shouted 'Stop!', so I stopped quickly. She said 'Quick! Call an ambulance!'
c I was walking along the street yesterday when it started raining and all my clothes got wet. So I went home and got changed.

● As a round-up, ask students to tell their stories.

> *Writing option*
> Students (or pairs of students) write a sentence from one of the stories. They pass it to another student (or pair), who adds a sentence either before or after it. Continue like this until a number of stories are built up.

3 Setting a scene

This exercise shows how we use the Past continuous for describing scenes in the past. This use is similar to the Present continuous (see Exercise 5.2).

> ➤ Focus on Form: Exercise 3
> ➤ Workbook: Exercise C

> *Key structures:* Past continuous tense; There was/were + -ing.
> *New words:* hold, lighted, couple, tune, nervously, dancer, intently.

1 Reading & gap-filling

● To introduce the exercise, look at the picture and get students to say what they can about it, e.g. *it's a bar, it looks dangerous, some people are playing cards.*
● Give time for students to read the story. Then go through it together, discussing what words should fill the gaps. Answers:

... *sitting* at the piano, *playing* a dance tune ... were *dancing* ... *holding* hands ..., *talking* together ... *playing* cards ... *sitting* alone, *looking* ... *standing* at the bar, *smoking* (*holding*) a large cigar and *watching* ...

2 Grammar focus: joining sentences

● Discuss how to join the sentences. Answers:

A tall man was standing by the window, looking across the street.
There was a thin woman in a white dress, sitting in a corner reading a newspaper.

> *Language note*
> In describing the past, we can add a series of phrases with *-ing* forms, just as we can in describing the present. Compare:
> *Present*: There's a man *sitting* on a chair, *reading* the newspaper.
> *Past*: There was a man *sitting* on a chair, *reading* a newspaper.

3 Activation: describing a scene

● In pairs or groups, students choose one of the pictures on page 108 and write a scene using sentences like those in the text. Encourage them to imagine other things beyond what they can see in the pictures.
● As a round-up, ask each group to read out their sentences.

> *Homework option*
> Students develop one of the scenes into a story.

2 Very short stories

when & while • so

1 Look at these two stories. How do we use *when* and *while*? How do we use *so*?

> **Story 1**
>
> I was lying on the beach yesterday when it suddenly started to rain, so everybody picked up their things and ran into the nearest café.

> **Story 2**
>
> While I was clearing out an old cupboard the other day, I found a 16th century map of Spain. So I took it to an antique shop, and they gave me £15,000 for it.

2 These sentences make three more stories. Which sentences go together? Tell each story using *when*, *while* and *so*.

A policeman knocked at the door.

I went out and turned them off.

The car broke down.

He told me my car lights were on.

I met my old friend Alex.

I was doing some shopping yesterday morning.

I was having supper at home one evening.

We decided to have lunch together.

We were driving to the theatre.

We missed the beginning of the play.

3 Now complete one of these stories.

a .... he heard a noise outside the window. ....

b I was driving along an empty road ....

c .... So I went home and got changed.

3 Setting a scene

-ing forms

1 Here is part of a novel. Fill the gaps with words from the box.

smoking	sitting
dancing	watching
standing	talking
holding	playing
looking	

2 Here are two other people the man saw. Join the sentences together.

> A tall man was standing by the window. He was looking across the street.

> There was a thin woman in a white dress. She was sitting in a corner. She was reading a newspaper.

Through the rain, I saw a lighted window and a sign which said 'Sam's Place'. I went in and looked around me.

An old man with grey hair was .... at the piano, ... a dance tune. In the centre of the room, in a space between the tables, a man and a woman were .... to the music.

There was a young couple .... hands in the corner, ... together in low voices. At another table, a group of six men were .... cards.

At a table by the door, there was a young woman .... alone, ... nervously around her.

Then I saw Mike. He was .... at the bar, ... a large cigar and .... the dancers intently. I walked over to the bar and ordered a drink.

3 The pictures on page 108 show other scenes from the story.

Choose one of the pictures and continue the description.

1 Past continuous

> He was reading a magazine.
> They were watching television.

Read the story. What were the other people doing when the lights went out?

At 10.00 last night, all the lights went out in our building.

At the time, I was reading a magazine.

 My parents …

 My brother …

 My sisters …

 My cousin …

 My uncle …

 My grandparents …

2 when & while

> I was having lunch when the phone rang.
> The phone rang while I was having lunch.

Match the sentences on the left with those on the right. Join them together using *when* and *while*.

What was happening?	*What happened?*
I was writing a letter.	I hit another car.
I was playing the guitar.	I broke a glass.
I was painting a wall.	A string broke.
I was driving to work.	My pen ran out.
I was washing the dishes.	I fell off the ladder.

3 -ing forms

> I saw him in the library. He was wearing sunglasses, and he was sitting at a table reading a magazine.

You are helping the police look for a man. The pictures show the times when you think you saw him. Say where he was and what he was doing.

Now cover the page. Can you remember what you saw?

How to say it

1 🔊 **Listen to *was* and *were* in these sentences. Practise saying them.**

I was having supper.
She was standing by the door.
They were holding hands.
We were talking about you.

2 🔊 **Listen to these sentences. Which one do you hear first? Write *1* or *2*. Then practise saying them.**

He's He was	standing in the corner.
We're We were	just having lunch.
There are There were	some people swimming.

Focus on Form

1 *Past continuous*

- Write these examples on the board:

> **All the lights went out.**
> **At the time ...   I was reading a magazine.**
> **   my parents were watching television.**

- Look at the pictures, and ask students to make sentences. Add them on the board. Answers:

My brother was washing his hair.
My sisters were playing cards.
My cousin was cooking (a meal).
My uncle was having a shower.
My grandparents were listening to the radio.

2 *when & while*

- Look at the examples, and show these two basic structures:

> **Past continuous + when + past simple**
> **Past simple + while + past continuous**

Note: We could also say *While I was having lunch, the phone rang.*

- Students match the sentences together, joining them with *when* or *while*. They could do this in pairs, or they could write the sentences.

- Go through the answers:

I was writing a letter when my pen ran out.
My pen ran out while I was writing a letter.

I was playing the guitar when a string broke.
A string broke while I was playing the guitar.

I was painting a wall when I fell off the ladder.
I fell off the ladder while I was painting a wall.

I was driving to work when I hit another car.
I hit another car while I was driving to work.

I was washing the dishes when I broke a glass.
I broke a glass while I was washing the dishes.

3 *-ing forms*

- Show how we can join sentences by repeating the *-ing* form of the verb:

> **He was sitting at a table. He was reading a magazine.**
> **He was <u>sitting</u> at the table, <u>reading</u> a magazine.**

- Look at the pictures. Ask students to say where the man was and what he was doing. Possible answers:

I saw him in a boat (on a lake), fishing. He was wearing an orange jacket and hat.

I saw him lying by a swimming pool, talking to a woman. He was wearing a swimsuit / swimming costume.

I saw him at the theatre, buying tickets. He was wearing a coat and holding some flowers.

I saw him at the station, carrying a suitcase and getting on a train. He was wearing a coat.

- Ask students to cover the picture. They try to remember what they saw.

How to say it

1 *Pronunciation of 'was' and 'were' in sentences*

- 🔲 Play the recording. Pause after each sentence, and focus on the reduced /ə/ sound in *was* and *were*:

/ai wəz ˈhævɪŋ/
/ʃi wəz ˈstændɪŋ/
/ðeɪ wə ˈhɒldɪŋ/
/wi wə ˈtɔːkɪŋ/

- Students practise the sentences.

2 *Distinguishing present and past forms (verb 'to be')*

- 🔲 Play the sentences. Pause after each one and ask students which alternative they hear. Then play it again to check. Answers:

He's standing in the corner.
We were just having lunch.
There were some people swimming.

- 🔲 Play both versions of the sentences. Students practise saying them. Focus on these differences:

/hɪz‿stændɪŋ/, /hi wəz‿stændɪŋ/
/wɪə dʒʌst hævɪŋ/, /wi wə dʒʌst hævɪŋ/
/ðɛərə səm piːpl/, /ðɛə wə səm piːpl/

T 82

20

This unit is concerned with three areas of language used in talking about people:
– physical description (height, facial features, hair)
– talking about people's ages
– describing personal characteristics.
The reading and listening activity is a personality questionnaire.

1 Famous faces

This exercise provides a natural context for describing what people look like: recalling the appearance of well-known people. It focuses on describing significant features (e.g. a moustache, a thin face) rather than detailed description for its own sake.

➤ Workbook: Exercise A, Listening

> *General adjectives*: tall, short, fat, thin, slim, well-built.
> *Facial features*: moustache, beard; small/large/hooked/straight nose.
> *Hair adjectives*: long/short, straight/curly/wavy, fair/dark; bald.
> (→ Beginner Unit 12.)

1 Introduction: identifying the pictures

● Look at the pictures and see if students know who the people were and where they were from. Answers:

1 Nelson Mandela (South Africa) 2 Indira Gandhi (India) 3 Joseph Stalin (Russia/USSR) 4 Margaret Thatcher (Britain) 5 Mao Tse-tung (China) 6 Abraham Lincoln (USA)

2 Matching task; listening to check; presentation of key vocabulary

● Look at the phrases, and ask students to say which people they go with. Use this as a way of showing the meaning of new words.

● 🔲 Play the recording. Pause after each speaker, and establish which phrases the speaker used (shown in italics below), and what else he said. Answers:

1 short, a small man, *short curly grey hair*, quite small eyes
2 a tall woman, wavy black hair with a white stripe, *a long thin face*, *a hooked nose*
3 *a big black moustache*, *thick black eyebrows*, black hair, a well-built man
4 *wavy fair hair*, a thin face, *a pointed nose*, wears earrings and a necklace
5 *a round face*, a small nose, *partly bald*, quite fat
6 tall, *a long thin face*, *a beard*, long hair

🔲 The tapescript is on page T85.

Language note: word order
When describing physical features, the normal order is *dimension* (length or size), then *shape*, then *colour*:
He had short, straight black hair.
She has a long, pointed pink nose.

● If you like, build up lists of words on the board under different headings, adding other items:

> <u>General</u>: *tall, short, fat ,thin, slim, well-built*
> <u>Face</u>: *thin, wide, fat, round; with a moustache/beard*
> <u>Nose</u>: *long, big, small, pointed, hooked*
> <u>Hair</u>: *long, short, straight, wavy, curly; fair, dark, grey; bald*

Language note
We say:
He *has* long/short hair.
He *is* bald.

3 Activation: pairwork game

● Divide the class into pairs, and ask students in each pair to look only at their own set of pictures. They describe the people in their pictures and decide which are the same as their partner's.

● When they have finished, students look at both sets of pictures and see if they were right.

Optional round-up phase
Look at the pictures together and get students to describe them.

4 Sentence writing & discussion

● Read the description of John Lennon. Then ask students to think of a famous person they know (alive or dead) and write a few sentences.

● Students read out their sentences. Ask other students if they agree with the description.

Alternative: guessing game
Students read out their sentences without naming the person. Other students guess who the person is.

20 People

1 Famous faces

1 These six people were all world leaders. How many of them can you recognise?

2 You will hear descriptions of the six people. Which phrases do you think you will hear in each description?

a round face   short curly grey hair

a big black moustache   partly bald   wavy fair hair   a pointed nose

a hooked nose   a long thin face   thick black eyebrows   a beard

▭ Now listen. What else do the people say?

3 Work in pairs. Find out if your partner has the same people as you.

Student A: Look only at the people on page 107.
Student B: Look only at the people on page 108.

4 Choose a famous person, and think about what they look(ed) like. Write a few sentences.

> I think John Lennon was quite tall and thin, and he had a long face and a long, hooked nose. He had long straight hair, and I think he had a beard and a moustache. He wore small round glasses.

Read out your sentences. Do other students agree with your description?

2 How old?

1 Use the table to talk about these people.

John's 42.

Kate's 27.

Tom's 15.

Eve's 84.

He's in his	(early)	teens.
	(mid)	twenties.
		thirties.
She's in her	(late)	forties.
		...

2 What about these people? How old do you think they are?

A Only one more year at university and you'll have to start looking for a job.

B I've been a teacher for 25 years now.

C I think I'm getting a bit old to have a baby now.

D She was born in 1915.

E I was just a baby during the Second World War.

F I'm buying him a razor for his birthday – he's just started shaving.

3 Here are some famous people. Roughly how old do you think they are in each photo?

3 Character adjectives

Both my parents get up early and work until late in the evening.

My mother never gets angry with us, but my father gets angry quite a lot, especially early in the morning.

My uncle gave me a new bike for my birthday, but my aunt only gave me a bag of sweets.

My grandfather found a gold ring in the street the other day, and he took it straight to the police station.

My grandmother can never remember where she left her glasses.

My older sister always watches the TV programmes she wants, and she always sits in the most comfortable seat.

My older brother never helps around the house – he spends all his time playing computer games.

My little brother always smiles and says 'hello' when he meets people.

My little sister always hides behind the sofa when we have visitors.

1 Read what the boy says about his family. Choose adjectives to describe each person. Use a dictionary to help you.

bad-tempered	honest
easy-going	lazy
forgetful	mean
friendly	selfish
generous	shy
hard-working	

2 Which adjectives describe you best? What about other people in your family?
Tell your partner.

3 🔲 You will hear three short scenes.

What happens in each one?

What can you tell about the people's characters?

2 How old?

This exercise introduces ways of describing people's approximate age.

> *Key expressions:* (in his/her) teens, twenties, thirties, etc.; early, mid, late.
> *Recycled language:* age.   (→ Beginner Study Pages C.)

► Workbook: Exercise B

1 Presentation of key expressions; practice

- Look at the table. To establish the meaning of the expressions, read sentences from the table and ask what they mean, e.g. *He's in his late teens* = He's about 18 or 19; *She's in her mid forties* = She's between 43 and 47.

- Look at the five people, and ask roughly how old they are. Answers:

  John is in his early forties. Kate is in her late twenties. Tom is in his mid teens. Eve is in her mid eighties.

2 Activation: making sentences

- Working in pairs or round the class, students make sentences from the table. Possible answers:

  A He's in his early twenties. B She's in her forties. C She's in her late thirties/ early forties. D She's in her eighties. E She's in her sixties. F He's in his early/mid teens.

3 Discussion: guessing people's ages

- In pairs, students look at the pictures and decide the people's age.
- Look at the pictures together. Then tell students their actual ages:

  Clint Eastwood: 31, 64. Elizabeth Taylor: 14, 31, 68. Michael Jackson: 10, 38.

> *Background notes*
> Michael Jackson (1958–), American rock singer; Elizabeth Taylor (1932–) British film star; Clint Eastwood (1930–) American film star and director.

3 Character adjectives

This exercise introduces a range of adjectives for describing people's character.

► Workbook: Exercise C

> *Adjectives:* bad-tempered, easy-going, forgetful, friendly, generous, hard-working, honest, lazy, mean, selfish, shy. *Recycled language:* the family (Unit 2).

1 Reading & presentation of vocabulary

> *Alternative*
> Read through the text straight away, and use it to present the adjectives.

- Either ask students to look up the adjectives in a dictionary, or go through them giving simple examples to show what they mean.

- Read through the text, and ask students to describe each person. Answers:

Parents: hard-working	*Aunt:* mean	*Older brother:* lazy
Mother: easy-going	*Grandfather:* honest	*Little brother:* friendly
Father: bad-tempered	*Grandmother:* forgetful	*Little sister:* shy
Uncle: generous	*Older sister:* selfish	

> *Vocabulary option*
> The list includes two pairs of opposites: *mean/generous* and *lazy/hard-working*. If you like, give the opposites of some of the other adjectives: *friendly/unfriendly*; *bad-tempered/good-tempered*; *easy-going/strict*; *shy/confident*; *honest/dishonest*; *selfish/unselfish*.

2 Activation: students talk about themselves

- Go through the list of adjectives, and tell the class which ones you think describe you (*I'm not very bad-tempered, I think I'm quite easy-going*, etc.). Then tell students a few things about your family (e.g. *My brother is very hard-working. He's a businessman, and he works 7 days a week*).

- Pairwork. Students say which adjectives describe themselves and other members of their family.

- As a round-up, ask a few students what their partner told them.

3 Listening & interpretation

> The tapescript is on page T85.

- Play the recording, pausing after each scene. Ask questions to guide students towards understanding each situation, e.g. *What does the man want? Are they friends or strangers? Does the other man give him money?* Establish these character adjectives:

  1 The second man is *generous*. 2 The woman is *friendly*, the man is *shy*.
  3 The first woman is *honest*, *friendly*; the second woman is *forgetful*.

> *Optional extension*
> Students choose one of the adjectives in the list, and write a short scene like those in the recording. They act out their scene, and other students interpret what is happening.

4 Are you a loner?

This combined reading and listening activity is a personality questionnaire about how sociable you are. Students do the questionnaire themselves, then listen to someone else doing it and give them a score.

> New words (reading): loner, company, seaside (adj.), alone, lonely; fun, social life, relax, desert island. *New words (listening)*: definitely, pretty (adv.).

1 Reading: answering a questionnaire; reading the key

- Look at the title, and check that students understand what the questionnaire is about (*a loner* = someone who prefers to spend time alone). Before doing the questionnaire, ask students quickly to say if they are 'loners' or not.

- Students answer the questions, working alone or in pairs. They should record their answers as they go. When they have finished, they add up their scores and read the description in the key that applies to them.

- As a round-up, ask how many students were in each category, and whether they thought the descriptions were accurate.

2 Listening & giving a score

- Play the recording, pausing after each section. Students listen and write down the person's score. Then discuss it together. Answers:

1a 2b 3a 4b 5a 6 Only swimming. Total score: 10 = Type A

> Tapescript for Exercise 1: *Famous faces*

1 Nelson Mandela isn't very tall and he has very short curly grey hair. And he has quite small eyes.
2 Indira Gandhi was a tall woman, and she had wavy black hair with a white stripe in it. And she had a long thin face and a hooked nose.
3 Well, Stalin had a big black moustache, and thick black eyebrows, and he had black hair. And he wasn't very tall, but he was quite well-built.

4 Margaret Thatcher has wavy fair hair, and a thin face with a pointed nose. And she always wears earrings and a necklace.
5 Mao Zedong had a round face and quite a small nose. And he was partly bald. And he was quite fat – at least when he was older.
6 Abraham Lincoln was tall, and he had a long thin face and a beard. And he had quite long hair.

> Tapescript for Exercise 3: *Character adjectives*

1 A Chris – I'm dying for a cup of tea. I don't suppose you could lend me 50p, could you?
   B Of course I'll lend you 50p. Look, 50p's not much good – why don't you have £5, that'll keep you going all day.
   A Oh …
   B You can pay me back whenever you want – doesn't matter.
   A Oh thanks, thanks very much.

2 A Hello. Gosh, it's very hot and crowded in here, isn't it?
   B Yes, it is a bit.
   A My name's Ann.
   B Oh. Um …
   A What's yours?
   B C-Chris.
   A Chris. Hi.
   B Hi.

3 A Excuse me, I say … Sorry, but you just dropped this £10 note.
   B What? Oh, oh, oh, oh thank you, oh dear, oh thank you very much.
   A That's all right. Just – I should put it in your purse if I were you.
   B Oh, oh dear, wait a minute – where's my – oh, here we are yes.
   A All right?
   B Yes. Yes, thanks very much. Bye.

> Tapescript for Exercise 4: *Are you a loner?*

OK. 'Where do you think is the best place to live?' The town centre, definitely. There's more to do, and you meet more people. I live in the town centre, and I really like it.
OK, question 2. Oh, I'd meet some friends for a drink. I think I'd want to be with close friends, not a lot of people I don't know very well.
Now, 'Which kind of holiday would you enjoy?' Um, probably a busy seaside town with lots to do. Yes, definitely, that's what I'd like. Not staying with my family in the country.
Number 4. 'You go to a friend's party …' Well, I like meeting people, but you can't just go up to people and say 'Hi', so I think I'd ask my friend to introduce me, yes.
5: 'You're alone on New Year's Eve. How do you feel?' Oh,

very lonely, I think. Last year I spent New Year's Eve just with my parents and my brother, and that was really boring, so, yes, I'd be really lonely on my own.
OK, 6. No, I wouldn't enjoy eating in a restaurant alone. 'Going on a long journey alone' – oh no, I'd want someone to talk to. Swimming alone, yes, that's all right – I think you get more exercise if you're alone. 'Going to the cinema' – well, I always want to talk about the film to someone while I'm watching it, so 'No'. 'Spending a weekend alone at home.' No, that's a long time, that's too long. A few hours would be OK, but not a whole weekend. And 'cooking a big meal just for yourself' – no. First of all, I don't eat much, and anyway if you cook a big meal, you want to eat it with other people, I think. So 'No'.

> *Language note*
> If you're *alone* (or *on your own*), it means you are not with other people (you may be quite happy about it).
> If you are *lonely*, you feel unhappy because you are alone.

> *Option: weaker classes*
> Read through the questionnaire first, presenting any unknown words. However, most students should be able to read the questionnaire without difficulty.

> *Note*
> *Two's company – three's a crowd*: this is a well-known saying. It means: you like to be with one other person, but no more than that.

4 Are you a loner?

Are you a LONER?

Do you like other people?
Or do you prefer your own company?
Answer the questions and find out …

1 Where do you think is the best place to live?
   a in the town centre
   b in a suburb
   c in the country, but near a town
   d right out in the country

2 It's your birthday. Do you:
   a have a big party?
   b meet some friends for a drink?
   c go out for a meal with a close friend?
   d go to bed with a good book?

3 Which kind of holiday would you enjoy the most?
   a staying at a busy seaside town with lots to do in the evenings
   b driving and camping with a group of friends
   c a quiet stay in the country with your family
   d going off alone on a walking holiday

4 You go to a friend's party and find you don't know any of the other guests. Do you:
   a make lots of new friends?
   b ask your friend to introduce you to a few people?
   c stay close to your friend?
   d sit in a corner quite happily?

5 You're alone on New Year's Eve. How do you feel?
   a very lonely
   b a bit lonely
   c you don't really mind
   d pleased

6 Would you enjoy any of these? Tick (✓) the boxes.

   ☐ eating in a restaurant alone
   ☐ going on a long journey alone
   ☐ going swimming alone
   ☐ going to the cinema alone
   ☐ spending a weekend alone at home
   ☐ cooking a big meal just for yourself.

KEY

Scoring Questions 1–5: a = 1; b = 3; c = 5, d = 7   Question 6: 1 for each tick (✓)

Type A (5–13 points)
You really love being with other people. Do you ever spend any time alone? Other people are a lot of fun – but remember that being alone can be fun too. Try it some time!

Type B (14–23 points)
You have a busy social life. You like other people, but you also like to keep a little time for yourself. Don't do too much – keep some evenings free to sit and relax quietly at home.

Type C (24–33 points)
You're rather quiet. You like being alone, but you're happiest with a close friend or relation. You don't like big parties very much. Your motto is 'Two's company – three's a crowd'.

Type D (34–41 points)
You're a real loner – you would probably be quite happy living on a desert island. But don't forget that there are a lot of other people in the world – and some of them are as interesting as you are!

---

1 Do the quiz and write your answers in the blue table.

   Now read the key. Are you a loner? Do you agree with the key?

2 🔲 Someone else does the quiz. Listen and write her answers in the red table.

   Work out her score. Is she the same type as you?

Your answers				Score
1 a	b	c	d	
2 a	b	c	d	
3 a	b	c	d	
4 a	b	c	d	
5 a	b	c	d	
6 ☐ ☐ ☐ ☐ ☐ ☐				
			Total score:	

Her answers				Score
1 a	b	c	d	
2 a	b	c	d	
3 a	b	c	d	
4 a	b	c	d	
5 a	b	c	d	
6 ☐ ☐ ☐ ☐ ☐ ☐				
			Total score:	

J Study pages

Focus on ... Nationalities

 Britain
 Ireland
 Spain
 Sweden

 Brazil
 Italy
 Canada
 India

 Morocco
 Mexico
 Germany
 USA

 China
 Japan
 Vietnam
 Portugal

 Greece
 Switzerland
 France
 Netherlands

1 Look at these representatives at the United Nations. What nationality are they?

Row 1: British, Irish, ...   *Row 4:* Chinese, ...
Row 2: Brazilian, ...   *Row 5:* Greek, ...
Row 3: Moroccan, ...

2 What nationality are these people? Which rows should they be in?

 Turkey
 Poland
 Hungary
 South Africa

3 Here are six famous people. Do you know their nationality?

 Luciano Pavarotti
 Yuri Gagarin
 Cleopatra

 Boris Becker
 Mahatma Gandhi
 Eva Perón

Pronunciation: Unusual words (4)

1 🔊 Try saying these words, then listen to check.

poetry	moustache
average	knock
secretary	biscuit
suitable	theatre
advertisement	customer

2 Write a sentence. Use at least two of the words from the box.

3 Read out your sentence.

Phrasebook Personal questions

Look at these people's answers.
What do you think the questions are?

 I'm a secretary.
 I'm Swiss.
 I'm nearly 18.

 Arabic and French.
 European history.
 In a small town near London.

🔊 Now listen. What else do the people say?

Have similar conversations.

You're a waiter from Madrid, in Spain. You're 30, and you speak Spanish.

You're a nurse from Recife, in Brazil. You're 23 and you speak Portuguese.

You're Chinese, and you study medicine in Singapore. You speak Chinese and you're 18.

Study pages J

Focus on ... *Nationalities*

This exercise focuses on words for nationalities, which are grouped according to their endings. It also recycles names of countries.

> *Key vocabulary:* nationalities: *-ian, -an, -ish, -ese* and irregular endings.

1 Presentation of nationality groups

- Look at the pictures, and get students to guess the people's nationalities. Show how they fit into groups according to their endings:

  Row 1: *-ish*: British, Irish, Spanish, Swedish
  Row 2: *-ian*: Brazilian, Italian, Canadian, Indian
  Row 3: *-an*: Moroccan, Mexican, German, American
  Row 4: *-ese*: Chinese, Japanese, Vietnamese, Portuguese
  Row 5: *Irregular*: Greek, Swiss, French, Dutch

2 Expansion: other nationalities

- Discuss what the nationalities are and what group they belong to. Answers:

  Turkish (Group 1)   Polish (Group 1)
  Hungarian (Group 2)   South African (Group 3)

- Give a few other countries that are important to the class (e.g. neighbouring countries), and discuss what the nationalities are called and which group they are in.

3 Extension: famous people

- Pairwork. Students say what nationality they think the people are or were. Then discuss the answers together, and ask what else students know about the people. Answers:

  Luciano Pavarotti: Italian (opera singer)
  Yuri Gargarin: Russian (astronaut, first person in space)
  Cleopatra: Egyptian (queen)
  Boris Becker: German (tennis player)
  Mahatma Gandhi: Indian (leader, led Indian independence)
  Eva Perón: Argentinian (wife of President of Argentina)

- As a possible extension, write the names of other famous people on the board (or ask students to think of them). Ask students what nationality they are or were.

Pronunciation: *Unusual words (4)*

> Words from previous units which may cause pronunciation problems.

1 Listening & practice

- 🔲 Ask students to try saying each word, then play the recording of it and get them to practise. Focus on:
  - the reduced /ə/ and /ɪ/ sounds in /ˈsekrətri/, /ˈsuːtəbl/, /ˈkʌstəmə/, /ˈævərɪdʒ/.
  - the silent *k* in /ˈnɒk/.
  - the multiple vowel sounds in /ˈpəʊətri, /ˈθɪətə/.
  - the unexpected stress and pronunciation of /ˈsekrətri/, /ədˈvɜːtɪsmənt/, /məˈstɑːʃ/ and /ˈbɪskɪt/.

2 Writing sentences

- Students write a sentence using words from the box, and including any other words they like, e.g.

  The secretary was eating a biscuit.
  I saw an advertisement for the new theatre.

3 Reading sentences aloud

- Students read out their sentences in turn. Focus on the pronunciation of the key words.

  Alternative: Dictation. Students dictate their sentence to the person next to them. As a check, ask students to read out the sentence they wrote down.

Phrasebook: *Personal questions*

This exercise practises everyday questions. It builds on language introduced in the Focus section.

> *Key language:* personal questions.

- Look at the replies. Ask students to guess the questions.
- 🔲 Play the dialogue to check. (Answers: see tapescript.) Establish what else the people say.
- Look at the situations, and establish what the people will say. If you like, build up dialogues on the board.
- Either students practise the dialogues in pairs, or two students have conversations in front of the class.

🔲 Tapescript for Phrasebook: *Personal questions*

1 A What do you do?
  B I'm a secretary. How about you?
  A Oh, I'm an accountant.
2 A What nationality are you?
  B I'm Swiss.
  A Oh, Swiss.
  B Yes. What about you?
  A I'm Canadian.
3 A How old are you, by the way?
  B I'm nearly 18. How about you?
  A Guess!
  B 20?
  A 21!

4 A What languages do you speak?
  B Arabic and French. What about you?
  A Me? I only speak English.
5 A So what are you studying?
  B European history.
  A Mm. That sounds interesting.
6 A Where do you live?
  B In a small town near London. Dorking, it's called.
  A Oh yeah, I know it.
  B Where do you live, then?
  A I live in Manchester.

Consolidation

while and during

This exercise focuses on the difference between while *and* during. *It picks up on language introduced in Exercise 19.2.*

1 Look at the examples and establish these differences:
  – we use *while* before a sentence (e.g. ... *he was having breakfast*).
  – we use *during* before a noun or noun phrase (e.g. ... *breakfast*, ... *his journey to work*).

2 Pairwork. Students fill the gaps in the sentences. Then go through the answers together. Answers:

  a during an important business meeting
  b during lunch
  c during the afternoon
  d while he was putting his coat on
  e during the journey home
  f while he was watching TV
  g while he was reading in bed
  h during the night

with

This exercise focuses on the use of with *for describing people's physical features and appearance. It builds on language introduced in Exercise 20.1.*

1 Look at the examples. Then look at the other pictures, and ask students to make similar sentences. Expected answers:

  The police are looking for a boy with short brown hair and blue eyes.
  The police are looking for a man with long grey hair, a moustache and a beard.
  The police are looking for a woman with curly black hair, sunglasses and long earrings.

2 On a piece of paper, students write a sentence about the person sitting next to them.

  Collect the papers. Read out sentences in turn, and see if the class can identify the person you are describing.

  Note: If most people in the class look quite similar, you could ask students to write a sentence about a well-known person (e.g. a singer, a politician, a local personality, a TV character).

Review

Giving directions

Review of language from Unit 14.

● Look at the map and ask students to follow the directions. Establish what the missing words are. Answers:

  Go straight *along/down* this road, *over/across* the bridge, and take the first turning *on* the right. Then carry *on* until you get *to* a kiosk. Turn left, go *past* the bank, and then turn right again *at* the post office. You'll see it *on* your left.

● Ask what the question was. Answer:

  Is there a bookshop near here?

have to and can

Review of language from Unit 17.

● Look at the pictures and read about Jim and Alex. Ask students to make sentences. Answers:

  Jim can drink coffee at his desk.
  Alex can't drink coffee at his desk.
  Jim doesn't have to wear a tie to work.
  Alex has to wear a tie to work.

● Get students to make other sentences. Possible answers:

  Jim can smoke at work. Alex can't smoke at work.
  Alex has to get up early. Jim doesn't have to get up early.
  Alex has to travel to work. Jim doesn't have to travel to work.

Jobs

Review of vocabulary from Unit 18.

● Working alone or in pairs, students think of jobs for each category and write them down.

● Go through the answers, and write vocabulary on the board. Possible answers:

  a secretary, manager, accountant, receptionist
  b doctor, nurse, cleaner, receptionist
  c shop assistant, manager
  d receptionist, manager, cleaner, waiter, cook
  e bus/train/taxi/lorry driver, (traffic) policeman
  f musician, singer, disc jockey
  g housewife, plumber, painter, window-cleaner
  h footballer, tennis player

Consolidation

while and during

1 Look at these examples. What's the difference between *while* and *during*?

> Carlos loves using his mobile phone. Yesterday …
>
> … he used it twice   *while* he was having breakfast.
>   *during* breakfast.
>
> … he used it six times   *while* he was going to work.
>   *during* his journey to work.

2 Look at these sentences. Fill the gaps with *while* or *during*.

Carlos also used his mobile phone …

a twice .... an important business meeting.

b twice .... lunch.

c four times .... the afternoon.

d twice .... he was putting his coat on.

e three times .... the journey home.

f twice .... he was watching TV.

g once .... he was reading in bed.

h and once .... the night.

with

1 To describe people, we can use *with*. Look at this example.

The police are looking for a girl. She has long black hair and glasses.

The police are looking for a girl *with* long black hair and glasses.

The police are also looking for these people. Describe them using *with*.

2 Write a sentence about the person next to you.

> The police are looking for …

Review

Giving directions

Read the answer. What are the missing words?

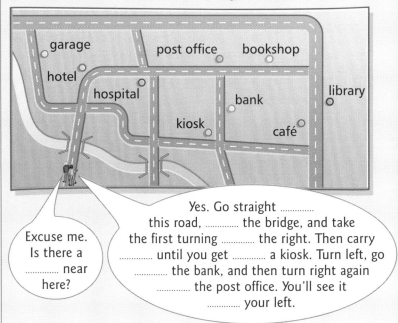

> Excuse me. Is there a .... near here?

> Yes. Go straight .... this road, ... the bridge, and take the first turning .... the right. Then carry .... until you get .... a kiosk. Turn left, go .... the bank, and then turn right again .... the post office. You'll see it .... your left.

What was the question?

have to and can

Make sentences from the table.

Jim and Alex are both accountants. Jim works from home. Alex works in a big office in the city centre, about 50 km from his home. So …

Jim	can can't	drink coffee at his desk.
Alex	has to doesn't have to	wear a tie to work.

What other differences are there?

Jobs

Think of two jobs …

a in an office   *e* connected with transport

b in a hospital   *f* connected with music

c in a shop   *g* connected with houses

d in a hotel   *h* connected with sport

Are your answers the same as your partner's?

21 Future plans

1 Intentions

going to

1 Look at these two people. Which are the man's thoughts, and which are the woman's?
Which could be the man's or the woman's?

When I get back home …

When I retire …

… I'm going to go round the world.

… I'm going to get up late every morning.

… I'm going to eat lots of good food.

… I'm going to buy a little cottage by the sea.

… I'm going to go to lots of parties.

… I'm going to see my girlfriend.

… I'm not going to type any more letters.

… I'm not going to wear a uniform.

What other thoughts do you think they might have?

2 Now choose one of these people, and continue their thoughts.
Write sentences with *going to* and *not going to*.

When I get to the hotel …

When I pass my driving test …

When the holidays start …

When I leave college …

When I get out of here …

When the children go to their grandparents …

3 Read out your sentences. Can other students guess whose thoughts they are?

21

This is the second of two units concerned with future time (the other is Unit 13: *What will happen?*). It shows students how to talk about intentions and plans, and deals with:
– the use of *going to*
– the contrast between *going to* and *will* for talking about intentions
– Present continuous tense with future meaning.

1 Intentions

This exercise shows a range of contexts in which people talk about their intentions and plans for the future. It introduces I'm going to *and* I'm not going to.

> ➤ Focus on Form: Exercise 1
> ➤ Workbook: Exercise A

> *Key structures:* going to, not going to.
> *New words:* retire, soldier, prisoner, type, driving test. (→ Beginner Unit 23.)

1 Reading & matching task; presentation of 'going to' & 'not going to'; making sentences

- Look at the pictures. Establish who the people are and what situation they are in:

  a soldier, in the army, about to come back home
  a secretary or office worker, about to retire

- Read the sentences and show these structures on the board:

  Point out that we use *going to* to talk about plans for the future, or things we intend to do.

I'm	going to not going to	+ verb

- Ask students which sentences could be the man's thoughts and which the woman's. Expected answers:

  a woman *b* man or woman *c* man *d* woman *e* man (or woman) *f* man
  g woman *h* man

- Ask students to suggest other sentences. Possible answers:

  Man: I'm going to see all my friends. I'm going to wear comfortable clothes. I'm going to watch TV in bed.
  Woman: I'm going to have a big party. I'm going to go on a long holiday. I'm going to go to lots of concerts.

2 Writing sentences

- Look at the pictures. Again establish who the people are and what situation they are in:

  someone travelling or on holiday, walking to a hotel in the rain
  someone learning to drive
  a pupil at school
  a student at college
  a prisoner in prison
  a mother with three children

- Students work in pairs or groups. Together, they choose one of the people, and imagine their thoughts about the future. They write sentences with *going to* and *not going to*.

3 Reading & guessing

- Students read out their sentences to the class. Other students try to guess who the person is.

> *Presentation option*
> Check that students know all the forms of *going to*. Build up a table on the board:
>
> | I'm
You're
He's/She's
We're
They're | (not) | going to ... |
> |---|---|---|

> *Alternative*
> Each pair or group chooses one of the people and writes one sentence. They pass their paper to another group, who add another sentence, and so on.

2 I'll probably …

When we talk about plans in English, we often use going to *to talk about definite plans, but* will (probably) *to talk about things we are uncertain about. This exercise shows how these two structures are used.*

> *Key structures:* going to, will. *Adverbs:* maybe, perhaps, probably.

➤ Focus on Form: Exercise 2
➤ Workbook: Listening

1 Listening & gap-filling; grammar presentation

- Look at the picture. Establish that the students are about to leave college, and are talking about their plans for the future.
- 🔲 Play the recording. Students listen and fill the gaps. Answers:

  A I'll probably go to Los Angeles. Maybe I'll find a job there.
  B I'm going to have a long holiday. I'll probably work in a café.
  C I'm going to study for a Master's degree. I'm going to teach at a university.

🔲 The tapescript is on page T90.

- Discuss which things the people are sure about. (Answer: the things they say with *going to*.) Establish these two ways of talking about future plans:

  > **Sure:**
  > **I'm going to have a holiday.**
  > **Not sure:**
  > **Perhaps | I'll go to Los Angeles.**
  > **Maybe |**
  > **I'll probably go to Los Angeles.**

> *Note*
> These structures are quite variable. The important point is that we do *not* normally say e.g. 'I'll see some friends' to talk about a definite plan; instead, we say *I'm going to see some friends.*

2 Activation: talking about future plans

- Either ask the questions round the class, or divide the class into pairs to ask and answer the questions.

3 Writing questions; asking & answering questions

- Write this structure on the board:

  > **What are you going to do …?**

  Ask students how it could continue, e.g. *in the summer, next weekend, when you leave school, after this lesson.*
- Students write a question to ask other students, who give a suitable reply.

3 Notice board

This exercise focuses on the use of the Present continuous tense to talk about things that have been arranged for the future. It also introduces a range of future time expressions.

➤ Focus on Form: Exercise 3
➤ Workbook: Exercise B

> *Key structures:* Present continuous tense. *Future time expressions:* tomorrow, the day after tomorrow, next (Tuesday), in (two weeks). (→ Beginner Unit 23.)

1 Grammar presentation; making sentences

- Look at the examples. Point out that we use the Present continuous tense to talk about things in the future that are *already arranged*.
- Look at the notice board. Students answer the questions. Expected answers:

  Tomorrow he's playing tennis.
  The day after tomorrow he's having supper with Ann / meeting Ann for supper.
  Next Tuesday he's going to the dentist / seeing the dentist.
  In two weeks he's going to a party, and he's taking his French exams.
  In two months he's going to a wedding.

> *Language note*
> We use *going to* to talk about things we plan to do; we use the Present continuous to talk about things that are already arranged. Compare:
> – We're going to have fish for lunch.
>   (= We've decided to have fish, this is our intention)
> – We're having fish for lunch.
>   (= We've already arranged it – we've probably bought the fish already)

2 Preparation for the pairwork activity: eliciting ideas

- Look at the topics and ask students to suggest possible activities. If you like, build up a list of activities on the board.
- Students write five activities in their diary. Then they ask and answer questions in pairs, to try to find a free day to go out.
- As a round-up, find out which pairs managed to find a day to go out.

> *Alternative*
> Students move freely round the class, trying to find people who are free at the same time as themselves.

2 I'll probably …

1 🔲 Three students say what they're going to do when they leave college. Listen and fill the gaps.

A .... Los Angeles.

.... a job there.

B .... a long holiday.

.... in a café.

C .... for a Masters degree.

.... at a university.

Which things are they sure about? Which things aren't they sure about?

2 Are you sure about your future plans? What are you going to do …

… tomorrow night?   … on your next birthday?   … when you retire?

3 Make up a question of your own. Ask other students.

3 Notice board

Present continuous

1 Today is Tuesday 8th May.

Look at this person's notice board.

This evening …

… he's going to the theatre.

… he's seeing 'The Tempest'.

… he's meeting some friends.

… they're having a drink.

What is he doing …

… tomorrow?

… the day after tomorrow?

… next Tuesday?

… in two weeks?

… in two months?

2 Think of activities that you might arrange for an evening. Use these ideas to help you.

sport   television   work   hobbies

going out   family   friends   food

Make a diary page for a week. Write five activities in the diary, and leave two evenings free.

Talk to your partner. Try to find an evening when you're both free to go to the cinema.

Monday	Evening class
Tuesday	Supper with Dave
Wednesday	

1 going to & not going to

> She's going to get up early.
> She isn't going to watch TV.

Sonia is taking an important exam next month, and she's decided to work as hard as she can. Talk about her plans using *going to* and *not going to*.

– go to parties
– answer the phone
– read a lot of books
– eat take-away food
– go away at weekends
– do a lot of housework
– have extra lessons
– stay up late

Think of one more thing she's going to do, and one more thing she isn't going to do.

2 I'm not sure

Look at these examples. Someone says what they're going to do at the weekend.

I'M SURE	I'm going to stay up late. I'm not going to do any work.
I'M NOT SURE	I'll probably watch the television.
	I might Perhaps I'll go to the cinema. Maybe I'll
	I probably won't go shopping.

Are you sure what you're going to do this weekend? Make true sentences. Use these ideas:

watch television	go swimming
see some friends	go to the cinema
eat in a restaurant	do some housework
visit relatives	go shopping

3 Asking about arrangements

> When?   What?   Where?   Who?
> How many?   How much?

> I'm playing tennis on .... with ....
>
> When are you playing tennis?
>   (I'm playing) tomorrow afternoon.
> Who are you playing with?
>   (I'm playing with) Kate.

Read these texts. What questions could you ask?

We're getting married next .... (1) in .... (2). We're inviting .... (3) people to the wedding. We're going to .... (4) for our honeymoon.

My father's retiring in .... (5), so my parents are moving to .... (6). They're buying a lovely little house right by the beach. And it's really cheap – they're only paying .... (7).

Tomorrow afternoon I'm .... (8) with .... (9).

Work in pairs. Ask and answer the questions.

How to say it

1 🔲 Listen to the phrase *going to* in this sentence. What happens when the speaker says it quickly?

I'm going to move into a new flat.

Practise saying these sentences quickly.

He's going to retire soon.
They're going to learn Spanish.
I'm going to have a big birthday party.

2 🔲 Listen to the intonation of these sentences. Practise saying them.

I'm going to work tomorrow.

They're going to get married.

Are you going to work tomorrow?

Are they going to get married?

Focus on Form

1 going to & not going to

- Look at the situation. Students make sentences round the class or write them down. Expected answers:

  She isn't going to go to parties.
  She isn't going to answer the phone.
  She's going to read a lot of books.
  She's going to eat take-away food.
  She isn't going to go away at weekends.
  She isn't going to do a lot of housework.
  She's going to have extra lessons.
  She isn't going to stay up late.
  or: She's going to stay up late (studying).

- Students write two more sentences, one positive and one negative. Then ask them to read out their sentences. Possible sentences:

  She's going to get up early.
  She's going to work every evening.
  She's going to get books from the library.
  She isn't going to go out in the evening.
  She isn't going watch TV.
  She isn't going to see her friends.

2 I'm not sure

- Remind students that:
  – if we're sure about our plans, we usually use *going to* or *not going to*.
  – if we're not sure, we can use *will probably*, *might* or *probably won't*.
- Ask students to make true sentences, either in pairs or round the class.

3 Asking about arrangements

- Read the example to show how the exercise works.
- Read through the texts and establish what the questions should be:

  1 When are you getting married?
  2 Where are you getting married?
  3 Who / How many people are you inviting?
  4 Where are you going for your honeymoon?
  5 When is he retiring?
  6 Where are they moving to?
  7 How much are they paying (for it)?
  8 What are you doing (tomorrow afternoon)?
  9 e.g. Who are you doing it/playing/going with? (*depending on the answer to 8*)

- Pairwork. Students ask the questions and make up suitable answers.

How to say it

1 Pronunciation of 'going to' in rapid speech

- 🔲 Play the sentence, and discuss what happens to *I'm going to* when it is said more quickly. It becomes reduced:

  /aɪm ɡəʊɪŋ tuː/ → /ʌm ɡəʊn(t)ə/.

- Play the other sentences and get students to repeat them quickly. Focus on the pronunciation of *going to*:

  /hɪz ɡəʊn(t)ə rəˈtaɪə suːn/
  /ðɛə ɡəʊn(t)ə lɜːn ˈspænɪʃ/
  /ʌm ɡəʊn(t)ə hæv ə bɪɡ ˈbɜːθdeɪ ˈpɑːti/

2 Intonation of statements and yes/no questions

- 🔲 Play the statements and questions and get students to repeat them. Point out that in the questions the voice rises higher and then falls more sharply.

🔲 Tapescript for Exercise 2: *I'll probably ...*

A I'll probably go to Los Angeles, because I've got a cousin who lives there – and maybe I'll find a job there and stay there for a year or two.

B First I'm going to have a long holiday. And then I'm not sure what I'll do – I'll probably work in a café or a bar for a time, to earn some money.

C Well, I know exactly what I'm going to do. I'm going to study for a Master's degree, and then I'm going to teach at university.

T 90

22

This unit deals with three areas of language used for talking about places in the world:
– saying where countries and regions are
– describing physical features and climate
– describing tourist attractions.
The reading and listening activity is about unusual websites on the Internet.

1 Where in the world?

This exercise teaches ways of describing where a country is, and introduces names of continents, oceans and regions of the world.

➤ Workbook: Exercise A

> *Key expressions:* Europe, Asia, Africa, America; northern, central; Middle East; Atlantic, Pacific, Indian Ocean, Mediterranean; border, coast.
> (→ Beginner Unit 16.)

1 Introduction: vocabulary presentation

- Check that students can pronounce the names of the continents and oceans: /ˈjuːrəp/, /ˈeɪʃə/ or /ˈeɪʒə/, /ˈæfrɪkə/, /əˈmerɪkə/, /ətˈlæntɪk/, /pəˈsɪfɪk/, /ˈɪndɪən/, /ˈəʊʃən/, /medɪtəˈreɪnɪən/. Locate them on the map. Answers:

  A North America B South America C Atlantic Ocean D Europe E Mediterranean Sea
  F Africa G Indian Ocean H Asia I Australia J Pacific Ocean

2 Reading & locating countries; making sentences

- Read through the descriptions, presenting any new words (e.g. *border, coast, partly*). Ask students to locate the countries. If students are interested, get them to suggest what countries they are. Answers:

  a 10 (Madagascar) *b* 5 (Finland) *c* 4 (Chile) *d* 3 (Panama)
  e 7 (Turkey) *f* 12 (New Zealand) *g* 8 (Egypt)

- Ask students to describe the other countries. Possible answers:

  1 (Canada) A large country in North America, north of the USA.
  2 (Mexico) A fairly large country in Central America, which has a border with the USA.
  6 (Hungary) A small country in Central Europe, which isn't on the coast.
  9 (Nigeria) A country in West Africa, on the Atlantic Ocean.
  11 (Thailand) A fairly small country in South-East Asia, on the Indian Ocean.

3 Activation: guessing game

- Give time for students to think of a country and prepare what to say. If you like, do this as pairwork.

- In turn, students describe a country. Other students guess what the country is.

Language note

We usually say *Northern/ Southern/Eastern/Western Europe.*

For other continents, we usually say *North/South/East/West: North America, South-East Asia.*

We also say *Central Europe, Central America, Central Africa,* etc.

Writing option

Students write a description of one or two countries. They then read out their description, and other students guess the country. If you like, let students use an atlas to help them.

---

1 Where in the world?

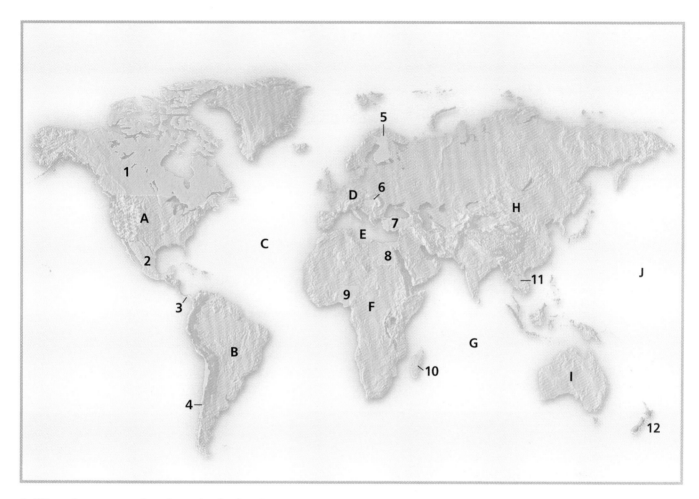

1 How do you say the places in the box?

North America	Europe	Asia	the Pacific Ocean	the Indian Ocean
South America	Africa	Australia	the Atlantic Ocean	the Mediterranean Sea

Can you match them with the letters A–J on the map?

2 On the map, twelve places are shown in yellow. Which of them is

a an island off the east coast of Africa, in the Indian Ocean?

b a country in Northern Europe, which has a border with Russia?

c a long, narrow country on the west coast of South America?

d a very small country in Central America, which has an Atlantic and a Pacific coast?

e a fairly large country in the Middle East, which is partly in Europe and partly in Asia?

f two islands in the Pacific Ocean, to the south-east of Australia?

g a country in North Africa, on the Mediterranean?

Where are the other yellow places?

3 Choose a country you know, and say where it is. Can other students guess its name?

This country is in south-western Europe. It has a border with Spain, and it's on the Atlantic Ocean.

Portugal.

2 What's it like?

FINLAND

HAWAII

EGYPT

1 You will hear people describing three of the places in Exercise 1.
  Which phrases do you think they will use about each place?

flat   a group of islands   thousands of lakes   very hot for most of the year

it hardly ever rains   volcanoes   beautiful beaches   quite a large population

mountainous   covered in forest   the valley of the River Nile   very cold in winter   desert

2 Listen and check your answers. What else do they say about each place?

3 Imagine someone asks you about your country. Say where it is and what it's like.

3 Tourist attractions

1 Imagine you're thinking of visiting the
  Great Barrier Reef. What other questions
  might you ask?

What is it?   Where is it?   How do you get there?   .... ?

Read the text on page 109.
Which of the questions does it answer?

2 Role-play

Student A: Choose a tourist attraction you know. Answer B's questions about it.

Student B: Imagine you're thinking of visiting this place. Ask A questions about it.

2 What's it like?

This exercise introduces vocabulary for describing a country or a region: natural features, climate and population.

➤ Workbook: Exercise B, Listening

> *Key vocabulary:* lake, mountain, beach, volcano, desert, forest, valley; mountainous, flat; population.   (→ Beginner Units 14, 16.)

1 Pre-listening activity; vocabulary presentation

● Look at the pictures and the phrases. Present any unknown items (if necessary, give well-known examples, e.g. the Sahara Desert). Focus on the adjectives *flat* (= no mountains) and *mountainous* (= lots of mountains).

2 Listening to check

● 🔲 Play the recording. Establish how the speakers use the phrases in Part 1, and what else they say. Answers:

Finland: is flat, has thousands of lakes, is covered in forest, is very cold in winter. (The temperature goes down to –40°.)
Hawaii: is a group of islands, has many volcanoes, has beautiful beaches, is mountainous, is covered in forest. (It has a very pleasant climate.)
Egypt: is quite flat, is very hot for most of the year, has quite a large population, most people live in the valley of the River Nile, most of the country is desert. (The land by the Nile is very fertile.)

3 Personalisation: describing your own country

● Ask students to use the language from Exercise 1 and from this exercise to describe their own country. Build up a description on the board.

> *Mixed nationality classes*
> Students prepare by writing a few notes. Then they sit with someone from a different country, and they simply tell each other about their own country.

3 Tourist attractions

This exercise gives practice in giving information about tourist attractions: where they are, what you can see or do there, how to get there, etc.

➤ Workbook: Exercise C

> *New vocabulary (reading text):* coral reef, off the coast, afford, helicopter, diving, glass-bottomed, species, turtle, whale, tropical. *Recycled language:* Present simple, there is/are, has got; yes/no and Wh- questions.

1 Making up questions; reading to check

● Look at the pictures, and talk about what they show. Introduce *coral reef.*
● Ask students what they think the answers to the questions might be. Ask them to think of other questions, and write them on the board. Possible questions:

What's the weather like? When is the best time to go there? Is it expensive to stay there? Where can you stay? What can you see there? Is it dangerous?

● Give time for students to read the text on page 109. Then read through it together, presenting new vocabulary as you go. Discuss which of the questions on the board the text answers.

> *Pairwork option*
> Students read the text in pairs and find answers to the questions on the board. Then discuss the answers together.

2 Preparation; asking & answering questions

● Choose a place you know, and take the role of a tourist agent or guide. Get students to ask you a few questions about it, and tell them what you know.
● Preparation. Students choose a place, and make a few notes.
● Pairwork. Students take it in turn to ask and answer questions.
● As a round-up, ask a few students what they found out from their partner.

> *Alternative: groupwork*
> Students prepare in pairs or small groups. Together they choose a place and 'pool' ideas about it. They then form new groups to ask and answer questions.

🔲 Tapescript for Exercise 2: *What's it like?*

1 Well, Finland is very flat. A lot of the country is covered in forest, and there are thousands of lakes. It's got quite a small population. And it's very cold in winter – it can go down to minus 40°.

2 Hawaii is a group of islands in the Pacific Ocean. The islands are quite mountainous, and they're covered in forest. Hawaii has got a lot of volcanoes and beautiful beaches, and it's very hot for most of the year.

3 Egypt is quite flat. It hardly ever rains and most of the country is desert, except for the valley of the River Nile, which is very rich farmland. It's very hot for most of the year, and it's got quite a large population.

4 www

This combined reading and listening activity is about the Internet. The reading is about unusual websites; in the listening, people talk about how they use the Internet.

> *Key words:* online, website, keyboard, screen. *Other new words (reading):* frog, message, traveller, at least, engine, save, fare, foreign, type in, programme, channel, linked to, monster, controls, insect, plastic. *New words (listening):* book (v.), encyclopaedia.

1 Vocabulary focus

- Check that students understand what the words mean: *online* = linked to the Internet; *website* = a place you can visit on the Internet (e.g. to get information); *keyboard* = the part of a computer with keys, where you type letters, numbers, etc.; *screen* = the part of the computer that you look at (like a TV screen).

2 Initial reading: scanning the text

- Read through the introduction, presenting any new words (e.g. *frog*). Give students time to scan quickly through the text and find the websites where you could find answers to the questions.

- Discuss the answers together. Answers:

  Weather in England: a 'Webcam' site (shows live pictures of Cambridge)
  Weather in the Sahara Desert: The Odyssey (shows pictures of West Africa)
  Drink in Russian: Foreign Languages for Travellers
  Pet frog: Frogland
  James Bond films: Digiguide (shows what's on TV this week)
  Flying across the Atlantic: British Airways (the view from Concorde)

- Look at the pictures, and discuss which websites they show. Answers:

  Webcam of Times Square, New York; V Car; Fiona's Shark Mania; Babelfish

> **Note**
> All these are real websites, which existed on the Internet when this exercise was written.

3 Detailed reading & discussion

- Students read through the text again at their own speed. As they read, they list the websites and give them marks out of 10 for interest and usefulness.

- Write the websites on the board, and give each one a 'class score' out of 10.

> **Pairwork options**
> 1 Students read the text with their partner, and agree together on what scores to give.
> 2 Students read the text alone, then get together in pairs and compare what scores they have given.

4 Listening & completing a table

- To introduce this part, ask students if they use the Internet, and if so what they use it for. If you like, build up a list of uses on the board.

- [cassette icon] Play the recording, pausing after each speaker. Students listen and complete the table. Answers:

  1 ... play games (chess, computer games)   2 ... buy things (books, CDs, clothes, holidays)   3 ... get information for school work (dictionaries, encyclopaedias, magazine articles, pictures).   4 ... send emails (to customers, friends, family)

> [cassette icon] Tapescript for Exercise 4: *www*
>
> 1 I find the Internet is very good for shopping. We use it more and more for buying books and CDs, and I even bought some clothes over the internet. The other thing you can do is book holidays over the Internet. We booked a cheap flight once, and it was very easy, and it was really good.
>
> 2 I use the Internet for games. I play chess with people all round the world. Last night I had a game with someone from Japan. I also download games from the Internet, so I can have any game I want.
>
> 3 I use the Internet for anything I need to help me with my school work. I use the online dictionaries, encyclopaedias and magazines. It's great because I can download pictures or articles and use them with my homework. It's very easy to use and it's free, so I like it.
>
> 4 Well, the main thing I use the Internet for is email. I've got a small business, and we don't really send letters very much any more. When I write to customers I usually do it by email, and my customers write to me by email. We probably send and receive four or five hundred emails a week. But of course I also use email to keep in touch with friends and family. I've got a daughter in Australia, for example, and she sends me an email almost every day.

4 www

1 All these words are connected with computers and the Internet. Do you know what they mean?

– online   – a website   – a keyboard   – a screen

2 *a* Look at the questions in the introduction. What websites can you visit to answer them?
  b What websites are shown in the pictures?

3 Look at all the websites in the article. Give each one a mark out of ten for interest.
  (10 = very interesting; 0 = not at all interesting), and for usefulness (10 = very useful;
  0 = completely useless). Show your marks to other students. Do you agree?

Do you know what the weather's like in England at the moment? Or in the Sahara Desert? Do you know how to ask for a drink in Russian? Or how to look after a pet frog? Are there any James Bond films on TV this week? And what's it like to fly across the Atlantic at 1,500 km per hour? It's easy to find answers to these questions if you're on the Internet, and if you know which website to visit ...

If you like travelling but you're feeling lazy, visit The Odyssey. On this website, you can follow a group of students who are travelling across West Africa. Every day you can read what they've done, see pictures of where they are, and (if you like) send messages to them.

Another good place for lazy travellers is the British Airways website. Here you can have the experience of flying in Concorde – or at least you can see the view from the windows and hear the sound of the engine – and save £4000 on the air fare.

Perhaps you're planning to visit a foreign country yourself, and need some help with the language. A site called Foreign Languages for Travellers is an online phrasebook. You can choose from 35 languages and 20 topics, and you can see the phrases on your screen and hear them at the same time. Or if you visit a site called Babelfish, you can type in a sentence in one language, and it will translate it for you.

Maybe you just want to stay at home and watch TV. If so, you can use a site called Digiguide to help you find what's on. It lists all the programmes on 80 channels. Just type in the name of the programme and it will tell you what channel it's on and at what time.

There are also lots of websites (called *Webcam* sites) which are linked to video cameras in different places around the world. If you go to a Webcam site, you can see what the weather's like in Cambridge, England, or watch what's happening in Times Square, New York. Or you can watch a live video of Loch Ness in Scotland, and see if you can see the Loch Ness Monster. One site, called V Car, is linked to a model car in San Diego, California. You can sit at your computer and drive the car yourself, using the controls on your keyboard and watching the car on your screen.

If you like sharks, visit Fiona's Shark Mania – it includes true stories about sharks, pictures of sharks, even poems about sharks. And then there is Frogland, for people who love frogs. Here you can see the Frog of the Month, and find out where to buy pet frogs and how to look after them. To feed your frog, you may need some live insects, and the best place for that is Online Direct Livefoods. You can order live insects from them over the Internet, and they will send them to you (by post) in plastic boxes.

Internet zone

---

4 Three people say how they use the Internet. Listen and complete the table

	Uses the Internet to ...	Examples
Speaker 1		
Speaker 2		
Speaker 3		
Speaker 4		

Focus on ... Nothing, no one, nowhere

1 What do you think the people in the pictures are saying? Match the questions with the answers.

Where are you going?	Nothing.
What are you doing?	No one.
Who are you talking to?	Nowhere special.

🔲 Listen and check.

2 Look at these examples.

I opened the door, but there was no one there.
there wasn't anyone there.

I waited, but she said nothing.
didn't say anything.

He has been nowhere interesting in his life.
hasn't been anywhere interesting in his life.

Sorry, I've got no money.
I haven't got any money.

3 How can you say these sentences differently? Change the phrases in blue.

a She gave me nothing for my birthday.
b We've got some bread, but we haven't got any cheese.
c They ate nothing for three days.
d There isn't anything to do in this town.
e I didn't meet anyone that I knew.
f They live nowhere near here.

Pronunciation: Consonant links

1 🔲 In these phrases, the consonants join together.

Try saying them, then listen to check.

parachute jumping	last Saturday
horse-riding	the last time
a post box	my parents' flat
a quiz show	bad-tempered
a good documentary	a pointed nose

2 Write a sentence. Use at least two of the phrases from the box.

3 Read out your sentence.

Phrasebook Arranging to meet

Fill the gaps in the conversation. Use these phrases.

Nothing special
I'd love to
Would you like to
Shall we meet
What are you doing

– .... on Friday evening?
– .... Why?
– .... come to a party?
– Yes, ...
– OK. .... at about 8 o'clock then?
– OK, fine.

🔲 Now listen and check. Where do they arrange to meet?

Have similar conversations.

Invite your partner to go to a concert on Saturday evening.

Invite your partner to go for a picnic on Sunday afternoon.

Study pages K

Focus on ... *Nothing, no one, nowhere*

This exercise focuses on the use of nothing, no one *and* nowhere. *It also shows the relationship between* nothing *and* not ... anything, no one *and* not ... anyone, *and* nowhere *and* not ... anywhere. *It builds on language introduced in Study Pages F Focus.*

> *Key structures:* nothing, no one, nowhere, not ... anyone, not ... anything, not ... anywhere.

1 Presentation of 'nothing', 'no one' & 'nowhere'

- Look at the pictures and the sentences. Establish what is going on in each situation, and ask students what they think the people are saying, e.g. *A teenage boy is going out, his father asks 'Where are you going?' He says 'Nowhere special'.*
- Play the recording to check. Answers:

  Where are you going? Nowhere special.
  What are you doing? Nothing.
  Who are you talking to? No one.

2 Presentation of *nothing*/*not anything*, etc.

- Show these forms on the board:

some	any	no
something	anything	nothing
someone	anyone	no one
somewhere	anywhere	nowhere

  (*Note:* We can also say *somebody, anybody, nobody.* They mean the same as *someone, anyone, no one.*)
- Make these points:
  – we use *some* forms in positive sentences (e.g. *I saw something*).
  – we use *any* forms in questions (*Did you see anything?*).
  – in negatives, there are two possible forms: *nothing, no one, nowhere* or *not + anything, anyone, anywhere.*
- Read through the examples to make this last point clear: the two alternatives mean the same.

3 Practice: changing sentences

- Go through the sentences. Ask students to give the alternative forms of the negative. Answers:

  a She didn't give me anything for my birthday.
  b We've got some bread, but we've got no cheese.
  c They didn't eat anything for three days.
  d There's nothing to do in this town.
  e I met no one that I knew.
  f They don't live anywhere near here.

> Tapescript for Focus on ... *Nothing, no one, nowhere*
>
> 1 A Where are you going?
>   B Nowhere special.
> 2 A What are you doing?
>   B Nothing.
> 3 A Who are you talking to?
>   B No one.

Pronunciation: *Consonant links*

> Phrases from previous units with joined consonants.

1 Listening & practice

- Play the phrases and ask students to repeat them. Focus on the way the end of one word links with the beginning of the next:

  /pærəʃuːt‿dʒʌmpɪŋ/   /lɑːst‿sætedi/
  /hɔːs‿raɪdɪŋ/   /ðə lɑːst‿taɪm/
  /pəʊst‿bɒks/   /maɪ pɛərənts‿flæt/
  /ə kwɪz‿ʃəʊ/   /bæd‿tempəd/
  /ə gʊd‿dɒkjʊmentəri/   /ə pɔɪntɪd‿nəʊz/

2 Writing sentences

- Students write sentences using phrases from the box, and including any other words they like, e.g.
  There's a post box opposite my parents' flat.
  I went horse-riding last Saturday.

3 Reading sentences aloud

- Students read out their sentences in turn. Focus on the pronunciation of the consonant links.

  Alternative: Dictation. Students dictate their sentence to the person next to them. As a check, ask students to read the sentence they wrote down.

Phrasebook: *Arranging to meet*

This exercise practises expressions used when arranging to meet someone. It builds on language from Unit 21.

> *Key expressions:* What are you doing ...?, Nothing special, Would you like to ...?, I'd love to ..., Shall we meet ...?
> *Recycled language:* Present continuous, time expressions.

- Ask students to fill the gaps in the dialogue. As you do this, present any new expressions.
- Play the dialogue to check.
- Look at the two situations with the class, and establish what the people will say.
- Either let students practise dialogues in pairs, or ask students to have conversations in front of the class.

> Tapescript for Phrasebook: *Arranging to meet*
>
> A What are you doing on Friday evening?
> B Nothing special. Why?
> A Would you like to come to a party?
> B Yes, I'd love to.
> A OK. Shall we meet at about 8 o'clock, then?
> B OK, fine. Where shall we meet, then?
> A Do you know the new café just opposite the museum?
> B Yes, I do.
> A Let's meet there. 8 o'clock?
> B OK. Great.

Consolidation

Using the Present continuous

This exercise focuses on three uses of the Present continuous tense. These were introduced in Exercises 5.1 and 5.2, and 21.3.

1 • Remind students of the three basic uses of the Present continuous which they have practised in this book. If you like, give a few simple examples, e.g.
   A *'now'*: I'm talking to you, we're sitting in the classroom.
   B *'around now'*: I'm going out a lot, I'm getting up very early this week.
   C *future*: I'm going to the theatre this evening; we're having chicken for dinner.
   • Look at the three conversations in turn, and establish which uses they are examples of. Answer:
   1 B 2 C 3 A

2 Students look at the sentences and decide which use they are examples of. Then go through the answers, and discuss different possibilities.
   Note: The idea of this is to give students a feeling for how the Present continuous is used with a variety of meanings.
   Expected answers:
   a A or B
   b C (or A if you're talking to someone in the street)
   c B
   d B (or C, if it's Monday, and you mean 'for the rest of this week')
   e C (or B, if talking on the phone at New Year)
   f A

It's …

This exercise focuses on the use of It's in impersonal sentences, to talk about the weather. It builds on language introduced in Unit 22.

1 Look at the examples. Elicit other expressions, and write them on the board. Possible answers:
   It's cold, It's warm, It's cool, It's windy, It's cloudy, It's foggy, It's snowing, It's wet, It's dry

2 Look at the pictures. Ask students to make sentences. Answers:
   It's hot and sunny.
   It's cool, cloudy and windy.
   It's cold and it's snowing.

Review

What happened? What was happening?

Review of Past simple and Past continuous tenses from Unit 19.

1 • To introduce the activity, write a Past continuous sentence on the board and ask students to complete it, e.g.

   > **I was just going to sleep when …**

   (Possible continuations: I heard a strange noise; someone came into the room; I saw a spider on the wall.)

   • Pairwork. Students complete sentences *a*, *b* and *c*. Then go through the answers, getting different suggestions from the class. Possible answers:
   a … my mobile phone rang. … the driver stopped and a stranger got in.
   b … it suddenly started raining; someone stole all our money.
   c … he found a wallet with £5,000 in it; he fell over and broke his arm.

2 Students continue the other sentences in the same way. Possible answers:
   a He was driving through the town when …; He was driving home from work when …
   b while he was working in London; while he was going by plane to New York.
   c The children were all jumping on the desks when …; Everyone was doing their homework when …

What's the matter?

Review of language from Unit 9 (Present perfect), Unit 12 (illnesses, aches and pains) and Unit 19 (accidents).

• Look at each picture in turn, and ask students to say what has happened or what is wrong with the person. Possible answers:
   a He's got a headache.
   b She has broken her arm/Her arm hurts.
   c She feels sick/ill.
   d She's got (a) toothache/Her tooth aches.
   e He's got a cold.
   f His back hurts/He's got backache.
   g He has broken his leg/His leg hurts/He has fallen over.
   h Someone has hit her in the eye/Her eye hurts.
   i He has cut his knee/His knee hurts/He has fallen over.
   j He's got a temperature/He's got 'flu.
   k He's got a stomach ache.
   l He has cut his face. His face hurts.

Adjectives

Review of adjectives from Unit 20.

1 Students complete the sentences. Answers:
   a wavy/curly *b* thin *c* short and fat *d* straight/pointed

2 Ask students to suggest suitable adjectives. Answers:
   a bad-tempered *b* mean *c* selfish *d* honest *e* lazy

Consolidation

Using the Present continuous

1 We use the Present continuous to talk about

   A things happening 'now' (at the moment we are speaking)

   B things happening 'around now' (not exactly at this moment)

   C things that we've arranged for the future.

   These are parts of telephone conversations. Are they A, B or C?

   Did I tell you? I'm going to evening classes ... Yes, I'm learning English ... Yes, I'm really enjoying it.

   Saturday? I'm seeing a friend in the afternoon, and we're going shopping together ... No, I'm not doing anything in the evening ... Yes, let's meet for a drink.

   Hello, Mary. Could you phone again later – I'm just making breakfast ... No, Joanna can't speak to you either – she's having a shower.

2 Look at these sentences. What is the most likely meaning: A, B or C?

   a I'm not feeling very well.

   b We're going to the theatre together.

   c I'm meeting a lot of interesting people.

   d He's working late this week.

   e We're spending New Year at home.

   f The children are watching TV.

It's ...

1 We often use *It's ...* to talk about the weather.

   It's hot.   It's sunny.   It's raining.

   What other expressions do you know like this?

2 What's the weather like in these pictures?

Review

What happened? What was happening?

1 Complete these sentences. Say what happened.

   a I was sitting in a taxi yesterday afternoon when ...

   b While we were lying on the beach last weekend ...

   c He was clearing out some cupboards in his bedroom the other day when ...

2 Now complete these sentences. Say what was happening.

   a ... a dog ran out in front of the car.

   b He first met his girlfriend ...

   c ... the teacher walked into the room.

What's the matter?

Some of these people are ill, and some have hurt themselves. What's the matter with them?

Adjectives

1 Complete these sentences.

   a His hair isn't straight. It's ...

   b Her eyebrows aren't thick. They're ...

   c She isn't tall and thin. She's ...

   d His nose isn't hooked. It's ...

2 What adjectives describe these people?

   a She gets angry a lot. She's ...

   b They never buy anything for anyone. They're ...

   c He only thinks about himself. He's completely ...

   d She never steals. She's completely ...

   e They never do any work. They're ...

23 Past and present

1 Things have changed

Present perfect

1 Read the woman's two letters: she wrote one a year ago, and she's writing one now.

A year ago

... Life's pretty boring here in England. I'm still in London with Mum and Dad (well, it's cheap!) and I'm working as a secretary. It pays quite well, but the hours are very long. I'm still going out with Bob, of course ...

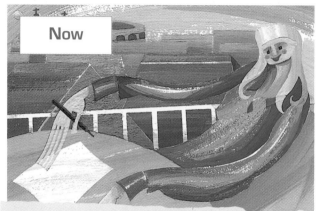

Now

... I'm in Italy, working in a hotel in Rome — just a temporary job as a receptionist. I've got my own flat, and I'm going out with someone called Riccardo, who I met at a party. He's really nice — he's teaching me Italian ...

What are the differences?

Last year ... she was in London.	*Now* ... she's in Rome.
... she was working as a secretary.	...
...	...

Now say what has happened between last year and now.

She's left London.   She's moved ...   She's met ...

She's changed her job.   She's stopped ...   She's started ...

2 How have these people's lives changed? Talk about them using verbs from the box.

A year ago   Now

A year ago   Now

start
stop
move
buy
sell
have

3 How has your life changed in the last five years? Write three things that you have done.

I've left school.
I've moved out of my parents' flat.
I've bought a computer.

23

This is the second of two units concerned with the Present perfect tense (the other was Unit 9: *I've done it*, which focused on the use of this tense for talking about recent events). This unit covers two further uses of the Present perfect:
– for talking about changes between the past and now
– for talking about experience.

1 Things have changed

This exercise introduces the Present perfect tense for talking about changes – i.e. saying what is different now from before.

> ➤ Focus on Form: Exercise 1
> ➤ Workbook: Exercise A

> *Key structure:* Present perfect tense.
> *Key verbs:* start + -ing, stop + -ing, move, change, leave, meet, become.

1 Reading & grammar presentation; practice of Present perfect forms

- Look at the extract from the woman's letter from last year, and establish the facts about her in the past (using the Past simple and Past continuous):

  Last year she was in London, she was living with her parents, she was working as a secretary, she had a boring life, she had a boyfriend called Bob.

- Look at the second letter, and establish the facts about her now (using the Present simple and Present continuous):

  Now she's in Rome, she's working in a hotel, she has a new boyfriend called Riccardo, she's learning Italian.

- Establish what has happened (using the Present perfect):

  She's left London. She's changed her job. She's moved to Italy. She's stopped going out with Bob. She's met a man called Riccardo. She's started going out with Riccardo.

- Write sentences on the board to show how we use the Present perfect tense to say what has changed between the past and now:

IN THE PAST	NOW
She <u>was</u> in England.	She <u>is</u> in Italy.
	She <u>has gone</u> to Italy.

> *Language note*
> We use the Present perfect when we are not interested in *when* things happened, just in *the fact that* they have happened (i.e. that things are different now from before).
>
> If we focus on 'when', we have to use the past tense: *She went to Italy in April.*

2 Activation: making sentences

- Look at each pair of pictures in turn, and ask students to make sentences. As you do this, check that students can produce Present perfect forms of the verbs in the box, and if you like, write these on the board. Possible answers:

  1 He's stopped smoking, he's stopped drinking beer, he's started doing exercise, he's lost weight, he's become thinner/healthier.
  2 They've moved to the country, they've bought a car, they've had a baby, they've bought a cottage in the country.

3 Personalisation: writing sentences

- To introduce the activity, tell students a few things that have changed in your life, e.g. *I've moved to a new flat, I've bought a computer, I've started reading 'The Times', I've got married.*

- Students write down things they have done, then show what they have written to the person next to them.

- As a round-up, ask a few students to read out their sentences.

2 Where are they now?

This exercise focuses on the relationship between the Present perfect and Present tenses. It practises questions with still *and* yet, *used for asking whether things have changed or not.*

───────────────
Key structures: Present perfect tense; Present simple and continuous; still, yet.
───────────────

1 Listening & gap-filling; grammar presentation; making questions

● Look at the picture, and read the sentences about the people in the photo.

● 🔲 Tell the class they will hear questions about what the people are doing now. Play the recording. Students listen and fill the gaps. Write the answers on the board:

> **Has she found a job yet?**
> **Is she _still_ living in that caravan?**

● Get students to suggest questions about Pam and Nick. Possible questions:

Are they still engaged? Have they got married yet? Are they still living in Madrid?
Does Nick still have long hair? Does he still play the guitar?
Is Pam still at university? Has she left university yet? Has she still got her motorbike?

2 Completing sentences

● Read the questions, and ask students to complete the answers. Possible answers:

a ... she's moved, she found a new one.
b ... I'm still reading it.
c ... they've woken up.
d ... I've eaten it.
e ... he's still looking for it.
f ... it's stopped.

3 Experience

This exercise introduces a slightly different use of the Present perfect: to talk about personal experience (i.e. things you have done at some time in your life).

───────────────
Key structures: Present perfect tense; I've never; Have you ever...?; Present perfect v. Past simple.
───────────────

1 Introduction; grammar presentation: Present perfect tense for experience

● Read the examples, and show the difference between:
  – *I've seen* a tarantula (= at some time in my life).
  – *I saw* a tarantula yesterday (talking about a particular time in the past).

● Students read the sentences and decide which choices are true of them. Then go through the answers together, and tell students your own answers.

2 Grammar presentation: questions & answers

● Look at the conversations. Ask students which verbs are Present perfect tense, and which are Past simple tense. Use this to establish that:
  – we use the Present perfect to talk in general about experience (*Have you seen a tarantula at any time up to now?*).
  – if we go into details of when, where, etc. we change to the Past simple (*I saw one yesterday, I once saw one at the zoo*).

3 Activation: asking and answering questions

● Students write a question of their own.
● Students take it in turn to ask and answer their questions.

➤ Focus on Form: Exercise 2
➤ Workbook: Exercise B

───────────────
Presentation option
Show how we can say the same thing in two different ways, using the Present or the Present perfect:
He's still living in London.
He hasn't moved yet.
She still smokes.
She hasn't stopped yet.
───────────────

───────────────
Language note
Note the position of *still* and *yet*:
still – before the main verb, but after verb *to be*:
She's still living in London.
They're still here.
yet – at the end of the sentence:
They haven't gone home yet.
───────────────

🔲 The tapescript is on page T98.

➤ Focus on Form: Exercise 3
➤ Workbook: Exercise C, Listening

───────────────
Language note
In this context we say *I've been to Scotland*, not ~~I've gone to Scotland~~. Compare:
He's *gone* to Scotland = he's still there.
He's *been* to Scotland = He's visited it (and come back again).
───────────────

───────────────
Alternative: class survey
Students move freely round the class, asking their question and answering other people's. They record the number of *yes* and *no* answers they receive. As a round-up, they report their results.
───────────────

2 Where are they now?

Questions • still • yet

1 Two friends are looking through some old photos. A couple of years ago …

… Sarah was looking for a job. She was living in a caravan.

… Pam and Nick were engaged. They were living in Madrid.

… Nick had very long hair. He was playing the guitar in a band.

… Pam was at university. She had a big motorbike.

📼 Listen to the conversation. Write the questions.

– What's Sarah doing now? .... ?

– No, not yet. She's still looking for one.

– And .... ?

– No. She's moved into a flat now.

What questions can you ask about Pam and Nick?

2 Complete the answers to these questions. Say what has happened or what is still happening.

a Is she still in the same flat? No, …

b Have you finished *War and Peace* yet? No, …

c Are they still asleep? No, …

d Is there any cheese left? No, …

e Has he found his passport yet? No, …

f Is it still raining? No, …

3 Experience

Present perfect • Past simple

1 Which of these things have you done in your life? Choose an answer.

I've seen / I've never seen — a tarantula.

I've eaten / I've never eaten — rabbit.

I've been / I've never been — to Scotland.

I've played / I've never played — basketball.

I've been / I've never been — in a helicopter.

2 Look at the conversations. Which verbs are in

– the Present perfect?   – the Past simple?

| Have you ever seen a tarantula? |

| Yes, I have. I once saw one in the zoo. How about you? |

| No, I've never seen one. |

| Have you ever been to Scotland? |

| No. I've been to England, but I haven't been to Scotland. How about you? |

| Yes, I've been to Scotland. I went there last summer. |

3 Choose one of the verbs and write a question. Ask other students your question.

Have you ever seen …?   Have you ever played …?   Have you ever been in …?

Have you ever eaten …?   Have you ever been to …?

Focus on Form

1 Changes & experience

We can use the Present perfect

A to talk about changes (how things are different from before):

Last year they were living in London, but now they've moved to Manchester.

He's left school – he's at university now.

B to talk about experience (things you've done in your life so far):

My brother's read all the James Bond books, and he's seen all the movies, too.

We've been to Florida three times, but we haven't visited Disney World.

I've never eaten octopus – is it nice?

Read the bubbles. Are the people talking about *changes* or *experience*?

a I've had lots of jobs –
I've been a waiter, I've worked in a bank, I've been a hotel receptionist and I've driven a lorry.

b I've bought a new car – it's much faster than my old one.

I didn't learn much French at school, but now I've started going to French evening classes, and I'm doing quite well.

c

d I've been up the Eiffel Tower – we went there two or three years ago.

e I've been windsurfing a few times, but I've never done a bungee jump.

2 not yet

> My brothers are still at school – they haven't left school yet.
>
> Katy's still living in London – she hasn't moved yet.

What haven't these people done yet? Use verbs from the box.

a They've still got that old car.
b Tom's still looking for a job.
c The children are still asleep.
d They're still engaged.
e She's still doing her homework.
f He's still in his pyjamas.

| find |
| finish |
| get dressed |
| get married |
| sell |
| wake up |

3 ever & never

ever	=	at any time
Have you ever been to Hawaii?	=	Have you been to Hawaii at any time?
never	=	not ever
My parents have never been abroad.	=	My parents haven't ever been abroad.

Think of three things that you've never done (and that you'd like to do). Write them down.

> I've never climbed Mount Everest.
> I've never been to Antarctica.
> I've never driven a Rolls Royce.

How to say it

1 🔊 **Listen to the these *-ed* endings.**

| changed | stopped | visited |
| climbed | finished | started |

Practise saying these sentences:

Have you finished that book yet?

He says he's stopped smoking.

She's changed the colour of her hair.

2 🔊 **Listen to the intonation of these sentences. Practise saying them.**

I've never been to Mexico.

I've never played basketball.

Have you ever been to Mexico?

Have you ever played basketball?

Focus on Form

1 Changes & experiences

- Read through the examples, which show the two main uses of the Present perfect tense.
- Give time for students to read the sentences in the bubbles and decide which of the two uses each one is. Answers:
  a Experience (= jobs he has done in his life so far)
  b Change (= Before he had an old car; now he has a new car)
  c Change (= Before he didn't know much French, now he's learning it)
  d Experience (= something she has done in her life – she's been up the Eiffel Tower)
  e Experience (= sports she has done and hasn't done in her life)

2 not yet

- Read the examples. Then look at the verbs in the box, and ask students to give the past participle forms. Write them on the board:
- Working alone or in pairs, students make sentences with *not ... yet*, using verbs from the box.
- Go through the answers together:
  a They haven't sold it yet.
  b He hasn't found one yet.
  c They haven't woken up yet.
  d They haven't got married yet.
  e She hasn't finished (her homework) yet.
  f He hasn't got dressed yet.

> *found*
> *finished*
> *got dressed*
> *got married*
> *sold*
> *woken up*

3 ever & never

- Read through the examples. Then ask students to write down three things they have never done. If you like, help them by writing prompts on the board, e.g.

> *I've never seen ...*   *I've never met ...*
> *I've never been to ...* *I've never driven ...*
> *I've never eaten ...*   *I've never played ...*
> *I've never drunk ...*   *I've never read ...*

- Students read out their sentences.

How to say it

1 Pronunciation of '-ed' endings

- 🔲 Play each group of words. Focus on the different sounds of the *-ed* ending, and also on the consonant clusters (underlined below):

  -ed = /d/: /ˈtʃeɪndʒd/, /klaɪmd/
  -ed = /t/: /stɒpt/, /ˈfɪnɪʃt/
  -ed = /ɪd/: /ˈvɪzɪtɪd/, /ˈstɑːtɪd/

- Play the sentences and get students to practise them.

2 Intonation of statements and yes/no questions

- 🔲 Play the statements and questions and get students to repeat them. Point out that in the questions the voice rises higher and then falls more sharply.

🔲 Tapescript for Exercise 2: *Where are they now?*

A What's Sarah doing now? Has she found a job yet?
B No, not yet. She's still looking for one.
A And is she still living in that caravan?
B No. She's moved into a flat now.

24

This unit is concerned with language for talking about the arts and
entertainment. This includes:
– the vocabulary of art forms, people and places (e.g. *play*, *actor*, *theatre*)
– talking about well-known people involved in arts and entertainment
– talking about TV programmes.
The reading and listening activity is a murder mystery.

1 Did you see … ?

This exercise is about going out to see things (e.g. concerts, exhibitions, films). It
introduces the basic vocabulary of art forms, the places where you can see them,
and people involved in them.

▶ Workbook: Exercise A

> *Key vocabulary:* film, painting, concert, play, opera; art gallery, museum, theatre,
> cinema, exhibition; actor, singer, band, orchestra. *Verbs:* see, watch, listen to, go
> to, go with. *Recycled language:* Past simple tense.

1 Introduction: identifying the pictures

● Look at the pictures, and talk about them with the class. Get students to say
what they show, who the people are, what they are doing, etc. Use this to
present the words in the list. Answers:

A *singers*, singing in an *opera* (in a theatre or opera house)
B people watching a *film* in the *cinema*
C a *museum* (an *exhibition* of dinosaurs)
D an *orchestra* playing music in a *concert*
E people looking at *paintings* in an *art gallery* (an *exhibition* of paintings)
F *singers* and a *band* playing in a (rock) *concert*
G *actors* performing a *play* in a *theatre*.

> *Language notes*
> An exhibition can be of paintings
> or other things:
> There's an exhibition of old
> cameras at the museum.
> I went to the Picasso exhibition at
> the National Gallery.
> An opera in English is what you
> go to see (e.g. *La Traviata* is an
> opera); the building is an *opera
> house*.

If you like, build up a list of things to see and places on the board:

You see …	at …
paintings	*an art gallery*
an exhibition	*a museum, an art gallery*
a concert	*a concert hall*
a play	*a theatre*
films	*a cinema*
opera	*a theatre, an opera house*

2 Activation: asking & answering questions

● Look at the questions and the answers in the bubbles. Point out that there are
two ways of replying:
– using the Past simple tense with a time expression (*I went … two
years ago*).
– using the Present perfect (*I've never been to …*).

● Pairwork. In turn, students ask and answer the questions. The idea is not that
they should talk a lot about each topic; they should just say if they've been to
each place and/or when they last went there (and possibly what they saw).

> *Optional lead-in*
> Get students to ask you the
> questions, and you give replies.

3 Extension: sentence writing & discussion

● Working alone, students choose one of the places they talked about (the one
that interests them most), and write sentences about it, following the model on
the page.

● In turn, ask students to read out what they wrote. Ask if anyone else saw or
wrote about the same thing.

> *Alternative*
> Students move freely round the
> class. They read out what they
> have written and listen to what
> other students wrote. If they find
> someone who saw the same thing,
> they discuss what they thought
> of it.

24 Arts and entertainment

1 Did you see ...?

1 Look at the pictures. What do they show? Use words from the box.

concert
play
singer
opera
museum
theatre
art gallery
exhibition
band
film
painting
actor
orchestra
cinema

2 When was the last time you ...

... went to a concert?   ... went to the theatre?
... went to an opera?   ... went to the cinema?
... went to a museum?   ... went to an art gallery?

Talk to your partner.

> I went to a concert last Saturday.

> The last time I went to the theatre was about two years ago.

> I've never been to an opera.

3 Choose one of the places you went to, and write a few sentences. Include answers to these questions.

Where was it?

When was it?

What did you see?

Who did you go with?

What was it like?

Try to find someone else who saw the same thing.

The last time I went to .... was ....
I went with ....
saw
I watched   ....
listened to
I thought it was ....

2 Famous people

Mozart   Van Gogh   Shakespeare   Elizabeth Taylor   Steven Spielberg

1 Look at these five people. Choose the best words to describe them.

actor   actress   composer   director   musician   painter   poet   singer   writer

What else do you know about them? Write two sentences for each person: one thing you're sure about and one thing you're not sure about.

Did other students say the same things?

> Mozart wrote a lot of symphonies. I think he was Austrian or German.

2 🖭 You will hear descriptions of two famous people. How quickly can you guess their names?

3 Work with a partner. Think of a famous person. What do you know about him/her? Write some sentences.

Read out your sentences to another pair. Can they guess who it is?

3 What's on TV?

1 Look at the list of programmes on page 109, and answer these people's questions.

> Which soaps are on tonight?

> Are there any quiz shows on TV tonight?

> I want to watch a good documentary. Is there one on?

> Which channel is the best for news?

> Are there any good films on this evening?

> Is there any football on this evening?

> Who are the Morgs?

> Who's on *My First Billion* tonight?

2 Work in groups. You've decided to spend the evening watching TV. See if you can agree about which programmes to watch.

> I'd like to watch ...

> Let's watch ...

> I think we should watch ...

3 Think about TV in your own country. What kind of programmes do you like? Which don't you like? What are your three favourite programmes?

soaps   sport   news programmes   comedy   documentaries   films   quiz shows   ...

2 Famous people

This exercise is a guessing game. It focuses on language for talking about artists of different kinds (e.g. painters, musicians, singers).

> *Key vocabulary:* actor, actress, composer, director, musician, painter, poet, singer, writer. *Recycled language:* Past simple tense.

1 Presentation of vocabulary; writing sentences

- Look at the people in the pictures, and ask students what kind of artist they are (or were). Use this to present new vocabulary, but do not go into other details at this point. Answers:

  Mozart: composer (also musician)   *Van Gogh:* painter   *Shakespeare:* poet/writer
  Elizabeth Taylor: actress   *Stephen Spielberg:* film director

- Read the sentences about Mozart. Then give time for students to write sentences about the other people.

- Take each person in turn, and 'pool' information about him/her from what students wrote.

2 Listening & guessing

- 🔲 Play the recording. Either pause from time to time to see if the class can guess the person, or ask students to raise their hand to stop the tape. Answers:

  1 Picasso   2 Beethoven

3 Writing & guessing game

- In pairs, students think of a well-known person connected with the arts (alive or dead) and write some sentences.

- In turn, students read out their sentences. The rest of the class try to guess who the person is.

3 What's on TV?

This exercise introduces language for talking about TV programmes.

> *Key vocabulary:* channel, programme; quiz show, sport, soap, news, comedy, documentary, film. *Recycled language:* making suggestions (I'd like to …, Let's …, I think we should …).

1 Reading: scanning a text to answer questions

- Read the questions and make sure that students understand them. Then turn to the TV listings on page 109. Working alone or in pairs, students find answers to the questions. If you like, give them a time limit (e.g. 5 minutes).

- Discuss the answers together. Answers (left to right):

  Films: Dancing Shoes (Ch. 2); True Grit (Ch. 2); Rocky 2 (Inter TV)
  Quiz shows: That's the question (TV Gold), Play it again, Sam! (Familia)
  My first Billion: Bill Gates (TV Gold)
  Documentaries: Focus (Ch. 1), Wildlife on One (Ch. 1)
  Football: Inter TV, 6.00
  Best channel for news: Channel 1
  Soaps: Downtown (TV Gold); Streetlife (TV Gold)
  The Morgs: A rock band (Familia)

2 Role-play discussion

- Divide the class into groups of four or five. Each group tries to agree together which programmes to watch during the evening.

- As a round-up, ask each group to tell you what they decided to watch.

3 Extension: speaking activity

- Go through the types of programme, and find out from students what they like. Encourage them to go into details about what they watch.

➤ Workbook: Exercise A

> *Background notes*
> Mozart: Austrian composer, wrote 41 symphonies, died when he was 35.
> Van Gogh: Dutch painter, painted *The Sunflowers*, cut off his ear, lived in France.
> Shakespeare: English, wrote plays and poetry, wrote *Hamlet*, lived in 16th–17th century.
> Elizabeth Taylor: British film actress, lived in Hollywood, played Cleopatra, got married 5 times (including twice to Richard Burton).
> Steven Spielberg: Jewish American film director, directed *Jaws*, *ET*, *Jurassic Park*.

> 🔲 The tapescript is on page T101.

> *Note*
> Students should order their sentences so they do not give away too much at the beginning (i.e. they should leave the most obvious things till last).

➤ Workbook: Exercise B, Listening

> *Language note*
> A *soap* (or *soap opera*) is a series like *Neighbours* or *Baywatch*, which follows the daily lives of characters who appear week after week.

> *Alternative*
> Ask each student or pair of students to look for answers to two questions only.

> *Alternative*
> Students write their favourite programme in each category (their favourite soap, their favourite TV sport, their favourite news programme, etc.). Then go through the categories together, and find out the 'class favourite' in each category.

4 Who shot the pianist?

This combined reading and listening activity is a murder mystery. The reading gives the story and the statements made by the four suspects. The listening is the solution to the mystery.

New words (reading): shoot/shot, murder, mystery, musical (n.), divorce (n.), gun, scream (v. and n.), upstairs, downstairs, covered in, follow.
New words (listening): shot (n.). *Recycled language:* Past simple and continuous.

Language note
Shot is used as the Past tense of *shoot*, and as a noun:
Someone *shot* Roger. I heard a *shot*.
Scream is used as a verb and as a noun:
She *screamed*. I heard a *scream*.

1 Reading; establishing the situation

- To introduce the topic, present the words *murder*, *shoot* (Past: *shot*) and *gun*.
- Read through the cartoon strip with the class, presenting any new words. Establish what we know about Roger Ray:

  He writes musicals, he has a wife and two children, he's a very unpleasant person.

Language note
A *musical* is a play or film with songs, like *West Side Story* or *Cats*.

- Consider each of the other characters. Discuss what we know about them, and why they might want to murder Roger Ray. Possible answers:

  Celia: his wife, a film star, wants a divorce because she's in love with Tom.
  Reason for murdering Roger: so that she can marry Tom.
  Jack: his son, 23 years old. Reason for murdering Roger: needs money.
  Sara: his daughter, 19, works for Roger and Tom as a secretary, has a boyfriend.
  Reason for murdering Roger: so that she can marry her boyfriend and still have money.
  Tom: writes musicals with Roger, his wife died 5 years ago, lives next door.
  Reason for murdering Roger: to marry Celia.

- Establish what happened at 10.30:

  Someone shot Roger Ray in the back.

2 Reading & discussion

- Give time for students to read the statements.
- Ask students who they think killed Roger Ray and why.

Pairwork option
After reading the statements, students discuss the solution in pairs.

3 Listening: the solution to the mystery

- 🔊 Play the recording. Establish who killed Roger Ray, how they did it, and how the detective knows. Answer:

  It was Tom. He came in from the back garden, shot Roger, went back out and threw the gun away.

  The detective knows because Tom says he heard a shot, although he also says he was in the next door garden. But no one else heard a shot, because the noise of the piano was too loud – they just say the piano stopped playing.

🔊 Tapescript for Exercise 2: *Famous people*

1 OK, this person was a painter. He was Spanish, but he painted most of his pictures in France, and he lived in Paris. He liked women – he was married four times. And his most famous painting was *Guernica*.

2 This person was a composer. He was German. He lived in the 19th century. And towards the end of his life he was deaf, but he still wrote music. And he wrote nine symphonies.

🔊 Tapescript for Exercise 4: *Who shot the pianist?*

Well, the important thing is that Roger Ray was playing the piano when the murderer shot him. And he was playing very loudly – both his children say so. So the question is: did anyone hear the shot? Well, Celia didn't hear it. She took Roger a cup of coffee after he stopped playing. Jack didn't hear the shot. He came down because he heard his mother scream. And Sara didn't hear it, either. Only Tom heard the shot. And that can mean only one thing: he heard the shot because he was in the same place as the gun. He wasn't in the garden, he was in Roger's study, holding the gun, and he shot Roger himself.

It was an easy murder. Tom was already in his garden. He put on an old pair of gloves, climbed over the garden wall and walked into Roger's study. Roger was playing the piano. He said hello, but he didn't stop playing. Tom went behind Roger, took out a gun, shot him in the back and put down the gun on the piano. Then he ran back into the garden, back over the wall into his own garden, and then he followed Sara into the street and back into Roger's house again. Of course, he took off the gloves first. When we looked in his garden, we found them lying in the flowers.

4 Who shot the pianist?

Reading and listening activity

1 Here's the first part of a murder mystery. What does it tell you about Roger Ray?

Why might these people want to murder Roger?

– Celia   – Jack   – Sara   – Tom

What happens one morning at 10.30?

1 Roger Ray and Tom **Turner write** musicals. Tom writes the stories, and Roger writes the music.

2 Roger lives with his family in a big house in London. He is married to film star Celia Dean.

Roger, I'm in love with Tom. I want a divorce.

Never! I'll never divorce you! Never!

3 His son Jack is 23.

Dad, I want to go round the world on a motorbike. Can I have some money?

No! If you want some money, get a job!

4 His daughter Sara is 19, and works for Roger and Tom as a secretary.

If you marry him, you'll never see any of my money! Never!

But Dad – Alex and I are in love!

5 Tom's wife died five years ago. He lives alone in the house next door.

Hey, Roger, I've got a great idea for a new musical!

Stay away from my wife, Tom Turner, or you'll never write a musical again!

6 Then one morning at 10.30 …

2 After the murder, a police detective interviews Celia, Jack, Tom and Sara. Read what they say.

I was in the kitchen making Roger a cup of coffee. He was in his study playing the piano, and he suddenly stopped playing. He often does that, when he's writing a new song. I took his coffee into the study, and found him dead. The door into the garden was open, and there was a gun on the piano. I picked it up, and it was still warm. And then I screamed.

I was in Tom's house, working in his study. I was typing some notes on the new musical. Tom was out in the garden. I could hear Dad playing the piano next door – he plays really loudly! Then the playing stopped, and I heard a scream. So I ran back home, went in the front door, and went into Dad's study. Jack and my mother were already there.

I was upstairs in my bedroom, using my computer, and Dad was making a terrible noise on the piano, as usual. Then he stopped playing, and a minute later, I heard a loud scream. So I ran downstairs, and went into Dad's study, and I found my mother standing by the piano. She was holding a gun in her hand, and Dad was lying across the piano, covered in blood.

I was at home. Sara was in the study, typing on the computer, and I was walking around the garden, thinking about the new musical. Next door, I could hear Roger playing the piano. Suddenly I heard a shot, and the playing stopped. Then someone screamed. I ran back into my study – Sara was gone – and followed her round to Roger's house.

Who do you think killed Roger Ray? How do you know?

3 🔲 Now listen to the detective's explanation.

Who killed Roger Ray? How? How does the detective know?

Final review

Shopping

1 You work in one of these six shops
   Choose a shop, and write down five things you sell.

a fruit stall

a chemist

a vegetable stall

a furniture shop

a kiosk

a clothes shop

2 Now think of five things you want to buy from other shops. Write a shopping list.

Shopping list
shampoo
bananas   carrots
table lamp   socks

3 Try to buy the things on your shopping list from the other shops.

How many things did you manage to buy?

Which job?

Present job?   Hard work?   Work with your hands?

Interests?   Money?   Work with other people?

Experience?   Qualifications?

Leisure activities?   Travel?   Work indoors? Out of doors?

Student A
You're not sure what kind of job you want to do. You go to the Jobs Advice Centre for an interview. Answer their questions.

Student B
You work in the Jobs Advice Centre. Interview Student A, and give him/her your advice.

True or false?

On a piece of paper, write ten sentences about yourself. Five should be true and five should be false. Choose topics in the box.

> your age
>
> your job
>
> your family
>
> your personality
>
> where you come from
>
> your leisure activities
>
> a problem you have
>
> languages you speak
>
> your favourite kind of music
>
> countries you've visited
>
> what you're going to do this weekend
>
> a book you're reading at the moment
>
> what you did yesterday evening
>
> something important that's happened to you recently

Give the paper to other students. Can they tell which sentences are true and which are false?

Final review

Shopping

This activity is a game, in which students try to 'buy' items from various shops. It revises vocabulary from Units 6, 8, 10 and 12. It focuses on the names of shops and items of shopping, but also practises asking for things, describing, choosing, etc.

1 Preparation: shops

- Explain that each student will be both a shop assistant selling things and a customer buying things from other shops. Go round the class, assigning one of the six shops to each student in turn. Then give time for them to write down five things they sell (e.g. *kiosk*: *cigarettes, magazines, newspapers, pens, postcards*).

2 Preparation: shopping lists

- Look at the example shopping list, and ask students where they could buy each item. Answer:

  shampoo: at a kiosk or a chemist's
  bananas: at a fruit stall
  table lamp: at a furniture shop
  carrots: at a vegetable stall
  socks: at a clothes shop

- Give time for students to write their own shopping list. They should write five items that they could buy at any of the other shops (but not their own shop).

3 Game

- Students move freely round the class, trying to buy the things on their list from other people's 'shops', and selling the items they have in their own shop.
- As a round-up, find out how many students managed to buy all the items on their list.

  Alternatives:

1 Groupwork. Students sit in groups of six, with each shop represented by one student. They buy and sell items within their group.
2 Whole class. Ask six students (one for each shop) to come to the front of the class. Other students try to buy the things on the list from them. Then call another six students to the front, and so on until someone has bought all the items on his/her list.
3 Whole class. At the beginning of the activity, choose six students to be shop assistants. They write a list of what they sell, and the other students write a shopping list. Then call the shopkeepers to the front of the class. In turn, other students try to buy the items on their list.

Which job?

This is a role-play activity, in which students give each other advice about jobs. It revises language from Units 16, 17, 18 and 23.

Preparation

- Explain the situation:
  - Student A wants advice about jobs.
  - Student B finds out what kind of person Student A is, what he/she is interested in, etc., and then suggests a suitable job.
- Look at the question prompts, and establish what Student B's questions might be, e.g.

  What is your present job? What do you do?
  What are you interested in?
  What work have you done before?
  What do you do in your free time?
  Do you mind doing hard work?
  Do you want to earn a lot of money?
  What qualifications do you have?
  Do you like travelling?
  Do you like working with your hands? Are you good at working with your hands?
  Do you like working with other people?
  Do you want to work indoors or out of doors?

Role-play

- Students sit in groups of four or five. One student is interviewed by the others, who ask him/her questions. They then suggest a suitable job.

  Alternative: Whole class. One student comes to the front of the class. The rest of the class 'interview' him/her. In turn, students ask questions like those you have prepared. Then ask the class what job they think would be suitable.

True or false?

This activity revises language from most units in the book. It gives practice in exchanging personal information in English.

Preparation; writing sentences

- As a preparation, look at each topic in turn, and ask students to suggest sentences they might make, e.g.
  your family: *I've got two brothers amd a sister. My father is a policeman. I'm married.*
- Give time for students to write five true and five false sentences about themselves. They should of course do this alone, and mix the true and false sentences together.

Reading the sentences; guessing which are true

- Students exchange sentences with the person sitting next to them, and they try to guess which are true and which are false.
- As a round-up, ask a few students what they found out about their partner.

  Alternative: Whole class. Collect the sentences, and then read them out in turn. Ask the class which they think are true and which are false.

Can you remember?

The pictures are from earlier units:

A	Unit 7	G	Unit 16
B	Unit 6	H	Unit 18
C	Unit 8	I	Unit 15
D	Unit 10	J	Unit 22
E	Unit 12	K	Unit 20
F	Unit 14	L	Unit 22

Alternative 1: Whole class

- Choose pictures in turn, and ask students to talk about them. Prompt them by asking questions, e.g. *What can you see? What are the people doing? What is the man going to do? Where is this? Why is it famous?*

Alternative 2: Pair or individual preparation

- Working alone or in pairs, students choose a picture, and prepare a few things to say about it. They can either prepare by talking to their partner or by writing notes.

- Ask students in turn to say what picture they chose, and to talk briefly about it. If you like, let other students in the class ask them questions about the picture or about the topic.

Alternative 3: Fluency game

- Give students time to look at all the pictures and quickly prepare something to say about them.

- Start with any picture, and choose a student. The student talks about the picture, saying as much as he/she can. When the first student can't say any more, another student continues, and so on. When no one can say any more about the picture, choose another picture and repeat the procedure. If you like, give a point to the student who says the last thing about each picture.

Additional material for Unit 9 Exercise 2

Copy the sentences below.

Either: Give a sentence to each student. He/She mimes the situation and other students guess the sentence.

Or: Let the class see all the sentences. In turn, students choose a sentence and mime the situation. Other students guess which sentence it is.

1 You've just had a shower.
2 You've won the lottery.
3 You've just got up.
4 You've lost your wallet.
5 You've cut your finger.
6 You've just broken a vase.
7 You've just finished a meal.
8 You've just written a letter.
9 You've just bought some flowers.
10 You've just seen a ghost.
11 You've got engaged.
12 You've bought a new coat.

Can you remember?

All of these pictures are from earlier units. Choose one of the pictures.
What can you remember about it?

A

LINDBERGH FLIES
FROM NEW
YORK TO PARIS
First non-stop
solo flight
across the
Atlantic

B

C

D

E

F

G

H

I

Scotland

England

Wales

London

J

K

L

Additional material

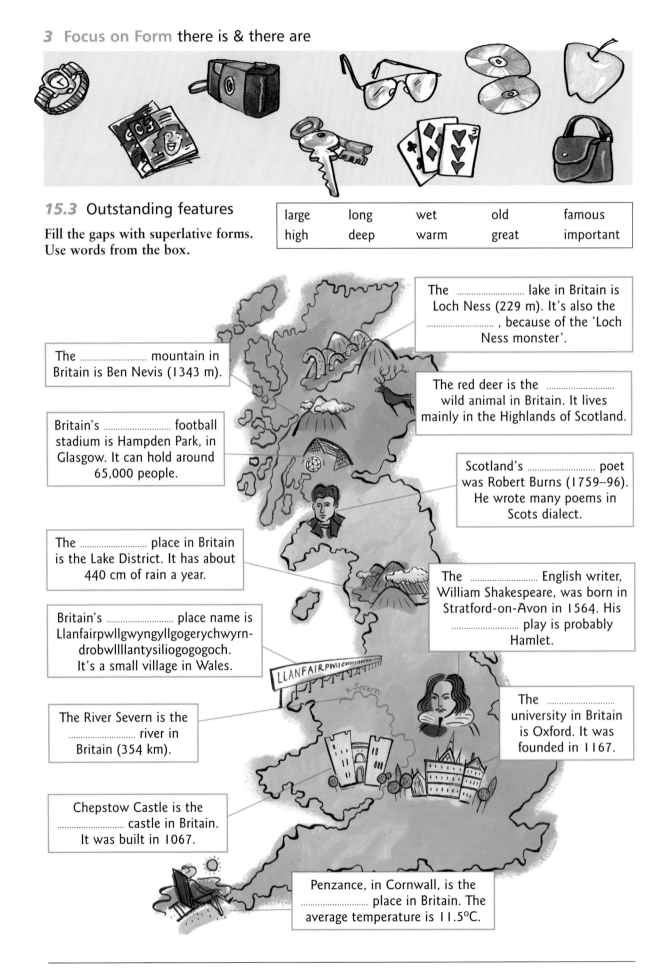

15.3 Outstanding features

Fill the gaps with superlative forms. Use words from the box.

large	long	wet	old	famous
high	deep	warm	great	important

The .... lake in Britain is Loch Ness (229 m). It's also the .... , because of the 'Loch Ness monster'.

The .... mountain in Britain is Ben Nevis (1343 m).

The red deer is the .... wild animal in Britain. It lives mainly in the Highlands of Scotland.

Britain's .... football stadium is Hampden Park, in Glasgow. It can hold around 65,000 people.

Scotland's .... poet was Robert Burns (1759–96). He wrote many poems in Scots dialect.

The .... place in Britain is the Lake District. It has about 440 cm of rain a year.

The .... English writer, William Shakespeare, was born in Stratford-on-Avon in 1564. His .... play is probably Hamlet.

Britain's .... place name is Llanfairpwllgwyngyllgogerychwyrn-drobwllllantysiliogogogoch. It's a small village in Wales.

The River Severn is the .... river in Britain (354 km).

The .... university in Britain is Oxford. It was founded in 1167.

Chepstow Castle is the .... castle in Britain. It was built in 1067.

Penzance, in Cornwall, is the .... place in Britain. The average temperature is 11.5ºC.

1.3 What do you know?

Student A

Make quiz questions.
Can Student B answer them?
(The right answers are in red.)

1 Pandas come from …

... Africa?
... China?
... India?

2 A baker sells …

... meat?
... fish?
... bread?

3 Americans celebrate
Independence Day …

... on 4th May?
... on 4th June?
... on 4th July?

Now answer B's questions.

15.2 General knowledge

Student A

Ask *Which …?* questions based
on these facts.

1 The temperature in Rio de
Janeiro in summer is about
29°C; in winter it's about 17°C.

The temperature in Hong Kong
in summer is about 28°C; in
winter it's about 15°C.

2 A human being has 32 teeth.
A crocodile has 64 teeth.

3 Mont Blanc is 4,807 metres
high.

Mount Kilimanjaro is 5,894
metres high.

4 The Kremlin was built in
1156.

Buckingham Palace was built
in 1705.

8.3 Everything in its place *Student A*

Study pages B Focus on … *Where things are*

1.3 What do you know?

Student B

Can you answer Student A's questions?

Now you make quiz questions. Can A answer them?
(The right answers are in red.)

1 Elephants come from …
   … Africa and China?
   … China and India?
   … India and Africa?

2 A greengrocer sells …
   … fruit and vegetables?
   … meat and fish?
   … papers and magazines?

3 Americans celebrate Hallowe'en …
   … on 31st June?
   … on 31st October?
   … on 31st December?

15.2 General knowledge

Student B

Ask *Which …?* questions based on these facts.

1 The United States of America is nearly 9.5 million square kilometres.

   Canada is nearly 10 million square kilometres.

2 The Greek alphabet has 24 letters.

   The Russian alphabet has 33 letters.

3 The Suez Canal is 162 kilometres long.

   The Panama Canal is 82 kilometres long.

4 The Atlantic Ocean is 3,300 metres deep, on average.

   The Pacific Ocean is 4,000 metres deep, on average.

8.3 Everything in its place *Student B*

5.2 There's a woman riding a bike

Study pages D Focus on ... *Both and neither*

A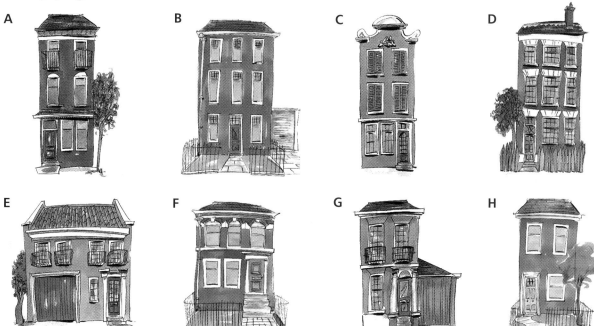
B
C
D

E
F
G
H

11.1 Find the differences *Student A*

20.1 Famous faces *Student A*

16.3 Spectator sports
Student A

1

2

3

4

19.3 Setting a scene

It was 10 o'clock when I got back to my hotel. I went into the lobby to get my key ...

The apartment wasn't locked. I opened the door slowly, and went inside ...

It was nearly 5 o'clock. I pulled back a curtain and looked down into the street ...

11.1 Find the differences *Student B*

20.1 Famous faces *Student B*

16.3 Spectator sports
Student B

17.3 Personal problems

My son steals

I think your son is crying out for more attention and love from you. Until he was 7, he was the only child, and he had you all to himself. Now, you say, you all do things together – that is, he has to share you with his little sister. Does he ever get to spend time alone with you, without his sister? If not, maybe he feels that you don't love him as much as you did before. Try to find some time every day especially for him – perhaps after his sister's bedtime – and ask your husband to do the same. If your son feels that he's an important part of your lives, perhaps he'll stop stealing – and he'll like his little sister more, too.

22.3 Tourist attractions

The Great Barrier Reef

is a huge group of coral reefs. It's more than 2,000 km long, and has more than 600 islands.

Where is it? Off the coast of Queensland, in north eastern Australia.

How to get there By boat from Queensland, or, if you can afford it, by plane or helicopter.

Where to stay About 20 of the islands have hotels – some of them *very* expensive! You can camp on some other islands, but bring everything you need with you.

What to do Diving, walking, fishing, trips in glass-bottomed boats.

What to see Coral; thousands of species of fish and birds; lots of turtles; some whales; a few sharks.

When to go This is a tropical area, and June and July (the local winter months) are pleasantly warm.

24.3 What's on TV?

Channel 1

6.00 News, weather
6.30 Sports news
6.45 Today. The main stories behind the news.
7.30 Focus: *The World Wide Web*. How is the Internet changing our lives?
8.30 Wildlife on One. The lions of the Sahara.

9.00 News, weather
9.15 Business week

Channel 2

6.00 Dancing **FILM** **shoes** (1942). Fred Astaire and Ginger Rogers star in this romantic musical.

7.45 News round-up
8.15 True Grit **FILM** (1969). Western starring John Wayne.

TV GOLD

6.00 The boys next door. Comedy series.
6.30 Detective! *Who shot the pianist?* Another murder mystery for Inspector Wallis.
7.30 That's the question. Quiz show with Matt Murphey.
8.00 News
8.15 My first billion. Interviews with very rich people. This week: Bill Gates.
9.00 Downtown. Jill falls in love – and Rod has a problem.
9.30 Streetlife. More soap from the City. Will Sue and Trev get back together?

INTER TV

6.00 Football, live from Milan.
8.00 Formula 1 motor-racing. All the latest news from Tokyo.
8.30 X-treme sports: Skateboarding and snowboarding.

9.00 Sports news
9.15 Rocky 2 **FILM** (1983) Sylvester Stallone stars as boxing hero Rocky Marciano.

FAMILIA

6.00 Cartoon time. American cartoons.
7.00 Top of the Charts. This week's top 40.
7.30 Band of the week: The Morgs in Concert.

9.00 News
9.05 Play it again, Sam! Music quiz. This week's guest is Susan Shields.

Tapescripts

1.1 Couples

1 Yeah, we like the same things, mostly. We both like music, so we listen to music a lot. Richard always goes to rock concerts, and I often go with him. And, yeah, we go out a lot together – we both like staying up late, so that's good.

2 Mark and I go out quite a lot – we have the same group of friends, so we all go out together usually. I get up early and go to bed early. Mark's more a late night person, I'd say – he often stays out really late.

3 John gets up early, which I don't do – I always get up late. And he usually works early in the morning, but I usually work late at night – so that's a bit of a problem, really.

2.1 Photo album

This is Julie and David and me. That's David in the middle – he's my boyfriend. And that's Julie on the left. She's my flat-mate – she's a secretary.

Now this is my grandmother. She's nearly 80 now. This picture was at a wedding, I think.

Oh, then this one, this is another picture of my boyfriend, David. And that's my brother, in the black jacket – he's 23, he works for television. And next to him is his girlfriend – she's an actress.

And this is me with my younger brother – he's 13.

2.4 Identical twins

Did you read about these twins from Minnesota? They're 40 years old, and they just met for the first time. They grew up in different families, never saw each other until … a few weeks ago, I think it was. And it turns out that they both have the same name, they're both called Jim. One of them married twice, the other one married three times – but their first wives were both called Linda, and their second wives were both called Betty. And they both have sons with the same name, and they both had dogs at some time, and their dogs both had the same name, they were both called Toy. They live in different towns, obviously, and they have different jobs, I think – yeah, one's a mechanic and the other one's a shop assistant. But they both drive the same kind of car – Chevrolet, I think it was. Oh yeah, and they both go to the same place in Florida for their holidays, the same beach even – though they never met there. Absolutely incredible.

Study pages A
Focus on … Personal data

OK, my name's Tim Dalton, that's D-A-L-T-O-N, Dalton. I'm English, and I was born on 28th June, 1982. My address is 163 Cannery Street – that's C-A-double N-E-R-Y, Cannery Street, and that's in Bristol, B-R-I-S-T-O-L, England. My phone number is 0117 650991. My car is a Honda Civic, C-I-V-I-C, Civic, and its number is W376 SBY, I think. Yes, it is. W376 SBY.

Study pages A
Phrasebook: Introductions

A Louise, I'd like you to meet my cousin, Richard.
B Hello, Louise.
C Hello, nice to meet you.
A And this is our neighbour, Mrs Green.
C Oh, how do you do?

3.3 Is there a swimming pool?

1 Oh yes, well, I love this hotel. I always go there. There's a very good restaurant. There's a nice bar, where you can sit and talk to people. And there's a good business centre in the hotel, with computers. And it's near the airport, so it's very convenient.

2 Well, it's not bad. The rooms are comfortable, but they're quite expensive. It's a long way from the centre of town. And there's a nice garden to sit in, but no swimming pool. And the restaurant's good, but again I think it's quite expensive.

3 Yes, I like staying there. The rooms are comfortable, they have big bathrooms. The beds are comfortable, too, which is good. You can also have breakfast in bed. I always have a room at the back, so it's nice and quiet. And there's a lovely garden at the back, too.

4.3 Tourist information

1 A How can I get to the airport?
  B The airport? You can get there by bus or by taxi.
  A How much does it cost?
  B The bus is £5, and a taxi is about £25.

2 A Excuse me, how can I get to the National Theatre?
  B The best way is by underground.
  A Right. How long does it take?
  B About 15 minutes. It isn't very far.

4.4 Airport

1 Well, I don't like flying very much, so I'm usually a bit nervous at airports. I like… I like to sit near the notice boards and listen to all the announcements, because I'm always worried that I'm going to go to the wrong place, or miss the plane.

2 I get a bit bored at airports. The flights are always late, and there isn't much to do, you just have to sit and wait. Sometimes I look around the duty-free shops, but usually I just take a good book to read, or listen to music, maybe, on my Walkman.

3 I always find airports very exciting places to be. I like the feeling of people travelling, going to far-away places. Yeah, it's really exciting. I like to walk around, see the planes taking off and landing, and just look at all the other people, see where they're going, what they're doing. Yeah, I really enjoy it.

Study pages B
Pronunciation: Small words (1)

1 It has tomato and onion in it.
2 She works for an American company.
3 It's in front of the café.
4 The plane leaves at midday.
5 Nice to meet you.
6 I come from London.
7 Tell them your name.
8 There are some magazines on the table.

Study pages B
Phrasebook: Buying a ticket (1)

A A ticket to Cambridge, please.
B Single or return?
A Return.
B That's £45, please.
A When does the train leave?
B 6.30, from Platform 3.

5.1 Imagine …

I'm in a plane, up above the clouds, and we're travelling to South Africa. And I'm with my girlfriend, she's sitting next to me, and I'm looking out of the window – I can see mountains, far below us. And my girlfriend is reading a book, and she's drinking a glass of fruit juice. And the other people on the plane are reading, and they're all wearing grey suits. But I'm wearing a white T-shirt with a big yellow sun on it.

6.1 Dishes

This is Murgh Korma, it's a curry dish from India. It's made with chicken, with yoghurt, onion, garlic and lots of spices. And you eat it with bread or rice.

Now this is Spaghetti Bolognese, a very well-known dish from Italy. The Bolognese sauce is made with minced beef and pork, tomato, onions, garlic and red wine.

This is Töltött Paprika, which is a very popular dish in Hungary. It's made with peppers, and they're filled with minced meat – pork or beef, usually – rice and onion, and spices. And it's cooked with tomato.

And this is Irish Stew – it's a popular dish in Ireland. It's made with lamb cooked with potatoes, carrots and onions.

This is Jambalaya, it's a dish from the USA. It's made with rice, onions, peppers and tomatoes. And it can have prawns, chicken, pork or pieces of sausage in it.

6.4 Unusual places to eat

A Well, I don't think Twins is real. How could you find so many identical twins to be waiters, waitresses, cooks? It says 'All 80 people who work there are twins'.
B Well, New York's a very big city.
A Yes, I know, but even so …
C Well, I think Colours isn't a real restaurant.
A Why not?
C Well, it says 'On Wednesdays everything is blue and purple'. What food do you know that's blue or purple?
A Fruit.
B Aubergines.
C Hmm. You can't just have fruit and aubergines on the menu.
A No, that's true. Well, what do you think?
B I think they're all real except Dracula's.
C Why?
B Because of this picture. I don't think it's a real restaurant.
C But it says 'restaurant' in the picture.
B Yes, I know, but I think it's from a film.
A Yes, a Dracula film.
B I don't think it's a real place. It doesn't look real, does it?
C But what about the Red Sea Star Restaurant? That's a bit strange, too.
A Why's that strange? There's a photo of it. That must be real.
C Yes, but who says it's a photo of a restaurant? It could be anything.
B Yeah, and the other thing is, it says it's 35 metres from land. So how do you get there? By boat or what?
A Well, they all seem rather strange, don't they? Maybe none of them are real.

Study pages C
Phrasebook: In a café

1 A Let's sit here.
  B Oh, yes.
2 B Excuse me. Could we see the menu, please?
  C Yes, of course. Just a moment.
3 C Now, what would you like?
  A I'd like a strawberry ice-cream.
  C Strawberry ice-cream.
  B And I'd like a coffee, please.
4 A Could we have the bill, please?
  C The bill. Yes, certainly. I'll bring it.

7.2 Did you have a good time?

A Oh hello! When did you get back?
B This morning. About 3 o'clock in the morning.
A Did you have a good time?
B Yeah, really good, yeah.
C How did you get there? By plane?
B No, I drove there.
C It's a long way to drive. Did you stop on the way?
B I stopped twice, for something to eat. That was all.
D Did you go to Vienna?
B Yeah, I spent about three days in Vienna.
D Where did you stay?
B Well, I had some friends there, so I stayed with them. They showed me round – it was really good.

7.3 Three days ago

A OK. When did you last go away for the weekend?
B Go away? Probably two months ago. I went to Scotland.
A And when did you last go out for a drink or a meal?
B Two days ago – on Wednesday. I went out to a Chinese restaurant.
A OK. When did you last go to the theatre, the cinema or a concert?
B Oh, well – I went to a rock concert at the weekend, so that was six days ago.
A And when did you last go out for a walk, a run or a swim?
B Well, again at the weekend. I went for a walk on Sunday – so that was five days ago.
A Right. When did you last go to a party, a club or a disco?
B Exactly a week ago. I went to a party last Friday.
A OK. And when did you last visit friends or relatives?
B Oh, about two hours ago. I went to a friend's house.
A OK. Thank you.

8.2 Rooms

1 It was quite a small room. It had a bed – a single bed – a cupboard, a television, a very small table and a chair. Oh, and there was one picture on the wall. And there was a phone beside the bed.
2 It was a very comfortable room. It had a sofa and an armchair, and a thick carpet. There was a television and a music system, and some bookshelves with all my books on them.
3 It was quite a large room, and it had chairs round the walls. And in the middle of the room there was a low table with magazines on it. And there were posters on the walls, and a clock.

8.4 Two ghost stories

This happened when I was about three years old. I don't actually remember it myself, but my parents told me about it later. Well, we had a cellar underneath the house where my mother did the washing, and I said I wanted to look in this little room at the side – we had a little room where we kept coal. And so we went inside, my mother and I, and it was empty and dark, and I said, 'Oh, look at that lady in the corner.' And I described an old lady in the corner – she had grey hair and she had a coloured apron, but I was the only person who could see this woman. And so we went upstairs very quickly, and my mother didn't want to go down to the cellar again for three weeks after that. And then later, my parents talked to the neighbours about it, and the neighbours said, 'Well, did you know that the woman who lived in the house before you was a rather strange old lady, and she had grey hair and she always wore a coloured apron. And she died in the cellar.'

Study pages D
Focus on … Both & neither

A Have the houses got three floors?
B One of them has got three floors, yes.
A And has one of the houses got a garage?
B Yes, one of them has got a garage.
A Hmm. What about trees?
B Both the houses have got trees.
A Both of them, right. So both of them have got trees, one of them has got a garage, one of them has got three floors … Have the houses got red doors?
B Yes, both of them have got red doors.

Study pages D
Pronunciation: Small words (2)

1 What was his name?
2 Where are you going?
3 You can get there by bus.
4 I was there a few days ago.
5 When does the train leave?
6 Where can I change money?
7 There are three bedrooms.
8 What was the film like?

Study pages D
Phrasebook: Finding a room

A Have you got any rooms free?
B Yes, we have. For how many people?
A Two.
B Do you want a double room or two single rooms?
A Two single rooms, with a shower.
B OK. Each room costs £50 a night.
A £50? Oh, dear. Have you got anything cheaper?
B No, sorry, that's all we've got.
A OK, thanks. Bye.

9.1 It's just happened

Hello. Yeah, I've just come out of the building, and I'm walking down the street to the station … Hello. I've arrived at the station now, I'm just buying a ticket … Hi. I've just got on the train – I'm having a cup of coffee … Hello, it's me again. I've just got off the train, and I'm coming out of the station … Hi. I've just gone into the supermarket – I'm buying some bread. Yeah, yeah, yeah, see you soon. Bye!

9.3 Have you …?

A Right, off we go.
B Have you turned the lights off?
A Yes, I have.
B Have you closed all the windows?
B Yes, yes.
A OK. Let's go then.
B Actually …
A What?
A I haven't closed the front door.

10.2 Can I try it on?

A Excuse me. What size is this jacket?
B It's 46.
A Oh, good. Can I try it on?
B Yes, of course. Here you are.
A Thanks … How does it look?
B Mmm. It looks very good. It really suits you. Does it feel OK?

A Yes, it's fine. It fits very well – it's really comfortable. How much is it?
B £65.
A Oh, that's not too expensive. I think I'll buy it.

10.3 When do you wear …?

1 I usually wear a tie at work. I don't wear one at home usually – only if we have very important visitors or something. But I nearly always wear a tie if I go out for a meal, or to the theatre or cinema or something like that.
2 I don't usually wear a tie, but if I go out to a party or a meal or a wedding, some occasion like that, yes, then I do wear a tie.
3 Well, unfortunately I have to wear a tie at the office where I work, but I hate wearing ties, and usually I put on my tie just before I get to the office and I take it off again when I leave the office. I certainly don't wear a tie at home, no.

10.4 The purple dress

It was terrible. I thought, 'What am I going to do? I must buy her another one.' So I went round all the expensive shops in town, and of course I couldn't find the same dress. So I went to catch the bus home. And by the bus stop there was another charity shop. And it was amazing, there was a purple dress in the window just like my cousin's, and it had a label saying £5. So I went inside and bought it. And the shop assistant said, 'Yes, a woman brought this in this morning. She said she only bought it yesterday, but when she got home, she found it wasn't the right size. So she gave it back to us.' So I took the dress to the cleaner's, and at the weekend I gave it back to my cousin. And she said, 'It's a funny thing. I was in town last week and I saw a dress just like this one. And do you know, it was in the window of a charity shop!'

Study pages E
Focus on … Mine, yours, …

1 A Is this coat yours?
  B No, I think it's hers.
  C Yes, it's mine.
2 A Whose is this?
  B I don't know – it isn't ours. Maybe it's theirs.
3 A Is this coat John's?
  B No, his is grey. That one's Sam's, I think.

Study pages E
Phrasebook: Paying for things

1 A That'll be £6.50, please.
  B Can I pay by cheque?
  A Yes. Do you have a cheque card?
  B Yes, I do.
  A That's all right, then.
2 A So that's £2 altogether, then.
  B Do you take credit cards?
  A No, sorry, we don't.
3 A That's £25, then.

B There you are. Could I have a receipt?
A Yes, certainly. Just a minute.

11.1 Find the differences

A Well, on the plate there are some bananas and an orange.
B What about grapes?
A No, there aren't any grapes.
B What's on the table?
A On the table there are some plates, and some bread, and a bottle of … wine, I think.
B Can you see any cheese in your picture?
A Yes. There's some cheese on the shelf.
B Are there any glasses on the shelf?
A Glasses? Yes. Three glasses.
B Any cups?
A No, there aren't any cups.

11.3 Complaints

1 Well, there's too much traffic, certainly, and too much noise from cars and lorries.
2 There aren't enough parks or trees, or green spaces generally.
3 Well, I think there are too many tourist buses, they make it very difficult to drive in the centre of town – in fact there are too many tourists in the summer, I think.
4 There's too much rubbish in the streets – they should clean the streets more often.
5 There aren't enough good clothes shops – I can never find anything I want to buy.

12.2 Cures

1 Well, I have very noisy neighbours in the flat above me, and they like dancing late at night. So I have a large cushion next to my bed, and I put the cushion over my head and I try to get to sleep. But if I still can't sleep, I take a broom and I bang on the ceiling. And then they always stop.
2 If you have hiccups, you should ask a friend to put his or her fingers in your ears, while you drink from a full glass of water.
3 This is my grandfather's cure for a cold. Get a bottle of brandy and a glass, and a hat. Then go to bed, and put the hat at the end of the bed. Drink a glass of brandy, then drink another glass, and keep drinking until you can see three hats at the end of the bed. Then go to sleep, and in the morning you'll be fine.

12.3 Going to the doctor

About a month ago I was at work as usual, I was at my desk working with my computer, and suddenly I felt really ill – I felt very hot and I had a headache and my eyes hurt a lot. So I phoned and made an appointment to see the doctor. And that evening I went to see the doctor, and he asked me a lot of questions, and he asked me to take my shirt off and he examined me. He looked at my eyes and

my ears. And in the end he said, 'Well, you've got the 'flu'. And he wrote me a prescription for some medicine, and he told me to go to bed and take the medicine three times a day and stay in bed for a few days. So anyway, I went to the chemist's to get the medicine, and then I went home and went to bed, just as the doctor told me. And, I stayed in bed for three days and slept. Well, sure enough, after that I felt better and I went back to work. But the funny thing is that I don't think I got better because of the medicine at all. I think I just needed three days away from my computer.

12.4 A long and healthy life

A This is quite wrong. You do get energy from meat, but also from eggs, milk, fish and many vegetables. You certainly don't need to eat meat to be healthy.
B Many people think you need eight hours' sleep. But in fact six hours is quite enough to be fit and healthy. And sleeping too long – nine hours or more – is actually bad for you.
C Bread, cheese, butter and crisps have a lot of calories, so they won't help you to lose weight. Maybe lunch in the restaurant was a better idea!
D It is true that, on average, people with partners live longer. But of course you have to be happy with your partner, and also have a healthy life.
E This is wrong. If you drink alcohol before you go to sleep, you sleep less well. You sleep very heavily for the first few hours, and you don't dream so much. And dreams are very important.
F It is true that if you have a heart problem, a small quantity of alcohol every day is good for you. But maybe your grandfather doesn't need half a bottle – just a glass or two would be better.
G In fact, that isn't true. If you do exercise regularly, you actually start to feel less hungry.
H Yes, it's true that if your parents and grandparents live long, then you have a good chance of living long – long life runs in families.

Study pages F
Focus on … For & since

A How long have you been here?
B Me? I've been here for about an hour.
A How about you?
C I've been here since 9 o'clock. I was one of the first people here.

Study pages F
Pronunciation: Small words (3)

1 Are you coming to the party?
2 What was his name again?
3 What can I do to help?
4 Where are we meeting them?
5 Can she swim?
  I think she can.
6 John! where are you?

Phrasebook: Making an appointment

A I'd like to make an appointment to see the doctor.
B Yes. Is it urgent?
A Fairly urgent, yes.
B OK. Can you come this afternoon?
A Yes, I can.
B OK. How about 4.30?
A Yes, that's fine.

13.1 Fortune telling

Well, you'll meet a tall dark stranger. At first you won't like him, but after a time you'll fall in love with him. But you won't be happy together, and you won't stay together very long. After a few months you'll leave him, and then you'll go on a long journey, and you'll go to live in a foreign country. You'll buy a house there, a small house by the sea, and you'll get married. You won't be very rich, but you'll be happy.

13.3 A bright future?

OK, the first one: 'Everyone will have enough food to eat.' No that won't happen – in fact I think people will probably have less food in the future. 'People will live 100 years or more' – maybe, it might happen. Rich people probably will live longer.
'We'll find a cure for cancer' – yes, I think we will, probably. I think it's happening already.
'There will be peace everywhere' – no, that certainly won't happen. I think there will always be wars.
'We'll discover a new kind of energy' – I'm not sure. That might happen – maybe some completely new way to travel. It's possible.
'There will be another world war' – yes, unfortunately, I think that will probably happen.
'We'll run out of oil and gas' – yes, certainly, that will happen.
'All the fish in the sea will die' – there are very few fish already, so I think it will probably happen.
'New diseases' – yes, I think that will probably happen. It happens now, so why not in the future too?
'Unfriendly aliens will attack the Earth' – no, that won't happen.

14.3 How to get there

1 Well, you go out of the station, and you come to a main road. Turn left there, go along that road to the end. Then turn left again, go under a railway bridge, and a bit further on you'll come to a garage. Turn left there, go down that road, and you'll see it on your left – it's a big building.
2 OK. Well, when you come out of the station you'll see a main road, all right? Turn right, go along that road, and carry straight on till you come to the main square – it's a big square, you'll see it. Then turn left, go past a church, and

you'll come to the river, OK? Now just before the river, there's a small road to the left. So go down that road, and it's about 100 metres down that road.

14.4 Los Angeles

Last year I went to Hollywood for two weeks. My friend picked me up at the airport and we drove in her car back to Hollywood. At first I was a bit disappointed, because it all looked rather untidy and dirty. But later on she showed me some of the sights. She drove me through all the very expensive areas like Belair, where the houses are absolutely enormous. And she took me to Universal Studios, where they make the great Hollywood films. We went to Disneyland, which is a little way outside Los Angeles, and we spent a whole day there – I really enjoyed it. And on another day she took me to see a place about 50 miles from Los Angeles, called Santa Barbara, which is a beautiful resort on the beach, and I swam in the Pacific Ocean. The people there were so polite and friendly, which I liked a lot. I had a wonderful time.

Phrasebook: Buying a ticket (2)

A: Two tickets for *Star Wars*, please.
B: Both adults?
A: No, one adult and one child.
B: That's £13, please.
A: What time does the film start?
B: At 7.30.

15.1 It's much better

a A The Regal Hotel's not bad, but the Metropole's much better.
  B Do you think so? Why?
  A Well, for one thing it's much quieter at night, the rooms are more comfortable as well – and I think the staff are more helpful. And it's cheaper.
b A I really like my new job. It's much better than my old one.
  B Is it? How?
  A Well, the work's more interesting, everyone's friendlier, and the hours are shorter, too.
c A I'm glad I moved into the city centre. It's much better than living out in the suburbs.
  B Really? Why's that?
  A Well, it's nearer my office, that's the main thing. But it's also more convenient for the shops and things, you know? It's livelier too, especially at the weekends.

16.1 Leisure activities

Louisa
I enjoy practising the piano, and doing the piano. I have a very good teacher called Miss Rowe. I learn the violin, and I enjoy that a lot. I collect shells and rocks, and I've got quite a lot of them. And I go swimming now and again, and I like bike riding.

Carsten
Well, I go running a lot – I live near a forest, so I go running in the forest. I listen to music, especially jazz. And I also cook – I like cooking for other other people, especially. Oh, and I also watch Formula 1 motor racing – that's a hobby of mine, too.

Josephine
I live very near the sea. All through the year I go for walks along the shore, and in the summer I go swimming every day. In the winter I like knitting – I make jumpers for my children and my grandchildren, and I enjoy doing different patterns. I spend a lot of time reading, mostly novels, and I'm very fond of poetry – I also write poetry now and then.

Patrick
I go to the theatre a lot, to see plays. I read a lot, I read a lot of books. I play golf sometimes, when I can. And I have an old house, which needs a lot of work, so I spend a lot of time at home painting the walls, mending things – looking after the house, really. I enjoy that.

16.4 A question of sport

1 Just three hundred metres to go now, and it's Comistar, then London Lady, and then coming up fast is Primo Valentino on the far side, and Primo Valentino is now in second place. Comistar, then Primo Valentino, and here comes Primo Valentino, he's going to win, just a few metres to go and it's Primo Valentino first, Comistar is second, and London lady in third place …
2 And this is Woods at the fifteenth, just off the green. This is a difficult shot, about six and a half, seven metres from the hole. And he hits it. And it's looking good, looking very good, and oh, it's stopped just short of the hole. And he'll be disappointed with that …
3 Murphy … to Berger … lovely little run up the right side, and now Owen, and it's still Owen, he's in the box, he's going to score, and – oh, what a save! A fantastic save from Seaman! The ball goes behind the goal, and it's a corner for Liverpool …
4 And they're away, and Green has made a very good start in lane 2, and so has Boldon in lane 5, and this is going to be very fast time, and Green is way ahead of the rest of the field, and it's a very fast time indeed. And Maurice Green has won the gold in the men's hundred metres – oh, and it's a new world record – an incredible time of 9.79 seconds …
5 So, 29 laps gone, 25 laps still to go, and it's still Mika Hakkinen in the lead, and Frentzen just behind in second place. And Hakkinen's lost control! He's taken the corner too fast, and he's left the track. Incredible! Mika Hakkinen is out of the race, so now it's Heinz Harald Frentzen in the lead …

Phrasebook: Asking where

1 A Excuse me, is there anywhere near here where we can play football?
  B Well, there's quite a big park just down that road. You can play football there.
2 A Excuse me, is there a park near here?
  B There isn't one very near here, but there's one down by the river. That's about 15 minutes away.

17.1 Renting a room

A Hello. 764 293.
B Oh, hello. I'm phoning about the rooms you have to rent. Is there still one free?
A Yes, there is, yes.
B Could you tell me a few things about it? Do I have to share the room with other people?
A No, you don't. They're all single rooms.
B I see. And what about visitors? Can I have visitors?
A Yes, you can, but only till 9 in the evening. They have to be out by 9.
B OK. Do I have to pay in advance?
A Yes. You have to pay one month in advance.
B I see. One other thing – can I keep pets in the room? I've got a small cat.
A No. You can't have pets, sorry.
B Oh, that's a pity. Well, I think I'll leave it, then. Thanks.
A All right, then. Goodbye.

18.3 A working life

Well, I studied economics at university, and then I got a job as an accountant in a local department store. It wasn't exactly what I wanted, but you know, it was a first job. Then after three years they promoted me to accounts manager, and I stayed in that job for a year, but then I got really bored, so I decided to leave, and I applied for other jobs in the area. But I couldn't find anything at all. So in the end I had to work as a waitress in a restaurant. Well, I wasn't very good at it, I was too slow and I kept breaking things, so after a few weeks they gave me the sack. And then just by chance I met an old friend who I knew at university, and he had a job in television. And he got me a job as a researcher for a TV programme called 'Business Today'. And then after a few months they decided they wanted younger presenters on the programme, so I got the job – and I love it.

18.4 Applying for a job

Part 1
A I'm so sorry I'm late. I couldn't find your office.
B That's all right. Sit down. Now. You're working at a hotel in Brighton.
A That's right.
B What kind of work do you do?
A Well, I'm a receptionist, so I answer the phone and sit at the reception desk, obviously, and give people their keys and … generally work as a receptionist.

Part 2
B Now at this hotel we do everything on computers, of course, so you'll have a computer at the reception desk. Do you have experience of computers?
A Well, I don't use a computer in my job at the moment, no – it's just a small family hotel – but we learned about computers at college, and I used a computer when I worked in an office, so I don't think that would be a problem.

Part 3
B Now, why do you want to leave your present job and come here?
A Well, as I said, the hotel where I am now is a very small hotel, and I really want to work somewhere bigger. Also the hours are very long.
B The hours are long. So you don't want to work long hours, then?
A Oh yes, I don't mind working hard. I just mean that the job's a bit boring, you know. There isn't really enough to do.
B I see.

Phrasebook: Renting things

A How much does it cost to rent a bike?
B It's £5 an hour, or £30 for the whole day.
A Do I have to pay in advance?
B No. No, you just give me a ten pound deposit.
A OK.

19.1 How did it happen?

1 I was on my way home from work. I was walking under a ladder, and someone was painting a window. And he slipped, and a can of green paint fell on my head.
2 I was going down some steps, and it was raining, and I slipped and went down about ten steps, and I broke my leg.
3 I was late for work and I was running for a bus when I tripped and I hurt my arm.
4 I was walking through the park when suddenly a huge dog came up to me and bit me on the leg.

20.1 Famous faces

1 Nelson Mandela isn't very tall, and he has very short curly grey hair. And he has quite small eyes.
2 Indira Gandhi was a tall woman, and she had wavy black hair with a white stripe in it. And she had a long thin face and a hooked nose.
3 Well, Stalin had a big black moustache, and thick black eyebrows, and he had black hair. And he wasn't very tall, but he was quite well-built.
4 Margaret Thatcher has wavy fair hair, and a thin face with a pointed nose. And she always wears earrings and a necklace.
5 Mao Zedong had a round face and quite a small nose. And he was partly bald. And he was quite fat – at least when he was older.

6 Abraham Lincoln was tall, and he had a long thin face and a beard. And he had quite long hair.

20.3 Character adjectives

1 A Chris – I'm dying for a cup of tea. I don't suppose you could lend me 50p, could you?
  B Of course I'll lend you 50p. Look, 50p's not much good – why don't you … look, why don't you have £5, that'll keep you going all day.
  A Oh …
  B You can pay me back whenever you want – doesn't matter.
  A Oh thanks, thanks very much.
2 A Hello. Gosh, it's very hot and crowded in here, isn't it?
  B Yes, it is a bit.
  A My name's Ann.
  B Oh. Um …
  A What's yours?
  B C-Chris.
  A Chris. Hi.
  B Hi.
3 A Excuse me, I say … Sorry, but you just dropped this £10 note.
  B What? Oh, oh, oh, oh thank you, oh dear, oh thank you very much.
  A That's all right. Just – I should put it in your purse if I were you.
  B Oh, oh dear, wait a minute – where's my – oh, here we are, yes.
  A All right?
  B Yes. Yes, thanks very much. Bye.

20.4 Are you a loner?

OK. 'Where do you think is the best place to live?' The town centre, definitely. There's more to do, and you meet more people. I live in the town centre, and I really like it.

OK, question 2. Oh, I'd meet some friends for a drink. I think I'd want to be with close friends, not a lot of people I don't know very well.

Now, 'Which kind of holiday would you enjoy?' Um, probably a busy seaside town with lots to do. Yes, definitely, that's what I'd like. Not staying with my family in the country.

Number 4. 'You go to a friend's party …' Well, I like meeting people, but you can't just go up to people and say 'Hi', so I think I'd ask my friend to introduce me, yes.

5: 'You're alone on New Year's Eve. How do you feel?' Oh, very lonely, I think. Last year I spent New Year's Eve just with my parents and my brother, and that was really boring, so, yes, I'd be really lonely on my own.

OK 6. No, I wouldn't enjoy eating in a restaurant alone. 'Going on a long journey alone' – oh no, I'd want someone to talk to. Swimming alone, yes, that's all right – I think you get more exercise if you're alone. 'Going to the cinema' – well, I always want to talk about the film to someone while I'm watching it, so 'No'. 'Spending a weekend alone at home.' No, that's a long time, that's too long. A few hours would be OK, but not a whole weekend. And 'cooking a big meal just for yourself' – no. First of all, I don't eat much, and anyway if you cook a big meal, you want to eat it with other people, I think. So 'No'.

Study pages J
Phrasebook: Personal questions

1 A What do you do?
  B I'm a secretary. How about you?
  A Oh, I'm an accountant.
2 A What nationality are you?
  B I'm Swiss.
  A Oh, Swiss.
  B Yes. What about you?
  A I'm Canadian.
3 A How old are you, by the way?
  B I'm nearly 18. How about you?
  A Guess!
  B 20?
  A 21!
4 A What languages do you speak?
  B Arabic and French. What about you?
  A Me? I only speak English.
5 A So what are you studying?
  B European history.
  A Mm. That sounds interesting.
6 A Where do you live?
  B In a small town near London. Dorking, it's called.
  A Oh yes, I know it.
  B Where do you live, then?
  A I live in Manchester.

21.2 I'll probably …

A I'll probably go to Los Angeles, because I've got a cousin who lives there – and maybe I'll find a job there and stay there for a year or two.
B First I'm going to have a long holiday. And then I'm not sure what I'll do – I'll probably work in a café or a bar for a time, to earn some money.
C Well, I know exactly what I'm going to do. I'm going to study for a Master's degree, and then I'm going to teach at university.

22.2 What's it like?

1 Well, Finland is very flat. A lot of the country is covered in forest, and there are thousands of lakes. It's got quite a small population. And it's very cold in winter – it can go down to minus 40°.
2 Hawaii is a group of islands in the Pacific Ocean. The islands are quite mountainous, and they're covered in forest. Hawaii has got a lot of volcanoes and beautiful beaches, and it's very hot for most of the year.
3 Egypt is quite flat. It hardly ever rains and most of the country is desert, except for the valley of the River Nile, which is very rich farmland. It's very hot for most of the year, and it's got quite a large population.

22.4 www

1 I find the Internet is very good for shopping. We use it more and more for buying books and CDs, and I even bought some clothes over the Internet. The other thing you can do is book holidays over the Internet. We booked a cheap flight once, and it was very easy, and it was really good.
2 I use the Internet for games. I play chess with people all round the world. Last night I had a game with someone from Japan. I also download games from the Internet, so I can have any game I want.
3 I use the Internet for anything I need to help me with my schoolwork. I use the online dictionaries, encyclopaedias and magazines. It's great because I can download pictures or articles and use them with my homework. It's very easy to use and it's free, so I like it.
4 Well, the main thing I use the Internet for is email. I've got a small business, and we don't really send letters very much any more. When I write to customers I usually do it by email, and my customers write to me by email. We probably send and receive four or five hundred emails a week. But of course I also use email to keep in touch with friends and family. I've got a daughter in Australia, for example, and she sends me an email almost every day.

Study pages K
Focus on … Nothing, no one, nowhere

1 A Where are you going?
  B Nowhere special.
2 A What are you doing?
  B Nothing.
3 A Who are you talking to?
  B No one.

Study pages K
Phrasebook: Arranging to meet

A What are you doing on Friday evening?
B Nothing special. Why?
A Would you like to come to a party?
B Yes, I'd love to.
A OK. Shall we meet at about 8 o'clock, then?
B OK, fine. Where shall we meet, then?
A Do you know the new café just opposite the museum?
B Yes, I do.
A Let's meet there. 8 o'clock?
B OK. Great.

23.2 Where are they now?

A What's Sarah doing now? Has she found a job yet?
B No, not yet. She's still looking for one.
A And is she still living in that caravan?
B No. She's moved into a flat now.

24.2 Famous people

1 OK, this person was a painter. He was Spanish, but he painted most of his pictures in France, and he lived in Paris. He liked women – he was married four times. And his most famous painting was *Guernica*.
2 This person was a composer. He was German. He lived in the 19th century. And towards the end of his life he was deaf, but he still wrote music. And he wrote nine symphonies.

24.4 Who shot the pianist?

Well, the important thing is that Roger Ray was playing the piano when the murderer shot him. And he was playing very loudly – both his children say so. So the question is: did anyone hear the shot? Well, Celia didn't hear it. She took Roger a cup of coffee after he stopped playing. Jack didn't hear the shot. He came down because he heard his mother scream. And Sara didn't hear it, either. Only Tom heard the shot. And that can mean only one thing: he heard the shot because he was in the same place as the gun. He wasn't in the garden, he was in Roger's study, holding the gun, and he shot Roger himself.

It was an easy murder. Tom was already in his garden. He put on an old pair of gloves, climbed over the garden wall and walked into Roger's study. Roger was playing the piano. He said hello, but he didn't stop playing. Tom went behind Roger, took out a gun, shot him in the back and put down the gun on the piano. Then he ran back into the garden, back over the wall into his own garden, and then he followed Sara into the street and back into Roger's house again. Of course, he took off the gloves first. When we looked in his garden, we found them lying in the flowers.

Reference section

1 Things people do

Present simple

We use the Present simple for

- repeated actions:
  I *get up* at 6 o'clock every morning.

- attitudes and feelings:
  She *likes* chocolate.

- things that are generally true:
  Penguins *live* in Antarctica.

Positive and negative

I You They	live don't live	here.	He She	lives doesn't live	here.

Questions

Do you Does he	eat meat?	Yes, I do. Yes, he does.	No, I don't. No, he doesn't.

When	do you does she	get up?

Frequency adverbs

always	usually often	sometimes	not usually not often	never

These adverbs normally come before the main verb:

She	sometimes walks doesn't usually walk	to work.

2 Family and friends

Family relations

Male	Female	M or F
father	mother	parent(s)
brother	sister	–
son	daughter	child(ren)
grandfather	grandmother	grandparent(s)
grandson	granddaughter	grandchild(ren)
uncle	aunt	–
nephew	niece	–
–	–	cousin

There are two general words for people in your family: *relations* and *relatives*.

English has no special words for male or female cousins.

Other people

neighbours = people who live near you.

next-door neighbours = the people who live next door.

flat-mate = someone who shares your flat.

room-mate = someone who shares your room.

my *boyfriend/girlfriend* = the person I'm *going out with*.

Verbs

Action	State
fall in love (with)	be in love (with)
get engaged (to)	be engaged (to)
get married (to)	be married (to)
get divorced (from)	be divorced

Study pages A

Personal data

Name: Thomas Kemp

Address: 18 Windsor Road, Manchester, MN6 8JT

Phone number: 0161 560435

Nationality: British

Date of birth: 17th July 1972

Possessive 's

Add *'s* after a singular noun:
my sister → my sister's car   Eva → Eva's husband

After plural nouns ending in -*s*, just add *'*:
my parents → my parents' car

After plural nouns that don't end in -*s*, add *'s*:
the children → the children's clothes

Common verb pairs

wake up	get up	get dressed
go to sleep	go to bed	get undressed

3 Talking about places

There is/are

Use *there is(n't)* before singular nouns.

Use *there are(n't)* before plural nouns.

Before plural nouns, we often use *some* or *any*.

There's There isn't	a TV in the room.

There are some chairs There aren't any flowers	in the room.

Yes/no questions

Is there a TV Are there any chairs	in the room?

have/has got

has got	*there is/are*
The house has got a large kitchen.	There's a large kitchen in the house.
The house has got three bedrooms.	There are three bedrooms in the house.

Positive and negative

The room	has got hasn't got	a balcony.

The rooms	have got haven't got	balconies.

Yes/no questions

Has the room got a balcony? Have the rooms got balconies?

4 On the move

Transport

go by train

go by bus

go by taxi

go by car
drive

go by bike
cycle

go on foot
walk

Journeys

The train *leaves* London at 3.00 p.m.

It *arrives in*
gets to Paris at 7.30 p.m.

The journey *takes* four and a half hours.

It *costs* £125.

Questions

How can I get to Paris?

How long does it take?

How much does it cost?

Describing transport

Opposite pairs of adjectives:

comfortable	uncomfortable
cheap	expensive
fast	slow
safe	dangerous
empty	crowded
reliable	unreliable

Study pages B

Place prepositions

The clock is …

in front of the
lamp.

behind the
lamp.

beside the
lamp.

above the
lamp.

under the
lamp.

between the lamp
and the plant.

early, in time, on time, late

If we get to the station *in time* (= early enough), we'll catch the train.

The train always arrives *on time* (= at the correct time). It's never *early*, and it's never *late*.

on, in, at

on: I go to school on Monday.
The plane leaves on Monday morning.

in: We eat late in the evening.
Are you at home in the afternoon?

at: I always get up at 6 o'clock.
She often works at the weekend.

5 Talking about now

Present continuous

We use the Present continuous to talk about

- things happening now, at the moment of speaking:
Ssh! *I'm reading* the newspaper.
- things happening 'around now':
He's learning German at school.

Positive and negative

I'm He's They're	(not)	having lunch.

Questions

Are you Is he Are they	reading?

What	are you is he are they	doing?

There is/are + -ing

There's a man. He's sitting on the grass.
→ There's a man sitting on the grass.

There are some children. They're playing football.
→ There are some children playing football.

Verbs of position

She's standing by the door.   He's sitting on the sofa.   They're lying on the beach.

6 Food and drink

Food

Types of food

Meat	beef, lamb, pork, chicken
Vegetables	onion, garlic, tomato, carrot, pepper, aubergine, mushroom, potato
Seafood	fish, shellfish, prawns
Fruit	apple, banana, orange, peach, melon

Common ingredients

flour, rice, sugar, cheese, butter, oil
salt, pepper, spices

Dishes

It's a Spanish dish.
It *has* cheese *in it*.
It's made with meat and rice.
The noodles *are cooked with* chicken and spices.

Good/bad for you

Fruit and vegetables are *good for* you. (= they're healthy)
Sweets *aren't very good for* you.
Cigarettes are *bad for* you.

Containers

a carton of orange juice   a bottle of beer   a jar of jam

a packet of spaghetti   a bag of flour   a can of tomatoes

Study pages C

like

After *like* we can use a noun or an *-ing* form:
She likes horses.
She likes riding horses.

Similar verbs: *love, don't mind, hate*

I	love like don't mind don't like hate	long journeys. flying. travelling by bus.

In a café or restaurant

Could I	see the menu, have the bill,	please?

I'd like	a cup of coffee, spaghetti bolognese,	please.

Expressions with *get*

get on/off a bus or train
get into/out of a car or taxi
get up in the morning (= get out of bed)
get dressed (= put on your clothes)
get engaged, get married, get divorced

7 The past

Past simple

We use the Past simple to talk about

- things that happened in the past:
  They arrived on Saturday.
  I got up early this morning.
- what things were like in the past:
  When I was a child, I lived in Australia.
  It was very cold yesterday.

Past tense of regular verbs: add *-ed* or *-d*.

Past tense of irregular verbs: learn the forms on page 128.

Positive and negative

I	liked		I	didn't like	
He	saw	the film.	He	didn't see	the film.

Questions

Did you				did you	
Did he	see the film?		When	did he	see it?

ago

We use *ago* to measure time back from now:

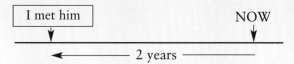

I met him two years ago.

I arrived *on Saturday*.	I arrived *three days ago*.
I was there *last week*.	I was there about *a week ago*.
I last saw her *in 1950*.	I last saw her more than *50 years ago*.

8 A place to live

Kinds of home

They live in …

a house.	a flat (an apartment).
a cottage.	a block of flats (an apartment block).

Their flat is on the third floor. → It's a third-floor flat.
Our apartment has 5 rooms. → It's a 5-room apartment.

Position

Their house is …

in the town centre.	on a main road.
in the suburbs.	on a square.
in the country.	near the airport.

Our apartment …

has a view of the park.
looks out on the park.
faces north/south/east/west.

Rooms and furniture

Room	Typical furniture
living room	armchair, sofa, carpet, curtains
kitchen	cooker, fridge, sink, cupboards
bathroom	bath, shower, washbasin, mirror
study	desk, (book)shelf, computer
bedroom	(single/double) bed, wardrobe

Describing rooms

Opposite adjectives

small	big/large
dark	light
comfortable	uncomfortable
tidy	untidy
quiet	noisy
clean	dirty

Study pages D

both and neither

Both (of) the men / Both of them	are wearing hats.
Neither of the men / Neither of them	has glasses.
One of the men / One of them	has a moustache.

this and last

They arrived *this morning* (= today).
They got married earlier *this week*.

I went fishing *last weekend*.
She went to India *last October*.

very, quite

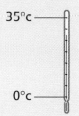

It's very hot.
It's fairly/quite hot.
It isn't very hot.
It's a bit cold.
It's rather/quite cold.
It's very cold.

9 I've done it!

Present perfect tense

We use the Present perfect to talk about recent events, or things that have just happened.

They've arrived.

I've just washed my hair.

Look – I've bought a new car

We use the Present perfect *without* a time expression. If we use a past time expression, we must use the Past simple. Compare:

Present perfect

They've just arrived.
I've washed my hair.
I've bought a car.

Past simple

They arrived at 3 o'clock.
I washed my hair last night.
I bought a car on Friday.

Positive and negative

| I've | closed the door. |
| She's | bought a car. |

| I haven't | closed the door. |
| She hasn't | bought a car. |

Questions

| Have you | closed the door? |
| Has she | bought a car? |

| What | have you
has she | bought? |

10 Clothes

He's wearing …  … a hat, a coat, a scarf, boots, and gloves.	She's wearing …  … a blouse, earrings and a skirt.	He's wearing …  … a jacket, trousers, a shirt and a tie.
She's wearing …  … a hat, a dress and high-heeled shoes.	He's wearing … … a T-shirt, shorts, sandals and sunglasses.	She's wearing … … a jumper, jeans and trainers.

Some clothes are plural: *trousers, jeans, shorts, sunglasses*. We can also say *a pair of trousers, a pair of shorts*, etc.

Clothes is a general word: it is only used in the plural.

Buying clothes

That jacket *suits* you. (= it looks good on you)
Is it *small, medium* or *large*? What *size* is it? It's *size* 14.
Try it on and see if it *fits*. (= it's the right size)
How much does it *cost*?

Study pages E

Possessive pronouns

I	my	mine
you	your	yours
he	his	his
she	her	hers
we	our	ours
they	their	theirs
John	John's	John's
Who?	Whose?	Whose?

I think that's *my* coat.
I think that coat is *mine*.

Are those *your* children?
Are those children *yours*?

This is *her* office.
This office is *hers*.

Whose book is this?
Whose is this book?

Paying for things

You can pay for things

- in cash
- by cheque
- by credit card.

Can I pay by credit card?

Do you take credit cards?

's

The 's ending can mean

is: She is my sister. → She's my sister.
has: She has won £1,000. → She's won £1,000.
possessive 's: This is John's car.

---

11 Quantity

some and any

Count	Non-count
I've got some books.	I've got some money.
I haven't got any books.	I haven't got any money.
Have you got any books?	Have you got any money?

We use *some* and *any* before plural count nouns and singular non-count nouns.

We usually use *some* in positive sentences, and *any* in negatives and questions.

Quantity expressions

Use *many* and *few* with count nouns, *much* and *little* with non-count nouns. Use *a lot of* (or *lots of*) with count or non-count nouns.

Count	Non-count
I buy *a lot of* clothes.	I eat *a lot of* meat.
I don't buy *many* clothes.	I don't eat *much* meat.
I buy very *few* clothes.	I eat very *little* meat.
How *many* clothes do you buy?	How *much* meat do you eat?

too and enough

Count	Non-count
I buy *too many* clothes.	I eat *too much* meat.
I don't buy *enough* clothes.	I don't eat *enough* meat.

Notice that we say:

He has too much money. (Not ~~too much of money~~)
She doesn't have enough time. (Not ~~enough of time~~)

12 How do you feel?

Parts of the body

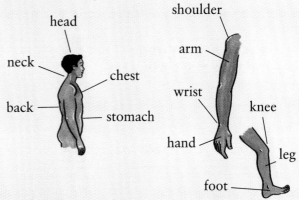

head, shoulder, neck, arm, chest, wrist, back, knee, stomach, hand, leg, foot

Aches and pains

pain is a noun: I've got a pain in my knee.
ache is a noun or a verb: I've got an ache in my wrist.
　　　　　　　　　　　　　My wrist aches.
hurt is a verb: My foot hurts.

We can also say:

a backache　　　　a headache
a toothache　　　　a stomach ache

Illnesses

With most illnesses, we use *have*:

have a cold　　　have 'flu　　　have a temperature

Going to the doctor

If you *feel ill*, you can *make an appointment* to see a doctor.
The doctor asks you questions and *examines* you.
The doctor writes you *a prescription*.
You take the prescription to the *chemist*.
You *take the medicine*.
If you're lucky, you'll *feel better*.

Study pages F

for and since

We use the Present perfect with *for* or *since* to talk about events that started in the past and are still going on now:

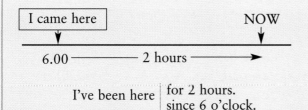

| I came here | | NOW |

6.00 ———— 2 hours ————→

I've been here | for 2 hours.
　　　　　　　 | since 6 o'clock.

a little, a few; very little, very few

a little/a few = some, but not a lot:

I drank *a little* water and ate *a few* biscuits, and I soon started to feel better.

very little/very few = almost none:

The refugees have *very little* food and *very few* clothes.

well

We use *well*:

- as an adverb: He sings very well.
  (= he's a good singer)

- meaning 'not ill': How are you today?
  Very well, thank you.

13 What will happen?

will and won't

We use *will* and *won't* to make predictions about the future:

You'll meet a tall dark stranger.
Don't worry – it won't hurt.

Positive and negative

They'll	get married.	There will	be a war.
They won't		There won't	

Questions

Will she get married?	Yes, she will. No, she won't.
Will there be a war?	Yes, there will. No, there won't.

| When will she get married? |
| What will she do? |

probably and might

They'll probably They might They probably won't	arrive today.

They might = perhaps/maybe they will
Probably comes <u>after</u> *will* but <u>before</u> *won't*.

14 About town

Places in towns

Activity	*Places to go*
eating/drinking	restaurant, café, bar
entertainment	theatre, cinema, concert hall
sport/exercise	stadium, sports centre, park, swimming pool
sightseeing	castle, museum, art gallery
religion	church, cathedral, mosque
night life	disco, nightclub

go + -ing: go swimming, go sightseeing, go shopping
go + for: go for a swim, go for a walk, go for a meal
go + to: go to the theatre, go to the cinema; go to a concert, go to a café; go to church.

Shopping

Ways of describing shops and shop assistants:

expensive	convenient	good quality
cheap	friendly	a good selection
crowded	helpful	a good atmosphere

Giving directions

Excuse me, can you tell me the way to …?
how can I get to …?

Go straight along this road.   Go on until you get to a main road.

Turn left at the church.   Go past the library.

Study pages G

if (first conditional) and when

After *if* and *when*, use the Present simple to talk about the future:

If When	I see her I'll give her the money.

Two-word verbs

wake up	Wake up! It's nearly 9 o'clock!
get up	I got up early and made breakfast.
stand up	Everyone stood up when the King arrived.
sit down	He came in and sat down on the sofa.
put on	She put on her glasses and read the letter.
take off	It's hot. I think I'll take off my coat.
try on	That's a nice jacket. Can I try it on?

Short answers

To give short answers, repeat the auxiliary verb (*is, was, does, has, did, will*, etc.).

Do you play chess?	Yes, I *do*.	No, I *don't*.
Did you like the film?	Yes, I *did*.	No, I *didn't*.
Was he at home?	Yes, he *was*.	No, he *wasn't*.
Is she staying here?	Yes, she *is*.	No, she *isn't*.
Have you got a bike?	Yes, I *have*.	No, I *haven't*.
Has he gone to bed?	Yes, he *has*.	No, he *hasn't*.
Will we be late?	Yes, we *will*.	No, we *won't*.
Can I try it on?	Yes, you *can*.	No, you *can't*.

15 Comparing things

Comparative and superlative

- One-syllable adjectives – add *-er*, *-est*:

fast	faster	fastest
large	larger	largest

- Two-syllable adjectives ending in *-y* – add *-er*, *-est*:

happy	happier	happiest
friendly	friendlier	friendliest

- Most other two-syllable adjectives and longer adjectives – add *more*, *most*:

helpful	more helpful	most helpful
interesting	more interesting	most interesting

- Irregular forms:

good	better	best
bad	worse	worst
much	more	most
little	less	least
far	further	furthest

Comparative structures

I'm	tidier / more intelligent	than my brother.

Which is	faster, / more expensive,	a BMW or a Jaguar?

To talk about a big difference, we can also use *much*:
I'm *much tidier* than my brother.
A BMW is *much more expensive* than a Fiat Uno.
My new job is *much better* than my old one.

Superlative structures

London is	the biggest / the most important	city in England.

Study pages H

Ability

Two ways to talk about ability:
I can swim quite well.   I'm quite good at swimming.
I can't sing very well.   I'm not very good at singing.

After *good at*, we can use a noun or an *-ing* form:

I'm	good at / quite good at / not very good at / no good at	cooking. / (playing) football. / writing letters.

16 Free time

Leisure activities

Outdoor activities

sailing	horse-riding	fishing	cycling

skiing	walking	camping	climbing

Indoor activities

cooking	knitting	painting	playing cards

writing letters	playing chess	playing the guitar	collecting stamps

go + -ing: go swimming, go horse-riding, go fishing
play: play cards, play golf; play the piano

Talking about activities you enjoy:

I	make cakes. / play chess. / go sailing.		I	like / enjoy	making cakes. / (playing) chess. / sailing.

Sports

Sports and activities they involve:

football	kick a ball, score a goal
basketball	throw a ball, score points
tennis	hit a ball over the net, score points

more, less and fewer

Less and *fewer* are both the opposite of *more*. Use *less* with non-count nouns and *fewer* with count nouns.

Joe has very *little* money and very *few* clothes.

He has *less* money and *fewer* clothes than Alex.

17 Rules and advice

must and *have to*

Must and *have to* mean almost the same. We usually use *must* when we *tell* people what to do; we use *have to* when we *talk about* this to other people.

You must stay in bed

I have to stay in bed.

mustn't and *don't have to*

You mustn't means 'Don't do it':
You mustn't tell her – she doesn't know yet.

You don't have to means 'It isn't necessary':
You don't have to pay to get in – it's free.

should and *shouldn't*

We use *should* if we think something is the right thing to do or a good idea:

You should write to your parents.
You shouldn't smoke so much.

Compare:

You mustn't cross the road. (= it's a rule)
You shouldn't cross the road. (= it isn't a good idea)

Positive and negative forms

You	must(n't) can('t) should(n't)	stay here.

I	have to don't have to	stay here.

18 A day's work

Places and jobs

Places	Typical jobs
hospital	doctor, nurse
office	manager, accountant, secretary
hotel	receptionist
restaurant	waiter/waitress
buildings	window cleaner, plumber, painter
the street	taxi driver, lorry driver, police officer
garage	mechanic
shops	shop assistant, hairdresser
night club	disc jockey, singer, musician

He *works in* a hotel.
She *works for* the Ford Corporation.
He *drives* a taxi.
He *mends/repairs* bicycles.

Good and bad jobs

She likes her job because …	He doesn't like his job because …
… it's interesting/useful.	… it's difficult/boring.
… she has long holidays.	… he has to work hard.
… she has a good salary.	… he works long hours.
… she can travel a lot.	… he has to travel a lot.

Careers

You *apply for* a job.
You *get* the job.
They *promote* you.
You *get the sack*. (= lose your job).
You *leave* your job and *look for* another one.
You *find* another job.
When you're 65, you *retire*.

Study pages I

someone, anyone …

Words beginning with *some-* follow the same pattern as *some* and *any*:

Positive	Negative/Questions
some	any
someone	anyone
something	anything
somewhere	anywhere

I've got something in my eye.
I can't see anything.
Can you see anything?

She lives somewhere in California.
I didn't go anywhere this summer.
Is there anywhere to play football here?

Verbs with prepositions

apply for	I applied for a job in a café.
pay for	Have you paid for that book?
wait for	We waited for the train for two hours.
look for	I'm looking for someone to help me.
look at	Do you want to look at my photos?
listen to	Ssh! I'm listening to the radio.
look after	Could you look after our cat while we're on holiday?
deal with	She has to deal with customers' questions.
work for	I work for a bus company.

19 Telling stories

Past continuous

We use the Past continuous to talk about

- the background to events in the past (things that were going on at the time):

  He *was having* a shower when the phone rang.

- scenes set in the past:

  The street was full of people. They *were singing* and *dancing*.

Positive and negative

I was She was They were	listening.		I wasn't She wasn't They weren't	listening.

Questions

Were you Was she Were they	listening?		Why	were you was she were they	listening?

when and while

when + Past simple:

He was having a shower *when* the phone rang.

while + Past continuous:

While he was having a shower, the phone rang.
The phone rang *while* he was having a shower.

Verbs describing accidents

bite – bit	cut – cut
break – broke	fall – fell
hit – hit	slip – slipped
hurt – hurt	trip – tripped

20 People

Physical appearance

What does he/she look like?

General: tall, short, fat, thin, slim.
Face: narrow, wide, round, square.
Nose: long, short, large, small, pointed, hooked, straight.
Hair: long, short, wavy, curly, straight, fair, dark.

He's bald, and he has a beard and a moustache.

She has glasses, earrings and a necklace.

Age

How old is he/she?

He's in his She's in her	early mid late	twenties. fifties.

He's in his teens / He's a teenager. (= 13 to 19)
She's middle-aged. (= between 40 and 60)

Character adjectives

Opposite pairs of adjectives:

generous	mean
honest	dishonest
friendly	unfriendly
hard-working	lazy
good-tempered	bad-tempered
selfish	unselfish
shy	outgoing

Study pages J

Nationalities

Ending in -ish

Spain	Spanish
Turkey	Turkish
Poland	Polish

Ending in -ian or -an

Germany	German
Italy	Italian
Egypt	Egyptian

Ending in -ese

China	Chinese
Japan	Japanese

Ending in -i

Iraq	Iraqi
Israel	Israeli

Other

France	French	Switzerland	Swiss
Greece	Greek	Netherlands	Dutch

while and during

while + sentence:

They arrived while we were asleep.
While I was having breakfast, I suddenly felt sick.

during + noun:

They arrived during the night.
During breakfast, I suddenly felt sick.

with

I saw a man.
He had a beard. → I saw a man *with* a beard.

I can see a boy.
He has fair hair. → I can see a boy *with* fair hair.

21 Future plans

going to

We use *going to* to talk about intentions or plans (things we have decided to do):

When I get home, I'm going to have a shower.
I'm going to wear my new dress tomorrow.

Positive and negative

He's They're	(not) going to	have a party.

Questions

Is he Are they	going to	have a party?

What	is he are they	going to do?

will

We can use *will* instead of *going to* if we are not sure. We usually add *perhaps*, *probably* or *maybe*:

When I leave college, I'll probably go abroad.
Perhaps I'll wear my new dress tomorrow.

Present continuous

We use the Present continuous to talk about things that are definitely arranged for the future. Compare:

We're going to have a party. (we're planning it)
We're having a party. (we've invited the people already)

Time expressions

We're going there	tomorrow. next Friday. in two weeks.

22 Around the world

Parts of the world

Continents

Europe	Africa	North America
Asia	Australia	South America

Oceans

Atlantic Ocean	Pacific Ocean	Indian Ocean

Regions

the Middle East	the Mediterranean
South-east Asia	the Caribbean

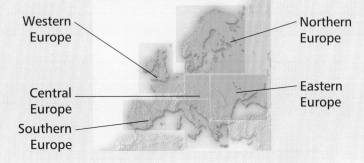

Western Europe · Northern Europe · Central Europe · Eastern Europe · Southern Europe

Features

mountain   volcano   hill   beach

desert   valley   forest   lake

Describing countries

It's mountainous/hilly/flat.
It's covered in forest.
It has a large/small population.

Study pages K

nothing, no one, nowhere

something	anything	nothing
someone	anyone	no one
somewhere	anywhere	nowhere

Positive: I can hear something.
Question: Can you hear anything?
Negative: I can hear nothing.
I can't hear anything.

Positive: I spoke to someone.
Question: Did you speak to anyone?
Negative: I spoke to no one.
I didn't speak to anyone.

Present continuous

- things happening 'at this moment':
  Look – they're coming out of the house.

- things happening 'around now':
  He's working very hard this year.

- things arranged for the future:
  I'm going to Tokyo on Monday.

Inviting people

Would you like to come to the cinema?

Yes, I'd love to.

Shall we meet in the main square?

23 Past and present

Changes

You can use the Present perfect tense to talk about *changes* (what is different now from before):

BEFORE   NOW
I was in London.   Now I'm in New York.

I've left London.
I've moved to New York.

still and *yet*

He's still living in London.

He hasn't moved to New York yet.

Are you still doing your homework?

Have you finished it yet?

Experience

You can use the Present perfect tense to talk about *experience* (things you have done at some time in your life):

I've been to Hong Kong several times.
I've never seen a tarantula.
Have you ever eaten octopus?

Present perfect and Past simple

We use the Present perfect without a past time expression. If we use a time expression, we must use the Past simple. Compare:

Present perfect	*Past simple*
She's found a new job.	She found a new job last week.
I've been to Hong Kong twice.	I went to Hong Kong in 1990, and again in 1995.

24 Arts and entertainment

Art forms

Art forms	*People*
stories, novels	writer
poetry	poet
films, plays	director, actor/actress, film star
paintings	painter
music	composer, singer, musician, band, orchestra

Art and *artist* are general words, but we often use them to talk about painting:

Botticelli was a famous artist.

Places

You go to see/hear ...	*at a/an ...*
paintings	art gallery, museum
music	concert hall
plays	theatre
films	cinema

You go to an art gallery to see an *exhibition* of paintings. You go to a concert hall to listen to a *concert* or an *opera*.

TV programmes

news programmes	comedy programmes
documentaries	quiz shows
films	soaps
sport	chat shows

Irregular verbs

Infinitive	Simple past	Past participle
be	was/were	been
become	became	become
bite	bit	bitten
blow	blew	blown
break	broke	broken
bring	brought	brought
build	built	built
buy	bought	bought
can	could	(been able)
catch	caught	caught
choose	chose	chosen
come	came	come
cost	cost	cost
cut	cut	cut
do	did	done
draw	drew	drawn
dream	dreamt	dreamt
drink	drank	drunk
drive	drove	driven
eat	ate	eaten
fall	fell	fallen
feed	fed	fed
feel	felt	felt
find	found	found
fly	flew	flown
forget	forgot	forgotten
get	got	got
give	gave	given
go	went	gone (been)
have	had	had
hear	heard	heard
hide	hid	hidden
hit	hit	hit
hold	held	held
hurt	hurt	hurt
keep	kept	kept
know	knew	known
lay	laid	laid
learn	learnt	learnt
leave	left	left
lend	lent	lent
let	let	let
lie	lay	lain
lose	lost	lost
make	made	made
mean	meant	meant
meet	met	met
pay	paid	paid
put	put	put
read /riːd/	read /red/	read /red/
ride	rode	ridden
ring	rang	rung
rise	rose	risen
run	ran	run
say	said	said
see	saw	seen
sell	sold	sold
send	sent	sent
set	set	set
shake	shook	shaken
shine	shone	shone

Infinitive	Simple past	Past participle
shoot	shot	shot
show	showed	shown
shut	shut	shut
sing	sang	sung
sit	sat	sat
sleep	slept	slept
speak	spoke	spoken
spell	spelt	spelt
spend	spent	spent
stand	stood	stood
steal	stole	stolen
swim	swam	swum
take	took	taken
teach	taught	taught
tear	torn	torn
think	thought	thought
throw	threw	thrown
understand	understood	understood
wake	woke	woken
wear	wore	worn
win	won	won
write	wrote	written

Phonetic symbols

Vowels

Symbol	Example
/iː/	tree /triː/
/i/	many /'meni/
/ɪ/	sit /sɪt/
/e/	bed /bed/
/æ/	back /bæk/
/ʌ/	sun /sʌn/
/ɑː/	car /kɑː/
/ɒ/	hot /hɒt/
/ɔː/	horse /hɔːs/
/ʊ/	full /fʊl/
/uː/	moon /muːn/
/ɜː/	girl /gɜːl/
/ə/	arrive /ə'raɪv/
	water /'wɔːtə/
/eɪ/	late /leɪt/
/aɪ/	time /taɪm/
/ɔɪ/	boy /bɔɪ/
/əʊ/	home /həʊm/
/aʊ/	out /aʊt/
/ɪə/	here /hɪə/
/eə/	there /ðeə/
/ʊə/	pure /pjʊɔ/

Consonants

Symbol	Example
/p/	pull /pʊl/
/b/	bad /bæd/
/t/	take /teɪk/
/d/	dog /dɒg/
/k/	cat /kæt/
/g/	go /gəʊ/
/tʃ/	church /tʃɜːtʃ/
/dʒ/	age /eɪdʒ/
/f/	for /fɔː/
/v/	love /lʌv/
/θ/	thick /θɪk/
/ð/	this /ðɪs/
/s/	sit /sɪt/
/z/	zoo /zuː/
/ʃ/	shop /ʃɒp/
/ʒ/	leisure /'leʒə/
/h/	house /haʊs/
/m/	make /meɪk/
/n/	name /neɪm/
/ŋ/	bring /brɪŋ/
/l/	look /lʊk/
/r/	road /rəʊd/
/j/	young /jʌŋ/
/w/	wear /weə/

Stress

We show stress by a mark (') before the stressed syllable:
later /'leɪtə/; arrive /ə'raɪv/; information /infə'meɪʃn/.

Acknowledgements

The authors would like to thank the following for their contributions to the new edition of *Language in Use Pre-intermediate*:

– for contributing to the reading and listening material: Michael Carrier, Paula Edmunds, Josephine Jones, Thomas Jones, Desmond Nicholson, Louisa Preskett, Patrick Rayner, Dr Lawrie Reznek, Diana Seavill, Ewa Simbieda, Carsten Williams, Andre Zaharias, Gabriella Zaharias.
– for designing the course: James Arnold and Stephanie White (Gecko Ltd).
– for commissioning artwork: Wendy Abel (Gecko Ltd).
– for the production of recorded material: Martin Williamson (Prolingua Productions) and Peter Thompson (Studio AVP).
– for picture research: Sandie Huskinson-Rolfe of PHOTOSEEKERS.

The authors would also like to thank the following at Cambridge University Press:

– Colin Hayes for his continuing support and help.
– Peter Donovan for organising the project.
– Jo Barker for overseeing the design of the course.
– Linda Matthews for control of production.
– Sue Wiseman and Val Grove for general administrative help.

Special thanks go to:

– James Dingle of Cambridge University Press, for his expert management of the various stages of the project, and his close involvement with the development of Pre-intermediate level.
– Meredith Levy, our editor, for her professionalism, good judgement and tireless attention to detail.

The authors and publishers would like to thank the following individuals and institutions for their extremely useful comments on the original Pre-intermediate course and for their helpful suggestions for revising the course material:
Dorothy Walker, Overijse, Belgium; Sidnea Nunes Ferreira, Cultura Inglesa, Blumenau, Brazil; Margareth Bassani, Curitiba, Brazil; M. Cristina Brieba, Santiago de Chile, Chile; Alena Lhotáková, Prague, Czech Republic; Aida Kassagby, The American University, Cairo, Egypt; Rachel Harris, Ville-la-Grand, France; David Barnes, Florence, Italy; Susanna di Gravio, International House, Rome, Italy; Paul Lewis, Nagoya, Japan; Maciej Kudla, Gdansk, Poland; Monika Galbarczyk, Warsaw, Poland; Mike Rogers, English 1, Seville, Spain; Heather Turin, Bell Language School, Geneva, Switzerland; Stephen Lewin, Australia Centre, Chiangmai, Thailand; Angela Clegg, Plymouth Language School, Plymouth, UK.

The authors and publishers are grateful to the following illustrators, photographers and photographic sources:

Illustrators: Kathy Baxendale: pp. 31 *mr*, 36 *b*, 39 *bl*, 105 *tr*, 106 *tr*, 117 *bl*; Liam Bonney: pp. 21 *m*, 50 *ml*; Linda Combi: pp. 33 *b*, 51, 62 *tl*, 94 *l*; Rachel Deacon: pp. 12 *t*, 31 *tl*, 40 *b*, 46 *tl*, 64, 74 *tl*, *mbl*, 78 *tl*, 79 *br*, 90, 95 *ml*, 98, 102 *bl*; Karen Donnelly: pp. 12 *b*, 21 *bl*, 23 *br*, 30 *tl*, 33 *m*, 39 *mr*, 45, 59 *b*, 63 *m* & *b*, 65 *t*, 69, 82 *mb*, 84 *tl*, 86 *l*, 104 *t*, 117 *tr*, 118, 119, 120, 121, 122, 123, 124, 125, 126 *mb*; David Downton: pp. 107 *bl*, 108 *bl*; Nick Duffy: pp. 10, 15 *tl*, 31 *bl*, 39 *br*, 41, 43 *t*, 44, 52 *t*, 55 *bl*, 57 *mtr*, 67 *tl*, 68, 76, 79 *tr*, 82 *ml*, 95 *mr*, 102 *tl*; Gecko Ltd: pp. 15 *tr*, 73, 87 *tr*, 91, 126 *mt*; Jo Goodberry: pp. 19, 65 *b*, 103 (I), 104 *b*; Jackie Harland: pp. 27, 28; Phil Healey: pp. 9 *b*, 13, 20 *tr*, 23 *tl*, 24, 26, 32, 42, 54 *tl*, *mb*, 63 *mt*, 71, 74 *mr*, 79 *bl*, 84 *mbl*, 87 *mr*, 97, 103 (A); Rosalind Hudson: pp. 18 *tr*, 52 *b*, 85, 87 *bl*, 103 (E); Paul McCaffrey: p. 81, 108 *t*; Louise Morgan: pp. 17, 18 *tl*, 22 *l*, 36 *t*, 38 *tl*, 43 *m*, 75, 105 *b*, 107 *t*; Pantelis Palios: pp. 9 *t*, 40 *t*, 50 *tr*, 57 *tr*, *mtl*, 59 *t*, 72, 100; Andy Quelch: pp. 37, 101; Rachel Ross: pp. 20 *tl*, 25, 95 *bl*, 106 *br*; Debbie Ryder: p. 60; Linda Scott: pp. 53, 58, 88; Holly Swain: p. 56; Sam Thompson: pp. 107 *br*, 108 *br*; Kath Walker: pp. 14, 22 *r*, 30 *r*, 38 *r*, 46 *r*, 54 *r*, 62 *r*, 70, 78 *r*, 86 *r*, 94 *r*; Sarah Warburton: p. 80; Emma Whiting: pp. 48, 67 *b*, 96, 107 *ml*, 108 *ml*.

Photographic sources: Ace Photo Agency/Roger Howard: p. 35 *m*, Ace/Mauritius: p. 44 *bmr*; Adams Picture Library: pp. 35 *br*, 44 *bl* & *br*, 99 *bm*; Allsport/Gary M. Prior: p. 69 (2), Allsport/Laurence Griffiths: pp. 69 (3), 103 (G), Allsport/Mike Hewitt: p. 69 (4), Allsport (UK) Limited: p. 69 (5); www.altavista.com: p. 93 *br*; theartarchive: p. 100 (2); E. Bradbury/Aspect Picture Library: p. 21 *br*; Mark Wagner-Aviation Images: p. 21 *tl*; Anthony Blake Photo Library: pp. 27 *tl*, 51 *bl*, Anthony Blake/Graham Kirk: p. 27 *tr*, Anthony Blake/Robert Golden: p. 27 *ml*; Portrait of Abraham Lincoln (1809–65), 16th President of the United States (b/w Photo). Private Collection/Stapleton Collection/Bridgeman Art Library: p. 83 *mr*; Camera Press/IMS: p. 27 *bl*, Camera Press/IMS/Bjorn Benkow: p. 69 (6), Camera Press/Richard Open: p. 83 *ml*, Camera Press/Curt Gunther: p. 84 (6), Camera Press Limited: pp. 83 *mc*, 100 (4); The J. Allan Cash Photolibrary: pp. 27 *mr*, 33 *tr*, 35 *l*; Cephas Picture Library/Christine Fleurent: p. 27 *mc*; Colorific Photo Library/Randy G. Taylor: p. 61 (A), Colorific/Black Star: p. 83 *tl*, Colorific Photo Library: pp. 83 *tm*, 84 (2), 100 (5); Donald Cooper/Photostage/Paul Scofield: p. 99 *br*; Sylvia Cordaiy Photo Library/Chris North: p. 21 *mb*; James Davis Worldwide: p. 61 (C); Dracula's Restaurant, Melbourne, Australia: p. 29 *t*; Copyright 1999, Earthcam, Inc., www.earthcam.com: p. 93 *tl*; Greg Evans International: pp. 33 *tl*, 92 *tr*; Mary Evans Picture Library/Douglas Dickens: p. 86 *tr*, MEPL: pp. 100 (1), 100 (3); The Ronald Grant Archive: p. 84 (3), Courtesy MGM/Ronald Grant: p. 84 (4), Courtesy Paramount/Ronald Grant: p. 109 (2) *b*; Robert Harding Picture Library: pp. 77 *t*, 103 (H); www.hellspark.com/car: pp. 93 *tr*, 103 (L); Hulton Getty Picture Collection: pp. 83 *tr*, 83 *b*, 86 *br*, 103 (K); The Image Bank/Eric Meola: p. 24 *br*, TIB/David Vance: p. 76, TIB/Jeff Hunter: pp. 92 *br*, 103 (J), TIB/Flip Chalfont: p. 99 *bl*; Images Colour Library: p. 24 *bl*; Simon Shepheard/Impact Photos: p. 21 *mt*, Frank Lane Picture Agency/H. Hautala: p. 92 *tl*, FLPA/P. Perry: p. 109 (1); London Features International/John Engstead: p. 84 (1); Simon Marsden/The Marsden Archive: pp. 37, 103 (C); Mirror Syndication International: pp. 13 *t*, 86 *tm*; Movieland Wax Museum, Buena Park, San Francisco: pp. 61 (E), 103 (F); Natural History Photographic Agency/A.N.: p. 93 *bl*; F. Blickle/Bilderberg/Network: p. 61 (F); PA News Photo Library: p. 84 (5); Pictor International: pp. 44 *bml*, 51 *bml*, 68 *bl* & *br*; Popperfoto: pp. 86 *tl*, *bl* & *bm*, 109 (2) *t*; Powerstock Zefa: pp. 19 *br*, 44 *btl*; Redferns Music Picture Library/ Paul Bergen: p. 84 (7), Redferns/ Henrietta Butler: p. 99 *tl*, Redferns: p. 99 *mr*; Red Sea Star Restaurant, Eilat, Israel: p. 29 *mt*; Rex Features Limited: p. 69 (7); Jules Selmes: pp. 8, 11, 16 *br*, 27, 28, 29 *mb*, 41, 44 *t*, 51 B, C, F, G, 67, 77 *m*, 89, 97; Sporting Pictures (UK) Limited: pp. 68 *tl*, 69 (1); The Stock Market/Mike Chew: p. 109 (4), TSM/ Torleig Svensson: p. 109 (5); Tony Stone Images/Peter Correz: p. 44 *btr*, TSI/Will & Deni McIntyre: p. 49 *b*, TSI/Monica Dalmasso: p. 51 *tl*, TSI/Thomas Zimmermann: p. 68 *tr*, TSI/Simon Bruty: p. 68 *tm*, TSI/Phil Cole: p. 68 *bml*, TSI/David Madison: p. 68 *bmr*, TSI/Doug Armand: p. 92 *bl*, TSI/Vito Palmisano: p. 99 *ml*, Tony Stone Images: p. 92 *tm*; Telegraph Colour Library/ Photomondo: p. 19 *t*, TCL/VCL: pp. 19 *bl*, 61 (B), TCL/Masterfile: p. 24 *t*, TCL/Laurent Delhourme: p. 49 *t*, TCL/VCL: p. 61 (B); TRIP/S. Surman: p. 61 (D), TRIP/Francesca Bondy: p. 99 *tr*; Debbie and Lisa Gantz, www.twinsworld.com: pp. 29 *b*, 103 (B).

t = top   *m* = middle   *b* = bottom   *r* = right   *l* = left   *c* = centre

We have been unable to trace the copyright of the material on pp. 13 *b*, and 35 *tr*, and would be grateful for any information that would enable us to do so.

Picture Research by Sandie Huskinson-Rolfe of PHOTOSEEKERS.
Cover design by Dunne & Scully.
Design, production, colour scanning and reproduction handled by Gecko Limited, Bicester, Oxon.
Sound recordings by Martin Williamson, Prolingua Productions at Studio AVP.
Freelance editorial work by Meredith Levy.